Philosophy of Law

2nd edition

Philo. ... nt for
stude ... hilos-
ophy ... ories
and c ... tes an
excep ... at the
dispu

Th ... sophy
of law

- V
  ti
- T ... y
  a
- C ... d sub-
  l ... st

Th ... in
Engli ... es to
rape, ... se in
2000, ... ed
Twin ... s
and ... e
ongoing controversy between postmodernism and defences of modernity.
These radical perspectives on legal theory and criminal law are compared
with those of the mainstream liberal tradition, giving students a more
complete picture of the current state of jurisprudence and philosophy of law.
The new chapters assess the value of both traditional legal theory and the
various critical perspectives, and study questions at the end of each chapter
help students explore the most important issues in philosophy of law.

Mark Tebbit is Lecturer in Philosophy at the University of Reading. He is also
a Member of Faculty at the University of Notre Dame (London Centre).

Philosophy of Law
An introduction

2nd Edition

Mark Tebbit

Routledge
Taylor & Francis Group

LONDON AND NEW YORK

First published 2005
by Routledge
2 Park Square, Milton Park, Abingdon, Oxon OX14 4RN

Simultaneously published in the USA and Canada
by Routledge
270 Madison Ave,. New York, NY 10016

Routledge is an imprint of the Taylor & Francis Group

© 2005 Mark Tebbit

Typeset in Times by
Taylor & Francis Books
Printed and bound in Great Britain by
Antony Rowe Ltd, Chippenham, Wiltshire

British Library Cataloguing in Publication Data
A catalogue record for this book is available from the British Library

Library of Congress Cataloging in Publication Data
Tebbit, Mark, 1950-
  Philosophy of law : an introduction / Mark Tebbit.-- 2nd ed.
     p. cm.
  "Simultaneously published in the USA and Canada."
  Includes bibliographical references and index.
  ISBN 0-415-33440-3 (hardback : alk. paper) -- ISBN 0-415-33441-1
(pbk. : alk. paper) 1. Law--Philosophy. I. Title.
  K230.T43A37 2005
  340'.1--dc22
                                    2005000798

ISBN 0–415–33440–3 (hbk)
ISBN 0–415–33441–1 (pbk)

Contents

Preface to 2nd edition

With the addition of new material in this edition, it is important to stress that this remains an introductory book aimed at philosophy and law students in the early stages of a course in the philosophy of law or jurisprudence. The main aim is still that of providing a basic grounding in the concepts and arguments that have been prominent throughout the history of philosophy and law, and to stimulate interest in wider reading in these areas. The dispute between natural law theories and positivism, along with the radical challenge represented in the early twentieth century by American legal realism, remains the central focus of the book, because these disputes have not been supplanted by the more recent radical challenges. With the extended treatment of the subject for this edition, however, I have included a general description and assessment of the contemporary critical onslaught on the mainstream, with a selection of representative themes from the most prominent of these critical theories.

There is no common factor behind the critical theories operating today, and they do not come in neat packages. Behind the diversity, however, the greatest single influence upon radical legal analysis is that of postmodernist philosophy, which by its very nature resists easy definition. 'Postmodern' and all the terms associated with it can be highly mystifying to the uninitiated. In the short chapters dealing with the attacks on 'modernity', I have done what I can to demystify these terms and explain with concrete examples the implications of postmodernism for legal theory. We are constantly assured in the media today that we now live in 'a postmodern world', that we are living through an irreversible shift in the direction of 'a postmodern culture'. This sometimes means no more than that some of us now are lucky enough to be living in a more tolerant and diverse political climate, or that all the old religious and moral certainties have gone. Postmodernism also does, however, have serious philosophical content, in as far as it represents a revolution in the philosophy of language and attempts to dismantle the philosophies traditionally associated with or derived from the Enlightenment. It is against this background that I have explained its impact on the mainstream legal theories.

Not all of the radical criticisms, however, are postmodernist in their basic orientation. Equally important is the more traditional radicalism of socialist and Marxist thinking on the law, in particular in their critiques of liberal individualism, the sometimes subliminal influence of which can be seen through the whole field of critical theories today. Just as most of the Marxist schools of thought, despite or perhaps because of the sharp decline of communism since the early 1990s, still stand on the side of 'modernity', so also do many of the feminist critical writings. The most valuable critical discussions have emerged from those who are engaged with the detailed analysis of legal concepts and legal reasoning. The rise of the Critical Legal Studies movement and those associated with it has also been significant in this respect. In presenting these criticisms as fairly and objectively as possible, what I have aimed at is a text that can be used to compare critical theories with mainstream thought, with a selective bibliography to point readers in the direction of deeper analysis. One point that should be noted is that the chapters on modernity and critical thought (Chapters 5, 9 and 13) presuppose familiarity with the arguments in the foregoing chapters.

The book is presented in three parts, each of which covers one of the main areas in which philosophical analysis has been prominent. Each of the chapters into which these parts are divided is followed by a set of study questions and selections for suggested further reading on issues dealt with in that chapter. The questions can be used in various ways. The main point is to indicate the kind of questions a student should be able to discuss at that stage of the book. They can also be used as formal essay titles and suggestions for essay content. They are loosely structured and need not be adhered to rigidly. The further reading recommendations, which are selected on the principle of diversity of opinion within the tradition, can be found in full in the bibliography at the end of the book.

Acknowledgements

Above all, I want to thank Rosalind Dunning for her constant encouragement and useful suggestions, especially on matters of law. I am also especially indebted to John Cottingham for his initial advice and constructive criticism. Comments on early stages of the draft by David Jabbari and Harry Lesser were also greatly appreciated, as were the comments and suggestions by a number of anonymous readers. The Reading University Philosophy Department as a whole, in particular the Head of Department, Mike Proudfoot, made this project possible. Special mention should be made of Dave Burnet and Hugh Maguire for valuable bibliographical suggestions. John Smallwood's legal advice was also greatly appreciated. The students who have taken my philosophy of law course at Reading and at Notre Dame, London, since the 1990s have also helped more than they realised. Patrick Dunn pointed out an inconsistency in the material in Chapter 10. Finally, I would like to thank all the philosophy and law lecturers who responded to my questionnaire in 1995.

Mark Tebbit
University of Reading
2005

Part I
What is the law?

1 Morality, justice and natural law

We all know what it means to break the law. It is perhaps the most fundamental fact governing our social behaviour that we understand the constraints
and the pressures to stay within the law and the consequences of not doing so.
The law is pervasive, controlling our lives in many more ways than we are
usually aware; nevertheless, in most commonplace situations we have a fairly
accurate knowledge of what the law requires and what it forbids. In those grey
areas in which this is not clear, you might seek legal advice about your rights
and obligations. In such situations, one thing you are unlikely to ask of a solicitor is where the law comes from, or, for that matter, why you should obey it;
such questions would be quite inappropriate. These, however, are among the
fundamental questions about the law. What exactly is the law? What does legal
validity mean? What is a legal system? What is the 'rule of law'? These questions have been asked by legal philosophers since the first appearance of
civilised legal systems, and the variation in answers has been of practical as well
as theoretical significance. The purpose of this first chapter is to introduce the
main points of disagreement on these questions and to explain some central
strands of traditional approaches to an understanding of the meaning of law.

Morality and law at variance

The issue that stands behind nearly every controversy in contemporary legal
theory is the problem of how law is to be understood in relation to moral
values. A distinctively modern claim that any student of the subject will
encounter almost immediately is the insistence that a systematic and
rigorous analysis of the law requires 'the separation of law and morality'.
This is frequently referred to as 'the separation thesis', and it is generally
held to be the defining characteristic of legal positivism. Despite its
apparent clarity, this thesis has been the source of much confusion and
dispute. What does it mean to say that the law and morality are separate,
that the law is one thing and morality is another? Before we proceed with the
analysis of the various perspectives on law, it will be helpful to consider
some ways in which law and morality appear to intersect and overlap, and
other ways in which they clearly diverge.

Within the present-day common law jurisdictions, there is a general expectation that the written law and legal judgement will at least roughly approximate to prevailing moral values and moral judgements. A victim of a fraudulent contract or a libel, for example, seeks legal redress in the expectation that the court will adjudicate in the same manner as would any fair-minded individual independently of the legal context. In this respect, it seems that morality and the law have a common purpose. Similarly, the system of criminal justice is expected to reflect popular norms of approval and disapproval. The primary function of the criminal law is commonly taken to be the protection of people from those who threaten or violate the interests of others. The most characteristic criminal offences are those that are commonly regarded as morally wrong: assault, murder, theft, burglary, fraud, criminal damage, and so on. In this respect also, it seems that the law is no more than the enforcement of a moral code, distinguishing right from wrong in much the same way. In short, if it is wrong, it must be illegal; if it is legal, it must be morally required or at least morally acceptable. To the extent that this is true, it can be said that there is a large area of overlap between morality and the law.

Closer examination, however, shows this to be a superficial assessment. There are in fact a number of distinct ways in which legal norms substantially diverge from moral norms. On the one hand, the law is in many respects *less* demanding than any serious moral code. The great majority of laws are prohibitions rather than positive commands, their main purpose being the negative one of establishing boundaries. The law generally does not require acts of charity or assistance that might be thought morally obligatory. In this sense, the law operates a minimal morality, based primarily on the need for restraint.

On the other hand, however, the law is in some senses *more* demanding than morality. In some relatively trivial respects, such as the requirements of bureaucracy or non-life-threatening traffic offences, it is arguable that one can break the law without doing anything morally wrong. What is often overlooked is that there are also more serious ways in which this can be the case. Legislation in the twentieth century has greatly extended the area of liability for harmful acts or omissions that are not directly intended and for which one would not normally be blamed. Whether or not this gradual extension of the 'duty of care' does actually reflect changing moral beliefs about responsibility is an issue about which more will be said in the course of the book. It is enough to say at this point that, on the face of it at least, the law has been ahead of popular perceptions of moral responsibility in this respect.

There is another distinct sense in which it can be seen that law and morality do not easily harmonise. Contemporary disagreement over such issues as the right to own firearms, the hunting of various kinds of animal, the stage of pregnancy at which abortions become unacceptable, the illegality of nearly every form of euthanasia, reveals an uneasy relationship between morality and the law. On such matters, the law cannot reflect the prevailing moral code, because there is no general agreement on the rights and wrongs at stake. In these contexts, the law must be out of step with morality, in the specific sense that it cannot match the prevailing moral beliefs of society as a whole.

The myth of the congruence between morality and law is also exposed by any reflection on the history of institutionalised injustice and the struggles for equality and human rights. Penal codes sanctioning excessively cruel or inappropriate punishment, the legal endorsement of slavery and the slave trade, the barring of religious and ethnic minorities from the professions, and the denial of civil rights to women have all been opposed primarily through pressure for legal reform. The Nazi Nuremberg laws, the laws establishing and upholding apartheid in South Africa and the US racial segregation laws have all been taken as outstanding examples of manifest incongruence between morality and law.

Many of these, of course, have been in step with the prevailing local morality of the day, and hence there is no necessary antagonism between the state of the law and the demands of contemporary moral perceptions or sense of justice. It is only from the standpoint of moral objectivism that it can be argued that the demands of justice rise above any particular social belief system, and that such laws can be judged in absolute terms as right or wrong. Moral relativists tend to argue that what usually happens is that with the advance of civilisation, the law comes into conflict with evolving moral norms, as these practices are increasingly perceived to be wrong; and that the law continues to protect outdated moral beliefs until it is reformed. Either way – moral objectivist or relativist – these examples show that there is at least a permanent tension between morality and the law, and that moral values never rest easily with the state of the law at any given stage of its development.

The positivist separation thesis insists that the law is one thing and morality, or the moral evaluation of the law, is another. This means that the connection between law and morality is contingent; laws do not always coincide with moral values or moral codes. There is no necessary connection between morality and the law. A law does not have to conform with any moral standard to be counted legally valid. One thing the separation thesis does not mean, however, is that legislators and judges are concerned exclusively with legal matters and should be quite indifferent to the moral rights and wrongs of the law. This may in practice be true up to a point, if the administration of a specific law is concerned more with the protection of sectional interests than with promoting justice, or if a judge believes that he or she is obliged to apply the letter of the law even when it is morally counterintuitive. These, however, are mistaken interpretations of the meaning of the separation thesis, the function of which is primarily to develop an accurate description of the reality of law. This is a crucial point in legal theory, and it will be developed and clarified in the following chapters. To understand the prime target of the positivist separation thesis, we need first to focus on the concept of justice and the natural law theories that were built on an absolutist interpretation of this concept.

What is justice?

The concept of justice is not only the most prominent theoretical concept in the philosophy of law, equalled in importance only by that of 'law' itself, it is also so regular a feature of common discourse about public life that virtually everybody has an immediate intuitive understanding of it. It is one of those concepts – like 'being' or 'truth' – that is so readily understood, especially in the context of its negation, 'injustice', that any questioning of its meaning tends initially to cause consternation. We can all give examples of an injustice, but when faced with the direct abstract question of what exactly is the justice that is being denied, it is difficult to know where to start. One good starting point is to ask what kinds of thing the quality of justice can be ascribed to, and to confine our answer in the first place to common usage of words.

What rapidly becomes clear is that justice, as a fundamental moral concept, can only be ascribed in situations involving consciousness, rationality and a moral sense. The suffering caused by hurricanes, earthquakes or elephant stampedes is not in itself an injustice. What might be thought an injustice is the failure to relieve such suffering, or to help some at the expense of others. Justice is an issue only where there is conscious, purposive activity. Whether this is the activity of natural beings such as legal officials and emperors, or supernatural agencies such as angry or benevolent gods, the presence of conscious purpose is a necessary condition for speaking of justice.

The kinds of thing that can be described as just or unjust fall into three basic categories: agents, actions and states of affairs that are created by the actions of agents:

1   In traditional usage, the quality of justice is commonly attributed to individuals as such, a 'just God', 'a just monarch' or 'a just man'. Although this usage is still extant, it is more common today to speak of persons with a greater or lesser sense of justice. We also use the term collectively to describe governments, which can have a general reputation for justice or for tyranny.

2   It is also more common in contemporary discourse to ascribe justice to particular actions and decisions rather than to people as such. A just action or decision is one that is sensitive to the rights of all those affected by it. An unjust action or decision is one that violates these rights.

3   The institutions typically held to exhibit the qualities of justice or injustice in varying degrees are those of a human society, a rule of law and a legal system. A society can be just or unjust in different ways: it can be organised in such a way that its benefits or burdens are distributed

unfairly, and 'an unjust society' can also be understood as one in which the discrimination against or persecution of minorities is commonplace. More specifically, a legal system – which is often assumed to be the very embodiment of the pursuit and protection of justice – can be just or unjust to a greater or lesser degree. Legal systems that fall into disrepute are those that, for example, suspend *habeas corpus* or pervert the rules of evidence. Legal systems can be defective in other substantive ways, by failing to provide just and accessible remedies for civil wrongs, or by failing to develop an effective system of criminal justice. More specifically again, an unjust law is one that is perceived to perpetrate a formal or substantive injustice. For example, laws that are retrospective in their effect are widely regarded as unjust, because the subjects of the law are unable to decide whether or not to obey. In such cases, the form of the law is unjust. If there were a law, for example, preventing women from owning property, it would also be unjust in substance because there are no objective grounds for believing that they lack the ability to administer it.

The above threefold classification can be supplemented by Aristotle's pioneering analysis, which remains a classical point of reference for legal theory. Aristotle (384–322 BC) divided justice into the distributive and the corrective (or 'emendatory'), the latter being subdivided into voluntary private transactions and involuntary transactions, the second distinction turning on the presence or absence of violence towards the victim of the injustice. This classification corresponds roughly to the distinction between social justice, civil justice and criminal justice.

Justice and equality

In the context of distributive justice, the problem of how the equality and inequality of status and entitlements between individuals are to be understood is paramount. Each political interpretation of what is to count as a fair distribution – whether rewards should be based on, for example, personal ancestry, individual worth and desert, effort or needs – has different implications for conclusions about political equality.

In sharp contrast, with both kinds of corrective legal justice, civil and criminal, the ideal of universal equality before the law is assumed. While it may often be true that legal practice falls short of the ideal, this equality in status between individuals who may be unequal in social standing or personal resources is one consequence of the first principle of formal justice, that 'like cases should be treated alike'. The relevant 'likeness' in this phrase lies in the actions and situations involved, rather than the types of people. This is not a timeless principle of formal justice, to be found in practice wherever there is a legal system; it is an ideal towards which civilised legal systems can generally be seen to be moving. It is a principle symbolised by the scales held by the statue of justice over the Old Bailey. The scales symbolise the essential aim of corrective justice as the restoration of a balance or equilibrium that has been tilted or broken. The scales also signify that all individual interests are weighed equally, while the symbol of justice blindfold signifies that all legal judgements will be made impartially, without favour or discrimination.

The development of formal justice

This aspiration to complete legal impartiality is one essential feature of what is known as the rule of law. If the justice in all kinds of human transactions is to be measured effectively, those transactions have to be governed by rules that are applied with as much consistency as it is possible to achieve. What this requires is the formalisation, and hence the depersonalisation, of justice. While the primitive human instinct for justice (for fair treatment, revenge, compensation) is inclined towards a holistic assessment of the merits of competing parties, or of the character of aggressors and victims, the development of legal justice must take the opposite direction. Moral principles and standards have to be formalised into unbending rules that then apply to the act, rather than the actor.

This formal conception of legal justice appears to many to run against the grain. It sometimes feels like an abandonment of real justice, which should surely take account of the full context and circumstances of a legal dispute or crime. The point of it, however, is that in the history of any legal system a stage is reached at which the influence of power and wealth on the administration of law is resisted and neutralised. When judicial independence is established, the ideal of impartiality – itself a precondition of equality before the law – can be developed. The outcome of such conflicts is a strong legal presumption in favour of the courts adhering to strict general rules, without which equality of treatment of parties would not materialise, leading to an arbitrary system of *ad hoc* decisions that would be no legal system at all.

The main purpose of corrective justice, then, in seeking to restore the equilibrium by penalising civil wrongs or criminal actions in proportion to the wrong or harm done, is to deliver this justice within the limits imposed by patterns of law that have already been established. This is one of the meanings of the phrase 'justice according to law'. Judges, it is generally held – especially in the light of the doctrine of binding precedent – are not free to arrive at what they in their conscience or individual wisdom believe to be the best decision; on the contrary, they are constrained to find the just decision *within the law*.

Justice, equity and the spirit of the law

Aristotle, who was writing both about the ideas of law and justice as such, and also about the realities of justice in the highly evolved legal system of ancient Athens, recognised the problems created by this systematisation of justice. While the strict application of general rules furthers the cause of judicial impartiality, its inflexibility does little for the adaptation of justice to individual cases that do not fall easily under such rules.

To counter the danger of justice becoming over-severe, Aristotle introduced the concept of equity (*epieikeia*), which he regarded as a quality intimately connected with, but distinct from and more precise than, justice. The equitable approach in law, for Aristotle, is aimed at the prevention of the unfortunate consequences of applying a general rule to a particular case that it does not, at a deep moral level, really cover. The feeling might be that while it is right in general that rule X should be applied, it does not really apply to this particular case Y, despite the formal requirements being fulfilled. For Aristotle, then, the function of the appeal to equity was to allow judges to temper the severity of legal justice, without departing from the constraints of law.

It is the *idea* of equity as a quality integral to law, rather than its place in the history of legal doctrine and practice, which is significant to disputes in the philosophy of law. The chequered history of its evolution, through Roman law and English common law, as the defining purpose of a higher court presided over by the Roman *praetor* or English Lord Chancellor, rendering 'equitable relief' to the victims of harsh justice in the lower courts, cannot be recounted here. What is of particular importance in this history is the role of conscience. The rationale behind the Chancellor's judicial intervention was to annul specific decisions, the outcome of which was unconscionable, or contrary to conscience.

If the spirit of equity is captured by the idea of an *ad hoc* overruling of the unconscionable, what does an 'equitable solution' mean? Does it imply that the equitable judge – for the specific purpose of this one case – casts aside the law in favour of a morally preferable standard? Or can this individualisation of justice be found within the ambit of law? This will ultimately depend, of course, on how we are to understand the concept of law. Does it exclusively consist of the explicit rules of 'black-letter law' as posited by a valid legal authority, or should it be taken in a wider sense to include the notoriously vague but irrepressible idea of 'the spirit of the law'? Those who are tempted to endorse the latter without further ceremony should bear in mind the conceptual problems here. 'Spirit' can be identified either with the justice with which the law is expected to be infused, or with the spirit of equity, which is to say that it can be contrasted either with a system of law that is indifferent to the requirements of justice, or with a rule-obsessed conception of justice that produces a repressively literalistic legal system. These are clearly two quite different senses in which 'the spirit of the law' can be interpreted.

Natural law theory and legal positivism

Despite these and other conceptual difficulties, the belief that justice is integral to law has been the guiding light of natural law theory since its inception. Firmly rooted in ancient philosophy and having undergone several significant revivals in the twentieth century, the evidence suggests that, despite its prescientific character and lingering religious connotations, the theory of natural law is not likely to disappear. In contemporary legal theory, however, legal positivism – the antithesis to natural law – is still in the ascendancy. It is the heart of this dispute that we need first to identify clearly.

The heart of the dispute with legal positivism

The exact nature of the conflict between natural law theory and legal positivism has always been, and remains, very difficult to pin down. While it is agreed on all sides that the dispute revolves around the question identified already, whether the concept of law must include the concept of justice, there is no general agreement as to the meaning of this conceptual inclusion. What does it mean to claim that justice is integral to law? There are two initial mistakes to be avoided here. The first common misconception is the drawing of a sharp practical contrast between a natural lawyer's concern with justice and human rights, and a positivist's supposed disregard of such matters. A further dimension of this mistake is the belief that positivists insist on obedience to the law, irrespective of how unjust it might be. The second, equally common, mistake is the assumption that the dispute is a purely theoretical one, with ultimately nothing substantive at stake at all. The truth of the matter is that there are substantive differences that cannot be resolved in a simplistic argument about which side values justice more highly.

The important point to note is that, given certain assumptions, each perspective appears to be wholly convincing. The two outlooks represent radically different ways of thinking, not only about the law, but also about the full range of ethical problems experienced in any kind of society. At the heart of the matter lies a conflict in intuition about the origin or source of law. Each confronts the question, 'What is law?' and each answers it in terms of where law comes from. Consider first the positivist answer to this question.

The legal positivist finds at the basis of law *a human convention*, something decided or stipulated at a determinate time, by flesh-and-blood individuals, for a particular purpose, with a specific function in mind. Law thus interpreted is an agreement in the sense that it is an outcome of decisions, rather than the issue of something beyond human control. The makers of these laws are people in a position of power sufficient to impose their will on the whole community, and the rules and sanctions thus put into effect might be implemented with or without consultation or consent. Either way, this is how laws are made; individual and collective decisions are the origin of law, and what law is can be explained in terms of what has been decided and laid down as law. These decisions or stipulations are essentially free creations. The laws thus created might reflect any interest or none, they may be steeped in wisdom and justice, or they might be widely regarded as tyrannical. Such considerations are irrelevant at the stage of definition of law; the question as to how good or bad the laws are has no bearing on their status as laws. This is a 'conventionalist' view of law.

Consider now the natural law answer to the same question. 'What is law?' is again answered in terms of where it comes from. At the end of all analysis, the natural lawyer finds at the basis of law something beyond human control or arbitrary decision. It is something that binds human lawmakers quite irrespective of what any individual or group wishes or decides; it is a force we feel impressed upon us whether we like it or not. Law is the outcome, not of human agreement, but of first principles or natural foundations, the value of which runs deeper than the usefulness or expedience of conventions. This is a 'foundationalist' conception of law, according to which laws are discovered rather than made. The actual human makers of positive law are constrained by objective considerations relating to the intrinsic nature of the laws, considerations of justice that are external to the will of the legislators. If they ignore these constraints, they are not making law at all.

Although these are two incompatible answers to the same question, there is a certain discordance here, which suggests that the disagreement could be accounted for if it could be shown that they are in fact answering subtly different questions. While question and answer both follow the form of a definition, the first appears to be descriptive, the second stipulative. The first answer focuses on authority and the mechanisms of power, while the second focuses on authority and legitimacy. This might suggest that positivists are talking about the actual nature of the law, while natural lawyers are speaking of reasons for law being binding. This suggestion, however, leads to a serious misconstrual of the significance of the dispute; it implies that when the argument is clarified, the positivist and natural law approaches can be understood to complement one another, with the one concentrating on analysis of law as it actually exists, and the other addressing questions about the ideal standards to which law should aspire. This misses the heart of the dispute, because the leading exponents of each tradition are undoubtedly at odds over the definition of law as it actually exists. For natural lawyers, the legal principles revealed by a purely descriptive account of law are inherently moral; for positivists, the law in its actuality is the practical expression of a political decision, the moral content of which is quite irrelevant.

Traditional natural law theory

The main difficulty in forming a concrete assessment of the merits and contemporary relevance of natural law theory lies in the sheer magnitude of its historical scope. Why, then, is it relevant today? The main reason lies in the strength and enduring appeal of the idea that the law is there to be found, which implies that there are natural limitations on what can be enacted or enforced as positive law, and still properly be regarded as law. This idea has persisted through all natural law's permutations from its early origins in ancient Greece and Rome, through to the present day. It is expressed today in the not uncommon belief that legal officials, councils and governments cannot act in a way that is contrary to natural justice or reasonableness. The idea takes a stronger hold when it is realised that, when they do in fact act in such ways, it is within the power of judges of the higher courts to rule them illegal, or – for example, in the USA – unconstitutional. On the face of it, then, there do appear to be natural constraints upon lawmakers. Let us consider now the origins and development of this idea.

The seeds of the fully developed classical natural law theory, which flourished in medieval Europe under the influence of St Thomas Aquinas (1225–74), were already clearly visible in the ancient world, in particular in the philosophies of Aristotle and of Cicero (106–43 BC). The idea that all legislation and judicial decisions are constrained by natural limitations, which are discoverable by reason, found expression in their postulation of a timeless 'higher law' governing all human transactions. What we have to consider is what sense can be made of this higher law, a law that is said to have greater authority than the laws that happen to be posited as the laws of the land.

As we have seen in the context of the equitable modification of law in the interests of particularised justice, Aristotle affirms the higher authority of equity. In a famous passage in which he uses as illustration Antigone's defiance of the tyrant Creon's law that her dead brother shall remain unburied, Aristotle writes of the higher law as by definition one that does not change, in contrast to the decrees of positive law, which are constantly changing:

> If the written law tells against our case, clearly we must appeal to the universal law, and insist on its greater equity and justice.…We must urge that the principles of equity are permanent and changeless, and that the universal law does not change either, for it is the law of nature, whereas written laws often do change.
>
> (Aristotle 1924: 1.18.2)

The assumption here is that there is a permanent idea of law that continues through a succession of generations and civilised societies, and survives any given manifestation or distortion of it. The edict at issue (the king commanding the non-burial of a dead brother) was one that excited a sharply focused abhorrence; it was in a peculiarly literal sense an *unnatural* law. This is why Aristotle chose it to dramatise the manifest injustice – and illegality in the light of natural law – of positive laws that are not in conformity with the laws of nature. Creon is deemed to have broken one of the natural limits that constrain the kind of laws which can be passed. This does not mean that it is not within his power to use the law to enforce his will but it does mean that his apparently legal proclamation is devoid of legal as well as moral authority. What makes it legally void is the higher law of nature.

This Greek idea that the laying down of the law by a properly constituted authority is not sufficient to establish its legality was echoed and reinforced by Roman natural lawyers. For Cicero, law is the highest product of the rational human mind, in tune with the elemental forces of nature. The validity of human law depends upon its harmonising with these forces. It was this blending of the ideas of reason and law with *nature* that contrived to suggest that, while it was possible for rulers to ignore the constraints of natural law, such actions ran against the grain of the natural order of things in a way that was unholy and blasphemous. In Cicero's uncompromising words:

> law is the highest reason, implanted in Nature, which commands what ought to be done and forbids the opposite. True law is right reason in agreement with nature. To curtail this law is unholy, to amend it illicit, to repeal it impossible.

> (Cicero 1928: Book 1)

This natural law idea, which is primarily negative in the sense that its purpose is to invalidate extreme abuses of legal power, became more powerful in the hands of the Christian theologians, who were able to ground the authority of human law and natural reason ultimately in the will of the one true God. For St Augustine (354–430), referring to extreme abuses of power, 'an unjust law is no law at all'. In similar vein, Aquinas asserted that a deviation from the law of nature is 'no longer a law, but the perversion of law'. It is in this negative sense that justice is understood to be integral to law; when the connection between law and justice is broken, the law is held to be invalid.

It should not be imagined, though, that the only moral authority behind the Christian natural law perspective is the unconstrained will of God. The idea that God is free to decree anything, good or bad, was in fact the basis of the positivistic challenge to natural law theory by the rival theological tradition headed by William of Ockham (*c.* 1285–1349). For the natural lawyer Aquinas, as much as for modern secular thinkers, reason is central to natural law; the will of God is constrained by the independent essences of good and justice.

In contrast to this negative idea that lays down the limits to what may be validly legislated, the equally important feature of Christian natural law theory lies in the binding together of the virtues of positive lawmaking with the moral precepts of Christianity. The essential purpose of the law is to promote and protect justice and just transactions between people. It is in this positive sense also that the connection between law and justice is held to be a necessary, conceptual one. Laws that conform with nature are inherently just laws, because they embody moral principles and prohibit actions that are unjust in the sense that they are contrary to the enjoyment of natural human goods. Thus, for Aquinas, the highest moral precept, 'to do good and avoid evil', is the source from which all the primary and secondary precepts are derived. Secondary precepts such as norms governing fair trade or the exchange of contracts are derived from the more fundamental precepts relating to the natural value of self-preservation. In this way the entire body of positive law, enforcing sanctions against actions such as violent assault, theft and fraud, can be justified by reference to first principles that are self-evident to reason. In short, the meaning of law and the meaning of justice are completely interwoven.

Study questions

General question: What connections and overlaps are there between morality and the law?

Further study questions: Which sense of connection between morality and law is required for natural law theory? What does the separation thesis separate? What is the difference between the ideas of justice and equity? Are either of them indispensable to the concept of law? Is the spirit of the law more important than the letter of the law? What is the heart of the traditional dispute between natural law theory and positivism? Is the pursuit of justice an essential feature of law?

Suggestions for further reading

For a general historical treatment of traditional theories of law, see Kelly (1992) and Lloyd (1964). For histories of English common law, see Baker (1990), Fleming (1994) and Harding (1966).

On the relation between law and morality generally, see Lloyd (1964: ch. 3), Lyons (1984) and Fletcher (1996: III). For general introductions to the natural law–positivist dispute, see Rommen (1947), D'Entreves (1951), Golding (1975: ch. 2), Lyons (1984: ch. 3), Golding and Edmundson (2005: ch.1), and Harris (1997: ch. 2). For more advanced studies, see further reading in Chapter 4 below.

Aristotle's writings on justice and equity are mostly contained in the *Nicomachean Ethics* (1985) and *Politics* (1948). The relevant writings of Cicero on law and justice can be found in the first book of *De Legibus* (1928). For Aquinas on natural law, see Aquinas (1948) and (1988a) or (1988b).

A good general book on justice is Campbell (1988).

2 Early positivism and legal realism

Although it is useful to classify most of the serious contributions to modern legal theory under the broad headings of legal positivism, natural law and legal realism, two important reservations should be noted. First, they have changed in various ways in response to legal and political events. Second, there is a lack of consensus on how even some of the leading theories should be classified. We can nevertheless paint the broad picture in terms of these three types of theory. This will be the purpose of the present chapter.

The rise of positivism: the philosophical background

As a distinctively modern school of legal thought, positivism was not established until well into the nineteenth century, primarily through the writings of Jeremy Bentham (1748–1832), the founder of modern utilitarianism. Legal positivism has evolved as a school of thought in its own right, but there is little doubt that it owed its origins, in substance as well as name, to positivist thinking as a whole, which grew out of the seventeenth-century revolution in philosophy and scientific method. Although 'positivism' as a general term is notoriously vague, it can be said to signify a body of doctrines associated with the belief that human knowledge is confined within the limits of what can be observed and recorded.

Positivism is rooted in the empiricist interpretation of the scientific revolution. On this view, what cleared the way for discovery and a deeper understanding of the world was a systematic concentration on appearances as they are given or 'posited' by our experience. This was taken to be the starting point for any claims aspiring to the status of genuine knowledge, and it was the basis of the empiricism of Bacon and Locke in the seventeenth century.

As a particularly rigorous form of empiricism, positivism was one of several directions that the new philosophy could have taken. Traces of it had always existed within the empiricist reaction to rationalistic interpretations of the world. In retrospect, many distinct features of positivism can be seen in ancient Greek and Roman philosophy, and more clearly in the medieval philosophy of William of Ockham. The spirit of positivism as exemplified by these forerunners and by those of the early modern period is perhaps captured by Ockham's celebrated 'razor', a methodological principle according to which it is illegitimate, for the purposes of explanation, to appeal to entities not strictly required by the explanation. In all our investigations of the natural world, there must be a presumption against theories that postulate a complex of unseen entities when a more simple explanation is available. This was not merely a deliberate bias against the unobserved; simplicity and economy are themselves regarded as explanatory virtues. The positivist assumption is that the more simple and economic the explanation, the more likely it is to be true.

In the wake of the scientific revolution, the spirit of positivism was present to some extent in all the leading philosophers and scientists, even in those such as Descartes or Leibniz who seemed at the furthest remove from the empiricist interpretation. As a coherent philosophy, it took shape slowly under the long-term influence of scientific discovery and the eighteenth-century philosophy of rational enlightenment. While distinct elements of well-formed positivism can be detected as early as Hobbes's philosophy as a whole, and in Berkeley's philosophy of science, it was not until Hume's sceptical onslaught on the rationality of the principles assumed by modern science and philosophy that positivism became a real force in European philosophy.

What are the basics of the positivist approach in modern philosophy? The first feature, common to all versions, is the guiding principle that, in the search for knowledge and truth, the evidence of the senses is paramount. Second, the doctrine of phenomenalism, which first appeared in Berkeley, stipulates that we are not entitled to assume the existence of anything beyond the appearances. With sound scientific method, there should be no distinction between appearance and essential reality. Third, there is a strong tendency towards nominalism in most positivist philosophers. This rests on the principle that takes the referents of a general term to consist exclusively in concrete individual instances of that term. Underlying these three features, we always find – at least implicitly – the normative principle that, in the absence of empirical evidence to the contrary, the simplest explanation is to be preferred.

The overall purpose behind this positivist enterprise was the exclusion of every trace of speculative metaphysics from investigations of natural phenomena, the understanding of which depended on the discovery of natural causes that were in principle observable. What was resisted was reference to any underlying essence or principle that was in its nature unobservable. This much is perhaps an obvious implication of the main features of the positivist programme. What is probably less obvious is that the same programme also implied, from the outset, a radical change in attitude to questions of human value. If all reference to things other than concrete, observable particulars were to be eliminated from science, and science is the only form of knowledge, then moral and aesthetic judgements about such qualities as 'worthwhile', 'elegant', 'commendable', and so on have also to be removed from the realm of knowledge and truth. One of the enduring positivist assumptions is that the objects of such value judgements are not given in experience in the sense that they are separable from the bare factual existence of particular things, and are therefore inaccessible to scientific investigation. The full impact of this exclusion of value by the scientific revolution as interpreted by positivism was not felt until it was spelt out in detail by Hume.

Hume's influence

The exact nature of the influence of David Hume (1711–76) on European philosophy has always been controversial, but there is a hard core that is undisputed. Our concern here is limited to the themes that are relevant to legal theory, in particular the rise of positivism and the eclipse of natural law. Hume's fundamental purpose in his philosophical writing was twofold: to challenge the traditional framework of moral philosophy in such a way that morality and law would be humanised by becoming more relative to human interests; and to undermine the overblown pretensions to knowledge of the rationalist philosophers of the Enlightenment. In carrying out this purpose, Hume inadvertently did much to establish the conceptual framework within which the transformation of every discipline into a rigorous science would be undertaken.

Hume stipulated two conditions for speaking good sense on any subject. The first – which is known as 'Hume's Fork' – is that all investigations should be confined to the reporting of experimental observation on the one hand ('matters of fact') and the rational elucidation of 'relations between ideas' (logical connections) on the other. The second condition is that such matters of fact should be understood in complete independence from any subjective evaluation of the factual subject matter (the much quoted 'separation of fact and value'). Reasoning that moves from matters of fact to matters of value results in confusion and nonsense. This is the philosophical source of the separation thesis in jurisprudence.

To these two claims, Hume added a third essential point concerning the nature of this reasoning. Contrary to the suppositions of his predecessors, Hume argued that the faculty of human reason is perfectly inert and morally neutral: 'It is not contrary to reason to prefer the destruction of the entire world to the scratching of one's little finger' (Hume 1972: 2.3.3, p. 157). The idea here is that reason has no bearing on human interests one way or the other. When this idea is applied to the first two conditions, the Humean implications for the human sciences become clear. If reason is morally neutral, the rational investigation of any kind of human behaviour or institution will make no reference beyond what is either empirically observable or logically demonstrable. The two cannot be combined. Second, the investigation will have nothing to reveal about the moral content of its subject matter. The moral worthiness of any human activity is not in itself open to rational analysis. Approval or condemnation may be felt by a subjective moral sense, but this is no more than the projection of an inner feeling onto an external object. The implications of Hume's austere proposals, when drawn out, would transform the very idea of law.

Bentham's utilitarianism and his attack on the common law tradition

The beginning of the decline of natural law theory can be dated quite precisely from the time of Bentham's scathing attack on Blackstone's (1723–80) *Commentaries on the Laws of England*. With hindsight, this can be seen as the historical turning point, the successful launching of modern legal positivism. His attack on the common law tradition was based upon his utilitarian philosophy, according to which all actions and institutions (including legal systems and laws) are to be judged solely in terms of their utility. A specific law, for example, is good or bad to the extent that it produces on balance more happiness than unhappiness, which Bentham measured in terms of pleasure and the absence of pain. On this way of thinking, the role of reason changes. It cannot distinguish just from unjust dealings without reference to consequences in terms of human welfare. The role of reason is removed from its central place in natural law theory and reduced to that of rationally calculating the external consequences of actions and laws in terms of the aggregate good that will come out of them.

Bentham had many specific complaints about common law theory and its practice, which was closely tied to the traditional natural law theories. He regarded much of what happened in the English courts as 'dog-law': that is, as the practice of waiting for one's dog to do something wrong, then beating it. His low opinion of the doctrine and practice of judicial precedent was illustrated by his likening of the doctrine to a magic vessel from which red or white wine could be poured, according to taste. This 'double fountain effect', whereby the decisions of judges are seen as capricious selection of whichever precedent suits their prejudice, was regarded by Bentham as the inevitable outcome of a legal system that is not controlled by principles of utility.

Bentham's overriding passion for legal reform required the kind of clarification that would mercilessly expose the shortcomings, the corruption and obfuscation which he found in the common law as it existed at the turn of the nineteenth century. This clarity, Bentham believed, could only be achieved with a rigorous separation of law and morality. As we have seen, the exact meaning of this 'separation thesis' has become deeply controversial. What Bentham himself meant by it was reasonably clear. If the law was to be subjected to systematic criticism in the cause of reform, it was essential that its workings should first be described in accurate detail. This was a matter of dispassionate factual reporting of the nature and workings of law, which he termed 'expository' jurisprudence. What he found obstructing this project of clarification was the blurring of the boundary between legal reality and value judgement.

This was precisely what Bentham accused traditional legal writers of doing. Blackstone, as one of the most eminent of these writers, was singled out by Bentham as a prime example of one who clothed moral preaching in the language of law. When law is analysed in such a way that each law is represented as the embodiment of a Christian moral principle and a perfect expression of 'reason', the result is the kind of vagueness and indeterminacy that is inherently resistant to radical reform on the basis of the utility of the laws. When, by contrast, law is analysed according to Bentham's expository principles, the way is prepared for a clear-headed 'censorial' jurisprudence, subjecting the law to moral criticism, based on the principles of utility, principles that for Bentham were fundamental to legal reform.

Austin's positivism and command theory of law

A common mistake made by newcomers to jurisprudence is the assimilation of the command theory to legal positivism. In fact, while both are concerned with the elucidation of the nature of law, the positivist separation of fact and value does not necessarily result in a command theory. Furthermore, versions of the command theory were formulated over a hundred years earlier than the rise of positivism, in the early modern theories of political sovereignty put forward first by Jean Bodin (1530–96), and later by Thomas Hobbes (1588–1679). A second misconception is that the command theory as it was developed in the nineteenth century by the pioneers of legal positivism, Bentham and John Austin (1790–1859), was nothing more than an elaborate expression of a common-sense view of the essential nature of law. It was, and remains, a controversial attempt to capture the essence of law.

Austin was the first to give the command theory of law a comprehensive, typically modern treatment within the framework of a positivist rejection of natural law, based on systematic conceptual analysis. By comparison, Bentham's analysis of the command theory, upon which Austin built, had been no more than a primitive sketch. Whereas for Bentham, the elaboration of a systematic science of law was but one of his many projects for enlightening and reforming the outlook of the educated classes, for Austin it was a single-minded project aimed primarily at the legal profession. What he sought was a coherent theory that would lay the foundations for a comprehensive understanding of law as a discipline which would place it on an equal footing with the other nineteenth-century sciences.

The hard core of Austin's analysis consists in the drawing of strict demarcation lines to separate the authentic subject matter of legal science from that which should be regarded as irrelevant to such a science. What Austin aims at, by a process of eliminative classification, is the criterion by which the boundaries of positive law should be set, in order to identify what are strictly and properly speaking laws. To this effect, Austin surveyed the full range of what in common usage goes under the general term 'law'.

The first move here is to identify and eliminate those senses of law that are to be regarded as an improper or inappropriate use of the term. These fall under two headings, laws by analogy and laws by metaphor. What is distinctive is Austin's decisive rejection of grey areas of legality: a law is either a law properly speaking, or it is not. Widely accepted rules that are only vaguely or by analogy regarded as laws, such as the rules of a code of honour or of international law, have no part to play in the elucidation of the nature of law. These are laws, not as a matter of hard fact, but by virtue of mere opinion. Those which are laws only metaphorically speaking, by which he means the laws of animal or human instinct and the general laws of nature, are eliminated on the grounds that there is an absence of will to be incited or controlled. In the operation of such laws, there is a different kind of necessity at work, one that qualitatively differs from the compulsion involved in human legislation. What we are left with in the category of laws, properly speaking, are those which do control an active will, the laws of God and the laws of human decree, both of which have the character of being general commands.

Austin's second move, having eliminated improper uses of the term, is to narrow down further the subject matter by getting rid of usages that do not denote laws which are to be regarded, strictly speaking, as laws. Although it is proper to speak of the laws of God, they are not laws strictly speaking because they are general commands laying down the moral requirements of utility. Of the human commands that are properly speaking laws, the ones that do not strictly qualify are those that have neither legal authority nor legal backing; an order from master to servant or from parent to child does not count as law.

The outcome of Austin's analysis, then, is a definition of what is to count as proper and strict law. In its most literal meaning, law 'may be said to be a rule laid down for the guidance of an intelligent being by an intelligent being having power over him' (Austin 1995: 18). At the heart of the law, we find the reality of the power held by some individuals over others. What completes Austin's analysis of law is his identification of the source of this legal power as the sovereign individual or body that takes no orders from any other source.

According to the theory of sovereignty at which Austin arrives, the laws that are properly and strictly speaking laws are those commands which are issued by a political superior to whom the majority of people in the society are in the habit of obedience, and which is enforced by a threatened sanction. In short, Austin's view of law is one of orders backed by threats. The three most important aspects of his concept of sovereignty are those that later excited the most criticism: it involves habitual obedience by the mass of society to a determinate sovereign individual or body, which itself is in no habit of obedience to any higher authority, its power being unlimited.

The significance of Austin's analysis of law is not obvious at a superficial reading. When the implications are absorbed, it can be seen how serious a blow it dealt to the traditional natural law outlook. The neutralisation of the laws of God is not particularly important in this context. What is important is that the practical reality of law can be understood with greater clarity when its essential nature as a human command with a determinate source is abstracted from the idea of law as a natural force rooted in the community. It is generally agreed that this shift of emphasis, from the common law idea of the community as the source of law to the image of law as the imposition of power, caught the legal mood of the times. It was only at a much later stage in the development of positivism that the weaknesses in this account became fully apparent. Before we consider the criticisms, we need to turn to another important development at the end of the nineteenth century.

Pragmatism and legal realism

Legal realism was a movement of thought among lawyers and academics that originated in the US law schools in the 1890s. Although it was closer in spirit to positivism than to natural law, the new realist movement, which reached the height of its influence in the 1920s–1930s, offered a perspective that was reducible to neither tradition. It should be understood from the outset that there was no single outlook shared by all the realists, and that there was no conscious attempt to formulate a technically precise concept of law. What nevertheless informed most of their writings was a broad conception of legal theory and practice that scandalised existing legal opinion at the time. Despite the great variety of opinion among the realists, it is possible to identify the prominent themes that taken together represent a third point of view, a pragmatic conception of law that threatened to undermine the plausibility of orthodox legal positivism as much as the traditional natural law outlook.

Who were the realists?

The initiators of realism in law were Oliver Wendell Holmes Jr (1841–1935) and John Chipman Gray (1839–1915). As the name suggests, realism was guided by the perception that the legal theories and doctrines as they were taught did not reflect the reality of the law as it was practised in the courts. What Holmes – in his seminal article, 'The Path of the Law' (1897) – and Gray, in his influential lectures of 1908, were proposing was a radical revision of the basis of legal theory to bring it into line with the actual realities of the legal process. As dissatisfaction with orthodox theory grew over the following decades, numerous legal writers followed in this realist vein.

The two leading lights of the realist movement as a whole were Karl Llewellyn (1893–1962) and Jerome Frank (1889–1957). In 1931, a decade of turbulence in the legal profession culminated in a polemic between Llewellyn and an eminent critic of realism, Roscoe Pound (1870–1964). The stand taken by Llewellyn was fairly representative of the sceptical temper of the movement as a whole. Jerome Frank represented the more radical wing of realism. *Law and the Modern Mind* (1930) was a frontal assault on what he saw as a systematic web of illusion and self-deception in the profession about the nature of law. Although many others are worthy of note, one in particular stands out. 'The Judgement Intuitive' (1929), written by a senior judge, Joseph Hutcheson, was an especially influential account of the realities of judicial reasoning. This was squarely within the realist movement, emphasising the widening gap between theory and practice.

Legal theory and judicial practice

One popular misconception is the belief that realists were hostile to legal theory, that they attempted to shift the focus of legal studies from theory to the practical realities of the courtroom and the history of case law. There is very little truth in this assumption. Even the most radical of the serious realists were interested, not in overthrowing theory, but in transforming it from a fixed body of dogmatic doctrines, rooted in tradition, into a more useful and dynamic approach to real legal problems in a time of rapid social and legal change in the USA.

The origin of this misconception was that the realist theory was indeed court-centred, and was more concerned with what the contemporary judges actually said and did than in what the textbooks told them they ought to say and do. What they were arguing here, however, was that the actual reasoning and practical justice handed down by real judges were the appropriate starting point for theory, rather than the *a priori* deduction of the meaning of law. This practical orientation in jurisprudence is analogous to the argument in the philosophy of science that theoretical speculation on the nature or spirit of the scientific enterprise should be grounded in the actual practice of working scientists.

The implications of the realist focus on actual legal cases went further than a reminder that theory should keep both feet on the ground. What it also implied, in different ways, was an understanding of the nature of law that was quite foreign to traditional ways of thinking. For John Chipman Gray, for instance, the decisions of judges and nothing else constitute the law. All else – the rules and principles of common law, the enacted statutes, the maxims of morality and equity, the dictates of custom, even the body of judicial precedent – is relegated to the status of *sources* of law, sources upon which the judges laying down the law can draw. For Gray, this was a strictly realistic assessment of the actual situation throughout legal history. Behind the rhetoric of a higher law, the will of the community or the command of the sovereign, what actually counts as law is the ruling of the judge, because this is what will be enforced. Gray's distinction between the nature and sources of law may seem arbitrary and implausible; it is difficult to accept the claim that a legal statute is not actually a part of the law until it has been tested in the courts. He did, however, make a persuasive case for his contention that much of the confusion in legal thinking stems from its failure to observe the distinction between actual law and its sources.

An even more spartan conception of law was suggested by Holmes's famous maxim that 'the prophecies of what the judges will do in fact, and nothing more pretentious, are what I mean by the law' (Adams 1992: 92). If this is taken literally, it means that for all practical purposes the law on any given issue actually consists only in the best predictions that well-informed lawyers can make about the way in which a case will be decided. It does not even extend to the decisions themselves, which in turn become no more than the basis for future predictions.

Neither of these pronouncements became dogma for the subsequent realist movement, but the hard-headed, unpretentious approach to legal analysis that they embodied did become the guiding spirit of the realism expounded by Llewellyn, Frank and many others. Holmes and Gray were both motivated by a desire to deflate what they saw as a persistent idealisation of law, the inevitable consequence of removing it from its actual practice. Many years later, Llewellyn's realist programme made central the need to recognise the fluidity of law and society, and therefore the futility of trusting established theoretical doctrines and fixed-rule formations. In place of such reverence for the past, Llewellyn proposed a shift of emphasis to the actual effects of judicial decisions.

The attack on certainty

The main feature of legal realism that can be traced directly to the influence of philosophical pragmatism is its frontal assault on what Frank termed 'the basic myth of certainty and fixity' in the law (Frank 1949: ch. 1). The first principle of the pragmatism launched by C.S. Peirce (1839–1914) was the recognition as illusory 'the quest for certainty' bequeathed by the rationalist Descartes and the classical empiricists from the early modern period. According to the dominant strain of thinking in the late nineteenth century, natural science was a raging success story, a steadily expanding accumulation of fully established unrevisable truths. Even for those who were more reflective about the foundations of this supposedly unrevisable knowledge, certainty as an ideal was largely unquestioned. The main philosophical question was how to place the sciences on a sound footing, or how certainty was to be attained. The Peircean rejection of certainty as the guiding ideal of science, a rejection that was soon to be vindicated by the upheaval and crisis in the mainstream sciences, was echoed by the legal realists. From Holmes to Frank, the reaction against the pursuit of the ideal of law as a certain science, requiring systematic rigour that would leave no room for error or indeterminacy, was the central feature of American legal realism.

The pragmatist attempt to remove certainty from epistemology was antifoundational. The range of issues this challenge raises is still nowhere near resolution, but the point to note here is that the denial of the need for certain foundations allows knowledge to be provisional. Traditionally it has been held that the first condition of knowledge is that what is believed must be true. Without truth, there is no knowledge. If a belief turns out to be false, then what was thought to be known was not known at all. This seems self-evident. And what also seemed self-evident was that for knowledge to be knowledge, the possibility of error must be ruled out: hence the importance of the quest for certainty.

What Peirce and later pragmatists were arguing for was the initially counterintuitive claim that knowledge does not require the elimination of every possibility of error. What we 'know' now may later turn out to have been mistaken, but this does not mean that we do not know it now. For many philosophers such reflections lead straight into scepticism, the denial that any of our claims to knowledge are sound. For the pragmatists, and others influenced by them, it leads to a far-reaching revision of our understanding of the character of knowledge and, notoriously, a redefinition of truth. For Peirce, the true opinion is the one destined to be believed by an ideal community of future scientists. For William James, the true opinion is the one that it is to our best advantage to believe. Although neither of these pragmatic concepts of truth, which seem too radical a departure from conventional usage, have gathered much of a following, the pragmatist rejection of certainty is nevertheless widely endorsed by the entire movement of anti-foundationalism in epistemology.

The movement against certainty in legal theory runs along parallel lines. Legal absolutism in the 1890s was as unconvincing to radical thinkers as the uncritical scientific positivism of this period was to philosophers who saw the weakness of its foundations. Holmes regarded the almost universal belief that the law could be determined and applied with scientific precision as explicable only in terms of 'the longing for certainty and repose', a natural impulse found in every area of thought. All his writing was directed at breaking down this illusion and its damaging consequences. The illusion of certainty that he and subsequent realists assailed was the comforting official belief that 'the law' was a fully formed pre-existing reality, a coherent body of rules ready to be applied by judges trained and sufficiently skilled in syllogistic reason to deduce the correct answer to any legal problem with complete certainty. For Holmes, the law thus understood became an imaginary 'brooding omnipresence in the sky', a reified power that guaranteed a spurious certainty and determinacy. The hard reality of law was in truth inherently indeterminate and uncertain, a more gritty affair involving the unpredictable balance of principles, policies and unspoken assumptions.

Jerome Frank's attack on the basic myth of certainty was more polemical and uncompromising. In Frank's writing, it becomes forthright and explicit that legal certainty is as undesirable as it is unattainable. Its absence is no cause for regret, but the pretence that law can be made fixed and unwavering was so pervasive that it stifled any understanding of the real nature of law. What Frank and many of his contemporaries were struck by was not merely the gap between theory and practice, but what he depicted as an astonishing self-deception at large in the interpretation of law as a fixed body of determinate rules, when it was plain for all to see that the opposite was the case, with rules adapted, changed and invented every day throughout the numerous jurisdictions of the USA. Although these were all rooted in common law, there was no denying that any particular decision was highly unpredictable.

Why was the belief in certainty so strong? Whereas, for Holmes, this contradiction required no more explanation than that the craving for certainty was a natural impulse, Frank sought the answer in Freudian psychoanalytic terms, in the unconscious yearning for the lost security of childhood, provided by the omniscient father figure. Frank believed that this almost universal creation of a chimerical certainty infected every aspect of legal theory in particular, because the law with its judges and judgements was peculiarly qualified to stand in for the father figure. Belief in 'the law' as a fundamental certainty fulfils a vital psychological need. The realist attack on this belief was inspired by the desire to uncover the reality of the workings of law that had been obscured by the myth of certainty.

The realist revolt against formalism

The pragmatist-inspired rejection of the ideal of certainty in law goes hand in hand with the hostility to the legal formalism that, in the perception of the leading realists, lay at the heart of modern legal analysis. 'Formalism' is a term with several distinct meanings and connotations in philosophy, mathematics and legal theory. What is relevant here is the realist interpretation of legal formalism as a tendency that has a damaging effect on both our understanding of law and the practical administration of justice.

Essentially, legal formalism is held to be a preoccupation with the outward forms of the law as it is written, at the expense of the inner content or substance of the law. This exaggerated emphasis on the formal was expressed by realists in a number of ways. The central point is that law is interpreted as a formally closed system, governed by strict rules of inference and demonstrative proof. This has two main implications: (1) as the narrowing down of legal reasoning to the form of the deductive syllogism, a formalistic approach is one that is guided by the belief that all legal problems can be resolved by framing them in syllogistic form, whereby major and minor premises yield a demonstrable conclusion; and (2) law is closed off to outside influences, so that its interpretation becomes a purely internal matter, to which other social factors are irrelevant.

The essential criticism is that the formalist approach makes the mistaken assumption that the law can be completely understood by studying and applying deductive formal logic. With syllogistic reason placed at the centre of law as a formally closed system, it becomes possible to resolve every problem in such a way that leaves no room for doubt. Holmes described this as the 'fallacy of logical form', the error in which lay in the refusal to recognise the non-logical forces at work in the determination of the content and growth of the law. The structure of the legal syllogism is such that the truth of the conclusion does not depend to any degree on the substantial content of any of the premises.

What follows from this essential criticism is a general picture of the formalist approach as 'a mechanical jurisprudence', according to which all problems of interpretation can be definitively resolved by meticulous attention to logical detail. It is mechanical because a calculating machine could do it: one could feed the question in at one end, and wait for the answer at the other. The chief danger, as Holmes saw it, lay in the modelling of the system of law on mathematics, imagining that the whole system can be deduced from general axioms, so that a judicial mistake can be seen as 'not doing one's sums right'. What this obsession with certainty leads to is a strong tendency towards literalism, focusing on the letter at the expense of the spirit of the law. It leads to a tendency to follow rules for their own sake; the natural consequence of this is the elimination of equity in the assessment of individual cases. The peculiar features of each unique case are to be found in the substantiality of the concrete circumstances of the case, not in the formal rules that can be made to fit the case. A mechanical jurisprudence – so the realist argument runs – trains the legal mind to abstract from these circumstances, to find the applicable rule that will provide the correct answer.

What were the realists urging against or in place of this formal mechanisation of jurisprudence? What would a non-formal, unmechanised jurisprudence look like? For Holmes, 'the root and nerve of the whole proceeding' is the judgement – often inarticulate and unconscious – that lies behind the logical form. What he is referring to here is not the judicial pronouncement on a case, but the individual act of judgement that precedes it, the judgement of the relative worth of competing claims, a judgement that comes before its rationalisation in logical form. What Holmes was arguing was that the real factors influencing these prelogical judgements – in particular, matters of social policy – are nearly always camouflaged by syllogistic reason. Holmes's 'realism' consists in his advocacy of making conscious and explicit what was damagingly left half-conscious and concealed by the logical rationalisations surrounding these judgements. It was the nature of this judgement, then, and the influences forming it, which needed to be brought into the light as the basis of a realist jurisprudence.

Realists of the later phase of the movement broadened the scope of these 'real factors' enormously, and focused on the nature of this judgement. Jerome Frank's provocative itemisation of the types of conscious and unconscious personal preference and prejudice at work in the judicial proceedings, attempting to explode the myth of judicial impartiality and objectivity, was seen by traditionalists as an attack on the integrity of the profession. Behind this polemic, however, was a serious and sustained assault on formalism.

This was nowhere more visible than in the realists' scrutiny of the manner in which judges formed their judgements and arrived at their conclusions. Joseph Hutcheson's account of 'the judgement intuitive' literally reversed the established assumptions about this thought process. Hutcheson confronted the security of the legal formalist mind, and its systematic application of general rules to yield a certain result, with the real human mind of the judge, in which the prominence of the faculty of imagination allows the natural process of *backward* reasoning to be given full rein.

In sharp contrast to the formalist belief that judges move carefully forward from premises to conclusion, reaching their judgement through a painstaking rational process, Hutcheson paints a vivid picture of the judge assembling all the relevant data and 'brooding over chaos', waiting for 'the flash of understanding which makes the jump-spark connection between question and decision' (Adams 1992: 201). The phrase of Hutcheson's that was to become highly influential was the idea of 'the hunching out' of a solution. What he maintained was that the inspired hunch, the flash of understanding, lay at the very heart of the process of discovery, and that it was precisely the role of this hunch which was suppressed by formalistic reason. On this account, the judgement is reached first, the rationalisation follows; the public or official reasoning of the judge is an elaborate justification of the decision already reached by other means. It is essential to note that Hutcheson's analysis was not intended as an attack on the judiciary, of which he himself was an eminent member. This intuitive process of reaching judgements he regarded as the link between the 'great judges' – those with most insight into legal problems – and the great discovering scientists such as Kepler and Galileo. What he was criticising was the failure, under the influence of a formalistic training, to use the intellect in this way.

This aspect of the attack on formalism and mechanism in law was taken up with alacrity by Jerome Frank. Reinforcing Hutcheson's assessment of the nature of creative legal reasoning, he argued that it was more important for lawyers to catch the creative scientific spirit than to imitate scientific logic. He insisted that the judgement in a court of law was no different in principle from judgements in any other context; that what it essentially involved was the working backwards from a vaguely formed conclusion to find the premises to substantiate it, the search continuing until the right conclusion is found. Referring to this feature of judicial reason as 'conclusion-dominance', he maintained that what was clearly evident in the practice of a lawyer-advocate, who is openly partisan for a conclusion favouring his or her client, was less evident but equally operative in the case of the 'impartial' judge. The fault, for Frank, lies not in the backward reasoning of the judge, but in the concealment of this reality by the myth of certainty and the pretence that the conclusion is the outcome of formal reason. What he advocates is a shift in focus from the study of legal logic to the study of the explicit and unconscious factors – political, social, economic and personal – which have the real influence on the judge's selection of the conclusion.

Realism and rule-scepticism

The rule-scepticism to which numerous realists in the 1920s and 1930s subscribed has been misrepresented and distorted more than any other feature of legal realism. Treated by many as a fantasy that flies in the face of the facts about the doctrine of precedent, dismissed by others as an eccentric exaggeration of the idiosyncrasies of unconventional judges, the genuine insights of the realist rule-scepticism have more recently been acknowledged once again.

The initial reaction to rule-scepticism, though, was hardly surprising. The sceptical attitude to the status and role of legal rules in the judicial process was the most significant and potentially damaging of the realist criticisms of traditional formalism and mechanical jurisprudence. Rule-scepticism, emerging from the attack on legal certainty, threatened not only to bring down the entire edifice of legal theory, but also to undermine the credibility of the law as an institution, a basic premise of both theory and practice being the idea of law as a coherent set of authoritative rules governing human transactions. What we need to be clear about, then, is what exactly this scepticism amounted to. Did it really threaten to undermine the law? Or was it proposing a viable alternative to law as understood and practised?

What does it mean to be *sceptical* about legal rules? The first question concerns the ontological status of rules. In what sense, if any, can legal rules be said to exist? Such questions have caused much confusion, because if scepticism means the doubting of the very existence of the rules – an attitude attributed to the supposedly extreme realists and dubbed 'rule-nihilism' – we have to ask whether such a claim even makes sense. The contents of statute book and case law are nothing but rules; the question of whether they are ignored or selectively applied is another matter. To say, for example, that there are no rules on inheritance or the validity of contracts would be manifestly absurd. Moreover, as H.L.A. Hart later pointed out, the very existence of the court of law presupposes the existence of secondary rules conferring legitimacy on the court (Hart 1961: 133).

Rule-nihilism, then, is easy to refute; however, it is doubtful that any of the realists seriously took this attitude. Frank explicitly repudiated such literal nihilism, arguing that this was the product of the formalist critics' inability to see any other alternative to their own absolutism. With this false alternative, either rules operate without exception, or there are no rules at all. As we shall see, the realist exposure of the mythical status of legal rules does not entail this nihilism. The basic argument is not that rules do not exist, but that rules are not what they appear to be.

Curiously, there is a hint – but no more than a hint – of ontological nihilism in Llewellyn's famous distinction between the paper rules officially adhered to and the real rules followed by the courts. That is to say, Llewellyn's rule-scepticism did amount to the claim that the ostensible rules – as mere paper, mere words – have no real existence or force. Even this, however, does not lead to the absurdity of denying that there are any actual rules prohibiting theft, or governing contracts or inheritance.

The second question concerns the *role* of legal rules. Given their real existence, what part do they play in the administration of law? Does the activity of judges consist in the simple application of the relevant rules to the case in hand, or do the rules play a more subordinate role than this? In answering these questions, we need to draw a contrast between a minimum and a maximum rule-sceptic thesis.

The minimum thesis is that judges do in reality – irrespective of official doctrine – have at least some discretion in at least some areas of law, to make decisions without reference to pre-existing rules. In so doing, the judges themselves make new rules. Advocates of this thesis believe that complete codification and predictability are neither possible nor desirable. What is desirable in some areas of law is flexibility and adjustment to circumstance. This is minimal rule–scepticism in the sense that it is sceptical of complete codification, and it is a very limited critique of formalism.

The maximum thesis is that judges do in reality – irrespective of official doctrine – have full discretion, in every area of law, to make decisions without reference to pre-existing rules. In so doing, the judges are not making new rules; they are merely deciding one unique case. Advocates of this thesis believe that the existence of rules exercises virtually no practical constraint on judicial decisions. The elaborate legal doctrine of precedent, of the binding nature of authoritative judicial decisions, is a pretence that conceals the truth of free creativity. This is uninhibited rule-scepticism, which constitutes a complete rejection of formalism.

Two preliminary points about these theses should be noted. The first is that the minimum thesis is only minimally sceptical of the prominent role played by rules. Its supporters include not only proto-realists like John Chipman Gray, but also those who were at most on the periphery of the realist movement, such as Pound and Cardozo, and positivists in the mould of H.L.A. Hart. Essentially, what it involves is no more than a cautious rejection of the extremes of formalism and mechanical jurisprudence. This is what it means to allow that there exists and should exist a certain amount of judicial discretion. Second, the maximum thesis should not be confused – as it so very often has been – with ontological nihilism, the view that legal rules are a complete mirage. The rules are there for all to see; however, advocates of the maximum thesis regard them as little more than a front or façade, the purpose of which is to cover the tracks of judicial innovation. The versions of rule-scepticism promoted by most of the realists lay somewhere between these two positions. Between the minimum and the maximum thesis, then, we need to formulate a moderate rule-sceptic thesis.

According to the moderate thesis, the role of rules in every area of law is radically suspect. Sometimes the rules are fully operative; sometimes they are not. All decisions, although not haphazard, are inherently unpredictable. The theory and practice of applying general rules, of using these rules to reason to a conclusion, and in so doing following precedent, do have some force, but not as great as imagined by formalist theory. In reality, judges at every level are able to select or disregard precedent to suit the conclusion already arrived at. On the moderate thesis, the idea that they are helplessly bound by the rules is indeed a myth.

It was in the spirit of this moderate thesis that Llewellyn drafted a list of what he regarded as the shared points of departure of twenty of the leading realists in the early 1930s. These included tendencies towards '*distrust* of traditional legal rules and concepts which purport to describe what courts or people are actually doing', and – crucially – towards 'distrust of the theory that traditional rule-formulations are THE operative factor in producing court decisions' (Twining 1973: 79–80). It was the limited extent and the uneven application of the rules that Llewellyn was highlighting. Rule-formulations were regarded as merely one operative factor among others, which may or may not be applied in any given instance. What he and others were resisting with this emphasis on distrust was the assumption that rules were necessarily, or by definition, the decisive factor influencing judicial decisions. The adoption of this moderate position, then, did not mean that all rules were to be regarded as bogus; what it meant was that a critical scepticism towards their actual authority should be maintained.

Frank acknowledged the realist direction of those who advocated the minimum thesis, but criticised their half-heartedness in this respect, arguing that they were still caught in the spell of the myth of certainty, and urging them to adopt a more thoroughgoing scepticism. His own position as a rule-sceptic was more ambiguous, seeming to oscillate between the moderate and the maximum thesis, between Llewellyn's critical scepticism and an outright denial of the efficacy of rules. Much of his writing is in the spirit of the latter, of uninhibited rule-scepticism, according to which rules are no more than aids for testing conclusions already reached, influences towards wise or unwise decisions, formal clothes in which to dress these decisions. In short, 'rules' of law are in truth guidelines rather than rules.

What is crucial here is Frank's understanding of the *status* of rules. He sees every rule as a formalised description of the past, as a useful abbreviated general description of the way previous courts have reacted and decided various cases. On his account, rules are not *established* by precedent, they are themselves merely compressed accounts of precedent in the abstract. They are informative of law, not constitutive of it. The determination of any actual concrete case adds another notch of authority to the traditional legal thinking on any given subject, but it is itself a part of the creative tradition. Every judge can either ignore this and fall against the tradition, thus reinforcing the formalist approach, or recognise it and contribute constructively to the continuing vitality of the tradition.

The pragmatics of justice

While it would certainly be an exaggeration to say that the realists were concerned entirely with the individualisation of justice, it is also true that their guiding purpose in opposing the formalist approach was the development of a perspective that would assist, rather than hinder, the ability of judges to arrive at just solutions to difficult cases. Behind this purpose lay the conviction that the attempt to operate the law as a closed logical system had a stultifying effect on the very idea of legal justice.

The formalist approach to justice was traditionally justified by the need to discover and maintain rules and principles that could be applied impersonally, without fear or favour, on the basis of the principle of equality before the law, that 'like cases should be treated alike'. The subjection of all to the rule of law, and the reluctance to make any exceptions, were believed – not unreasonably – to be indispensable to the development of a just legal system. This was felt to express the inner meaning of justice, that the same rules be applied to everyone. In short, justice is best provided by a 'government of laws, not men'.

It was against this picture of formalised justice that the realist rule-scepticism reacted. The realists had a pragmatic attitude to justice in as far as they regarded this picture as an unattainable idealisation of law. In the real life of the law, there is no certainty, no guarantee that the legal process will deliver just solutions to every problem. This absence of certainty is due, not primarily to the human fallibility of judges and juries, but to the fact that any real legal system will always contain indeterminacies. What the realists were trying to expose and dissolve was the illusion that a sophisticated modern legal system, perfectly formalised and idealised, is the perfect vehicle for legal justice.

What Frank saw in this was the elimination of the human factor, specifically the marginalisation of the spirit of equity. If justice is to be real, it has to be individualised to the circumstances of each concrete case. As we saw earlier, the idea of equity as the necessary correction to justice administered too literally originates in Aristotle. Frank argued that the tradition emanating from Aristotle's account of equity distorts it by removing it from the ambit of law, by representing it as an unfortunate necessity disrupting the regular procedure of law, in the interests of a wider sense of justice than is allowed by law. Frank's challenge to this interpretation, which has been very influential, reverses its assumptions. The spirit of equity, he argues, is not an expedient to be wheeled in for the odd occasion, it is inseparable from the rest of what we call law. Furthermore, as the superior aspect of justice, it is found at the very heart of the law (which, for Frank, it should be remembered, is what actually happens in its main arena, the courts) because 'as against Aristotle and Pound it would be wiser to go to the other extreme and to say that the law is at its best when the judges are wisely and consciously exercising their discretion, their power to individualise cases' (Frank 1949: 141).

With the abandonment of the quest for certainty, the problem of the objectivity of justice also diminishes. Hutcheson's model judge, the realist waiting for the flash of inspiration and 'hunching out' solutions intuitively, rather than applying the deductive syllogism, has 'a roving commission to find the just solution' (Adams 1992: 203). In contrast to the lawyers, who are partisan for their clients, the judge is partisan for justice. This is what Hutcheson argues against those who see the model judge as the one who dispassionately applies the rules to find the correct decision. The justice of the pragmatic decision is relative to the moral judgement of a real individual, who depends primarily on understanding and experience, using formal reason only to check and reinforce the decision. The justice rendered by the strict application of pre-existing rules is an abstract justice that makes no real contact with the interests of the competing parties in the legal dispute.

A final point about the pragmatic nature of justice concerns the opening up of the deliberations of the judge to outside influence. The idea that the intrusion of non-logical, extra-legal considerations of social policy should be made explicit and legitimate, for the sake of the continuing vitality of the law and its interaction with a changing society, was first made forcefully by Holmes. This idea has influenced the whole of modern jurisprudence, not just the legal realists. Its general character is essentially forward-looking. For the realists it meant an instrumentalist focus on probable outcomes of legal rulings, rather than a retrospectivist reverence for past decisions. What they were advocating was a future-directed honesty about the social objectives of the judiciary, reflecting contemporary views of morality and justice in a changing world.

Conclusion

The crucial feature in the history of the idea of law between Aristotle and the early twentieth century was the transition from the concept of law as an embodiment of justice to the distinctly modern idea of law as morally neutral fact. This was a transition from a philosophy for which the role of natural reason was central, to a positivist philosophy of law as descriptive science, for which the dictates of reason were quite incidental to the subject matter of this science. The eternal ideals of the higher law were giving way to an understanding of law as human-made expressions of entirely earthly powers.

It is easy to see why the hard-headed factual approach of Bentham and Austin rang true in an age of scientific materialism. Austin's concept of law as a structure of commands appealed to the nineteenth-century scholars and lawyers who were looking for the truth behind the idealised rhetoric of natural justice. From a secular point of view, natural law looked increasingly like a relic from more spiritual societies. Many of the features of this positivism were adapted and developed by the early American realists. Holmes especially – with his 'cynical acid' stripping the legal reality down to its bare mechanisms – did much to impress the spirit of positivism upon American legal theory. At the same time, however, there was an anti-formalist strain in realism from Holmes to Frank, which worked against positivism and created the space for a distinctive and new approach to law that was freed from the grip of both the traditional theories.

Study questions

General question: Were the early positivists successful in exposing the weaknesses of natural law theory and common law thinking?

Further study questions: What were the essential features of Austin's legal positivism? Explain Hume's influence on the separation thesis. How might one defend natural law theory against positivism? To what extent was the new legal realist movement merely an American version of legal positivism? Explain and critically examine the realist revolt against legal formalism. Which version of rule-scepticism, if any, do you find the most convincing? How might one defend natural law theory against legal realism? All things considered, how realistic was American legal realism?

Suggestions for further reading

On Hume and positivism in philosophy generally, see Kolakowski (1968). For Hume and the fact–value separation, you should read Hume (1972: 3.1.1). A good concise commentary on Hume is found in Woolhouse (1988: ch. 8). On Bentham's legal positivism, the main text is Bentham (1970). For commentaries, read Hart's essay in Summers (1971) or Hart (1982) and (1983: ch. 2). Dinwiddy (1989: ch. 4) and Postema (1986) are also useful. Austin's primary text is Austin (1995). There are useful commentaries in Harris (1997: ch. 3) and Riddall (1991: ch. 2). For a more advanced comment on Bentham and Austin, see Cotterell (1989: ch. 3).

Full studies of American legal realism include Rumble (1968) and Twining (1973). The essential primary source to read is Holmes (1897). Other important sources are Gray (1921), Frank (1949) and Llewellyn (1930). Novick (1989) is an interesting biography of Holmes. Important commentaries include Golding and Edmundson (2005: ch. 3), Friedmann (1944: ch. 25), Dias (1985: ch. 21) and Cotterell (1989: ch. 7). Hart (1961: 132–44) is a significant analysis of rule-scepticism. For a useful collection of American pragmatist writings, see Thayer (1982).

3   Modern positivism and its critics

It is probably no exaggeration to say that virtually all of the problems and disputes in contemporary jurisprudence and philosophy of law – even at their most technical – either concern or can be traced back to the perennial attempts to clarify the conceptual relation between morality and the law. As we have seen, this is no easy matter, not least because there has never been general agreement on the scope of either morality or law. Contemporary responses to the 'What is law?' question, then, revolve around an examination of the senses in which concepts such as those of 'legality', 'legal validity' or 'legal system' must include or exclude considerations of moral content, moral validity or moral evaluation.

It is also the meaning of this inclusion and exclusion that is at issue. The claim that legal analysis can and must be undertaken without reference to moral concepts (content, validity, justification, justice, rights) can mean either (1) that a temporary separation 'for the purposes of study' (as urged by Llewellyn) is desirable for a truer vision of law; or (2) that the separation represents a distinction within the object of study itself, suggesting a world of hard, objective legal facts, on the one hand, and a world of legal possibilities, ideals to which all laws and legal systems should conform, on the other. On the first interpretation, the 'exclusion' of moral issues from jurisprudence is an intellectual abstraction that allows that the undivided reality of law is still out there. On the second interpretation, the 'exclusion' is more than theoretical; the law itself, the object of legal science, is interpreted as being divided into separate zones of pure fact and pure value. Either way, we arrive at the familiar distinction between descriptive and normative jurisprudence, but the distance between these two interpretations of the distinction is of the utmost importance.

The meaning of the separation thesis is one of the main points at issue in the development of contemporary theory, and in the debates between the followers of Kelsen, Hart, Fuller and Dworkin. Even when the law–morality question does not arise directly, the dispute is traceable back to it. When, for example, one legal philosopher after another presses for a more accurate factual description of a specific legal system, a stand one way or the other has already been taken on the law–morality question.

Legal validity

Although a great part of contemporary theory has focused on the question of the authentic source of legal validity, there has been a sometimes bewildering lack of consensus on what exactly the claim to legal validity involves. It is not the wide range of reference that is in doubt. The term 'legally valid' (or 'invalid') can be applied to a legal system as a whole, to a particular putative rule of law, a document such as a will or a contract, an official action such as a judicial direction or order, or the implementation of a punitive sanction. It is quite appropriate to speak of any of these in terms of validity and invalidity.

The problem arises when we ask exactly what is meant by the ascription of legal validity to any of these things. Initial attempts to elucidate tend to run into circularity or regress. A will or a contract is valid if it satisfies certain specified formal conditions; however, these in turn have been stipulated by a valid authority. Similarly, a valid sanction is one that is allowed or required by law, as laid down by a valid authority. A valid rule of law is one authorised by another rule. One general implication is that valid rules or actions cannot be legally challenged; this is what it means to be legally valid, which is to say that they are *binding*. But what exactly does this mean? Does it mean that there is an obligation to comply with it? Within the context of law, it would certainly seem so. No legal official is free to make an independent moral assessment of a legally valid order or to ignore a legally valid document, any more than a citizen is free to break any laws he or she disapproves of or finds inconvenient. In a wider context, the obligation is by no means clear. One is legally bound to obey a valid law, but is there any moral obligation? Is the claim that a law is valid equivalent to the claim that it is morally valid or justified?

The Nazi legality problem

The problem of disentangling formal validity from moral obligation came under close scrutiny after 1945, with the defeat of Germany and the dismantling of the Nazi state. There were a number of closely linked issues here. First, there was the question of the legal authority of the new courts established at Nuremberg for the purpose of war crime trials. Second, there was the question of how to regard the status of the Nazi legal system and its statutes and orders between 1933 and 1945. Third, there was the question of how the new West German Federal Constitution (1949) provided the authority for retrospective judgement of individuals whose actions had been legal under the authority of the previous regime. Each of these questions raises problems for theories of legal validity and for the morality–law separation thesis.

It is well known that the most prominent defence at the Nuremberg trials for war crimes and crimes against humanity was that the defendants were doing their duty in carrying out orders validly issued by their superiors in accordance with existing law. Although in reality the reasons for rejecting the legitimacy of this defence may well have been pragmatic, the explicit reasoning by the Nuremberg judges was complex. The essential point is that, although there was no explicit reference to the higher law of natural law theory, the authority of standards of conscience independent of existing positive law at the time was indispensable. This, it seemed, was the only way in which the 'following orders' defence could plausibly be rejected. Yet these rulings themselves had to be seen to be carrying the full authority of law, otherwise it would appear that the courts were importing extra-legal standards and imposing 'victors' justice' on the vanquished. It was not sufficient to denounce the content of Nazi rules of law and military orders as morally abhorrent; the actions of the accused had to be shown to be *criminal*.

Thus it was tacitly conceded that the content of rules and orders was in some sense and to some extent relevant to legal validity. This was a significant concession to natural law theory on a crucial point at issue with legal positivism. The belief was growing, especially in Germany, that the experience of Nazi law had discredited positivism as a legal theory, on the grounds that there are laws, the content of which is so foreign to any conception of justice that they do in fact lose their status as law. The Austinian precept that law is one thing, its merits and demerits another, was believed to be undermined by the unprecedented departure from the ideal of the rule of law in Nazi Germany, the 'demerits' of which had become central to assessing the regime's claims to legality.

This line of argument against positivism, however, has never been regarded as decisive. One response is that the systematic abuse of legal power on this scale is a special case, and that it is only in such extreme cases that reference to content must be made. This response is unsatisfactory; serious injustice sanctioned by various legal systems is a matter of degree. The second, more important positivist response is that the argument confuses legal validity with justification. The stamp of legal validity, this response goes, does nothing to confer moral legitimacy on a legal system, an individual rule of law or a specific order, a commercial transaction or anything else. Legal validity is concerned solely with the identification of formal criteria, and as such is morally neutral. As we shall see, much depends here on what is meant by 'morally neutral'. We must turn now to a consideration of the essential claims made on behalf of positivism by its two leading exponents, Hans Kelsen (1881–1973) and H.L.A. Hart (1907–95).

Legal normativity: Kelsen's formal theory

Of all the leading contributions to the history of legal positivism, Kelsen's stands out as the most uncompromising. Rigorously scientific and thoroughly conventionalist in his assumption that all laws are human artefacts, Kelsen refined a 'pure theory of law' with its subject matter quite purposefully sealed off from outside influence. Taking his cue from Hume, and working in parallel with the positivist Vienna School, with which he was loosely associated, Kelsen applied the is–ought dichotomy to law in a way that was distinctive and radical. In moral theory, he developed a version of emotivism that led him to the view that moral ideals, especially that of justice, are essentially irrational, and hence entirely unsuitable for any kind of scientific analysis. The main object of scientific jurisprudence, for Kelsen, was the uncovering of the logical form behind the confusion of empirical appearances. He conceived this discovery of logical form as a project of rational reconstruction of the law as a unified whole. In this, he was influenced by Kantian epistemology rather than by the empiricist models of science. As a science, the object of study was held to be law as such, rather than any particular legal system; what he was seeking was the purely formal structures of any possible legal system. In this enterprise, Kelsen was emphatically opposed to any kind of natural law theory; justice and the higher law had no place in scientific jurisprudence. In short, he was attempting to push the positivism of Bentham and Austin to its logical conclusion, while detaching it from its objective utilitarian basis, and in so doing to root out the hidden presence of natural law assumptions in modern legal theory.

Kelsen's 'pure' theory of law is pure in two senses:

1 *The purification of subject matter*. In order to establish law as an independent science, it is necessary to strip it down to what is distinctively legal. To focus on the purely legal dimension of law – specifically legal validity – all the moral, political, sociological and psychological dimensions must be displaced from the science. The ideal sought here is a purely distilled conception of the object of legal science.

2 *The purification of the investigation*. In order to undertake this scientific investigation effectively, the investigation must itself be value-free. The science of law is 'pure' in the sense that it is free of ideology. In pure theory, there is no approval or disapproval, either implicit or explicit. The ideal sought here is a purely distilled conception of the investigating subject, the legal scientist, understood as a purely formal observer.

Taken in combination, these two conceptually interlocked senses of purification – of law itself and of its methodology – lead to a focus on the pure form of laws and the legal system. In this sense, Kelsen's theory is formalist. It involves the suspension or bracketing out of the concrete content of the laws that link up into a legal system. The concrete content – the social function, the political purpose, the justice or injustice of the laws – is irrelevant to the investigation of the formal structure of this link up.

So what is Kelsen's image of law? How does he understand the formal legal reality laid bare by this positivist method? When purified of all extraneous elements, what comes into view – in any legal system – is one rationally connected structure of norms, in the shape of a pyramid. These 'norms' have to be understood as specifically legal 'oughts', which are distinct from either moral oughts or legal rules. Legal rules as rules are not logically linked with one another. Legal norms are the oughts of which legal rules are the visible manifestation. The 'formal-logical' connections that give the legal system its unity apply to norms rather than rules, and it is these connections that the formal analysis reveals.

Thus, it is in these logical connections between legal norms that Kelsen seeks the meaning of legal validity. To this effect, the language of law is formalised by recasting every rule in terms of a legal ought, each of which is expressed as an 'imputational connective' ('if X conditions obtain, then Y sanctions ought to be applied'). This is the inner structure of any possible law. The directive to apply specified sanctions, whenever given conditions obtain, is addressed to a line of legal officials enforcing any kind of law along the full length of the legal process.

Each norm can only be validated by referring it to a higher norm (in the hierarchical pyramid), 'higher' in the sense of being more general. Thus, each norm is validated logically by being a more specific instance of another norm. The formal connection, hence the validity, abstracts from the concrete content of the norm. Any statement containing a legal norm can be validated or invalidated in this way. Thus, for example, a norm which requires that anyone who insults the government should be executed would be validated by a more general norm according to which all enemies of the state should be executed.

Kelsen's basic norm

If the formal validation of any particular legal norm must always lie in the identification of another legal norm, it clearly faces a problem of infinite regress. This leads us into the central and most controversial feature of Kelsen's pure theory. If norms are always referred to other norms, what is the ultimate source of their legal validity? It is not sufficient to say that validity is derived from the fabric of the normative order, that this order is purely formal and that content is irrelevant. The continued reference to norms further up the hierarchical structure inevitably raises the question of what stands at the top of the structure, the apex of the pyramid, the most general norm. What is it that gives the legal system its rational unity? Kelsen's answer is that the existence of any legal system must assume or presuppose a basic norm (*Grundnorm*). This norm he describes as 'hypothetical', in the sense that we can only hypothesise its existence.

The basic norm, then, is the most general norm hypothesised as the norm behind the final authority to which all particular valid norms can be traced back. This is the only norm that cannot itself be questioned or validated. It is in this sense that its validity is presupposed or tacitly assumed in any legal activity – for example, the relevant actions of a court official, a police officer, a solicitor, a gaoler – which acknowledges the validity of particular norms. It should be noticed especially that the basic norm is not the actual constitution – of the USA, the UK, Germany or wherever – which would be the empirical object of *political* science. It is what Kelsen terms the *logical* constitution that takes the form of an ought-statement that the constitution 'ought to be obeyed'. It is this norm that is presupposed as the basic one underpinning or tying the entire structure of the legal system. Another sense in which it is presupposed is that by its very nature it has never actually been posited or laid down as an act of will. In this sense, Kelsen insists, the basic norm can only be an act of *thinking*, and as such cannot be regarded as a norm of positive law.

Criticisms of Kelsen's pure theory of law come from every angle. For traditional defenders of the higher law of natural justice, the theory is seen as the high tide of dehumanising positivism. Also, as an expression of relentless formalism, seeking out the most abstract patterns in the law and deliberately excluding all sociological factors, the pure theory is clearly at the far end of the spectrum from American legal realism. It has also been attacked from within the positivist camp for its supposed ambivalence about the value-free nature of the normative science it proposes, and accused of sliding back towards the very natural law theory that it is supposed to be rooting out.

Does Kelsen equivocate between a specifically legal concept of the validity of norms and a morally evaluative analysis of validity? Many critics believe that he does. Much of the confusion, however, is due to the normative language he is using. It often sounds as though Kelsen is describing a moral obligation when he is not. 'One ought to behave as the constitution prescribes' (Kelsen 1970: 201) is typical. When he distinguishes a state execution of a criminal from murder, by tracing the norm requiring it back to the authority of the constitution and the basic norm that this should be obeyed, it sounds as though he is justifying it. But in fact this is a purely descriptive account of why the execution is legally valid, while other acts of killing would be counted as murder. Kelsen is at least explicit in his declared *intention* to separate legal validity from any moral connotations: 'The science of law does not prescribe that one ought to obey the commands of the creator of the constitution' (ibid.: 204). Also, he insists that

> the contents of a (specific) constitution and the national legal order created according to it is irrelevant – it may be a just or unjust order; it may or may not guarantee a relative condition of peace....The presupposition of the basic norm does not approve any value transcending positive law.
>
> (ibid.: 201)

In short, Kelsen is committed to legal positivism, to the strict separation of law and morality in the relevant senses, and indications to the contrary are misleading.

H.L.A. Hart's concept of law

While Kelsen's theoretical purification of law has continued to exert a significant influence, the theory of law that has made the greatest impact on
contemporary positivism was the one developed by H.L.A. Hart in the
1950s. Hart's *The Concept of Law* (1961) is the single most influential book
of this period. What he was attempting here, from within the positivist
camp, was to apply the radical insights of the new linguistic philosophy to
the central problems of jurisprudence in such a way that would place it on a
sound theoretical footing and do justice to the complexity of law. Hart
acknowledged the value of Bentham and Austin's pioneering efforts at clarification, and admired their uncompromising exposure of the weaknesses of
classical common law and natural law thinking, but he saw in their commitment to the command theory – which he accepted as expressing a partial
truth about some areas of law – a serious obstacle in the path of genuine
understanding of the law as a whole.

Hart's attack on the command theory

In confronting the well-entrenched Austinian tradition in English jurisprudence, Hart was also turning against the older positivist way of thinking
about law, in particular the basic tenet that law is essentially the expression
of a will, rather than an articulation of a pre-existing good. This belief was
the origin – in ancient and medieval philosophy – of the command theory
running from Hobbes to Austin and beyond. Before Hart, it appeared that
an outright rejection of this tenet must result in the abandonment of positivism. One of Hart's striking achievements was to show that this was not
true, that it was both possible and necessary to detach positivism from
command theory in order to reveal its true explanatory strength.

It was not that the command theory had previously gone unchallenged.
The critiques by John Chipman Gray and Jerome Frank, for example, did not
go unnoticed, but were not absorbed by the mainstream. As we have just
seen, Kelsen was also sharply critical on the grounds that command theory is
misdirected and confused the analysis with psychology. His own formalistic
version of positivism, however, did not break with the command theory, when
suitably depsychologised and aimed at legal officials rather than citizens.

For Hart, by contrast, the solution was more radical. What he aimed to
show was that Austin's analysis, purporting to provide the key to unlock the
secrets of jurisprudence, was fundamentally misguided. The command
theory was, for Hart, seriously defective; it did not reflect the reality of any
possible or actual legal system, and its explanatory power was very limited.
It was not something to be renovated by adjustment; it needed to be
supplanted by a new explanatory hypothesis about the nature of law.

Among Hart's most effective arguments, there are two that stand out,
each pointing to his own proposed concept of law. The first concerns the
range of areas of law that the theory of command backed by sanctions as

the essence of law purports to explain. There are many such areas, observes Hart, involving rules that cannot plausibly be construed as orders or commands in the required sense. Rules such as those controlling the legality or otherwise of contracts, marriages or wills are not rules, the disobedience of which is followed by a sanction. They are rules that facilitate social transactions, and the consequence of the failure to observe the legal formalities is that the transaction is null and void. To construe – as Austin does – these rules creating facilities as tacit commands, and the nullification of the transaction as a sanction, is a distortion of their power-conferring function. The command theory, then, is defective *as explanation*.

Hart's concept of a legal system

The second argument concerns a distinction between types of legal rules that are wholly different in kind. This is the argument that runs through Hart's conceptual analysis of social practices with which he attempts to rebuild the positivist theory of legal validity, having rejected the command theory. Arguing that what is missing from Austin's analysis is the concept of an accepted rule, Hart unfolds his own analysis that aims at a more sophisticated understanding of the social practice of following a rule.

He distinguishes first between social rules that constitute mere regularity of behaviour, such as social conventions of etiquette, and rules that constitute *obligations*, in the sense that there is insistent demand for conformity. Second, he argues, we then have to distinguish between obligations based on the prevailing moral code, which are enforced only by social approval and disapproval, and obligations that take the form of rules of law and are enforced by physical sanctions.

Third, the crucial distinction is drawn between different types of legal rules, which Hart calls primary and secondary. *Primary* rules of law are said to be those that are essential for any kind of social existence, those that prescribe, prevent or regulate behaviour in every area with which the law is concerned. These are all the rules constraining anti-social behaviour: rules against theft, cheating, violence, and so on. As such, they constitute the great bulk of the positive laws in which the legal system consists. But any legal system must comprise more than this; it must also include what Hart called *secondary* rules, the function of which is exclusively addressed to the status of the primary rules. The secondary rules are fundamentally different in kind from the primary rules. They bring primary rules into being, they revise them, they uphold them, or they change them completely. Hart argues that the creation of secondary rules marks the transition from a prelegal society to a legal system. Without the secondary rules, the essential function of which is to create, identify and confer legitimacy on the primary rules, there would be no way of resolving doubts or disputes about them, no way of changing or adapting them to new circumstances, no one to authorise punishment for breaking them.

The most fundamental of these secondary rules Hart calls 'the rule of recognition'. This is the rule to which the authority of all the primary rules is referred. It is a secondary rule that settles doubts and uncertainties, and provides the authority to resolve them. As such, it is the all-important source of legal validity, from which the legality of any law, minor by-law or legal document, or the legitimacy of any court of law and the proceedings therein, any action by a legal official, is ultimately derived.

This basic rule, Hart maintains, can appear in any number of forms or guises. It can be written or unwritten, spoken or unspoken. It might be the rule that 'whatever the sovereign says is law'. It might be the way in which the primary rules are uttered or enacted. It might be a formal document or a constitution. In the UK, it happens to be the rule that 'what the Queen in Parliament enacts is law'. Whatever form the rule of recognition takes, it is essentially a socially accepted fact in any given legal system, every one of which must have one if it is to qualify as a legal system, rather than a prelegal assemblage of unvalidated primary rules.

Hart and Kelsen

There are, of course, clear parallels between Hart's rule of recognition as the source of legal validity and Kelsen's basic norm. They both serve the same vital function in grounding the positivist interpretation of the idea of a legal system. The rule of recognition, like the basic norm, is the linchpin that gives the system unity, and every other rule must be referred to it. The differences, however, are as great as the similarities. Hart's basic rule is a (secondary) rule of law, not a Kelsen-style norm, or 'ought-statement'. As such, it is a social fact, rather than a hypothetical norm that is presupposed by all legal activity. As a social fact and a rule of law, it is itself a part of the legal system, whereas the Kelsenian basic norm lies outside of the system. There is also a different reason for its validity being unchallengeable. For Hart, it is a meaningless question to ask whether or not the rule of recognition is valid. The demand for a demonstration of its validity, he says, is equivalent to demanding that the standard metre bar in Paris be correct. Legal validity is measured against this basic rule of law; it cannot be measured against itself.

Hart and legal positivism

We have to be clear about the sense in which Hart was a legal positivist. His concept of law was certainly a radical revision of what had previously been known as positivism. This was due largely to its association with the command theory. Hart firmly believed, as we have seen, that there was continuity as well as discontinuity between himself and the Austinian tradition. What he objected to in the command theory was that it concealed the real structure of law as the interplay between different types of rules, as revealed by his own analysis. He did not, however, regard the command theory as a complete distortion. As noted above, the rule of recognition might well be the fact that the will of the sovereign is supreme. Thus, Hart's criterion for the unity of a legal system is more general than Austin's.

With the command theory displaced, Hart's idea of a positivist approach to law is defined by its commitment to two theses: the morality–law separation thesis and the thesis that analysis of legal concepts should be the main task of jurisprudence (Hart 1983: 57–8). However, one of the features of Hart's theory for which he is best known is his defence of the 'minimum content thesis' (Hart 1961: 189–95), according to which there are a number of natural features of humans living in society that to some extent determine the content of law as it must exist if it is to be viable as an institution consistent with the minimal purpose of human survival. Natural human vulnerability, for example, makes laws prohibiting violence absolutely basic. The environmental fact that resources are always limited dictates the need for laws protecting the security of land and the basic needs of life. The fact that most people are 'neither angels nor devils' makes law necessary and at the same time possible. These and other 'truisms' about human life point to the conclusion that laws must have a bare minimum of moral content if they are to serve their function as laws at all.

Hart presented this minimum content thesis as consistent with his 'rule of recognition' version of positivism, but not with the command–positivist thesis that law is the effective enforcement of the will of the sovereign. Contentiously describing his thesis as 'the core of truth' in the natural law idea, he claims that it constitutes 'a reply to the positivist thesis that law may have any content' (Hart 1961: 195). What he is explicitly repudiating here is the Austinian version of the separation thesis. On his own version, the content is constrained by a natural connection between law and basic natural needs, but the conceptual connection between law and morality or justice is decisively rejected.

This is a subtle version of positivism. It is not, as many have mistakenly believed, a version of natural law, however minimal.

Fuller's secular version of natural law

Lon L. Fuller (1902–78), a distinguished Professor of Law at Harvard from 1939 to 1972, contributed more than any other individual to the revival of natural law in the postwar years. Inspired by a deep antipathy to the positivist concept of law, but equally unimpressed by the dead weight of the traditional natural law approach, he developed an original humanistic perspective based on the idea that law itself, as a human institution, naturally generates a specifically legal morality that is the proper starting point for the solution to the problems of legal theory. Fuller's early criticism was directed at classical positivism, but from the 1950s on it was increasingly directed at his contemporaries Kelsen and Hart, with whom he was engaged in an extended controversy over the basic question of the nature of law.

How and why Fuller regarded his own position as a modern version of natural law theory is the main question we will need to consider here.

Natural law and secularism

The idea that natural law can be detached from religious ethics, that it can flourish without an ultimate authority in the will of God, has never been entirely absent from natural law theory. What has always been uppermost is the place in the theory occupied by the natural faculty of reason. Even in Aquinas's natural law theology, the role of reason is pivotal as the source of legal validity. It was ventured as early as the fourteenth century by the Ockhamist Gregory of Rimini that offences against reason would still be sinful, even if God did not exist. The famous declaration by Grotius in the seventeenth century, that 'even if that which cannot be conceived without the greatest iniquity, that God did not exist, were true, natural law would still have binding force', echoed and reinforced this idea, and paved the way for the secularisation of the Enlightenment. Many legal thinkers of the eighteenth century, while detaching themselves from Christian orthodoxy, were still committed to the foundational ethical principle of natural law.

Nevertheless, the survival of natural law theory into the twentieth century, against the tide of scientific positivism, owed a great deal to the tradition of Aquinas and the influence of the Roman Catholic Church. The idea that human behaviour is and should be controlled by objective ethical standards derived from a higher law, ultimately sanctioned by the will of God, was still central to early twentieth-century natural law thinking.

Fuller's attraction to natural law theory was a purely rationalistic one, which owed nothing to the 'higher law' of the traditional theory. Along with his insistence on putting God out of play, he rejected the idea of law itself, in Holmes's famous aphorism, as 'a brooding omnipresence in the sky', a pre-existing moral order to which lawmakers have to submit. In contrast to this 'higher law' analysis, Fuller saw law as an entirely natural, human creation, but one that was subject to the same kind of 'natural laws' as other human crafts, such as carpentry or engineering. Just as there are unskilled methods by which tables or window frames cannot be crafted, there are ways in which laws and legal systems cannot be constructed. This 'good carpentry' metaphor was central to Fuller's entirely secularised version of natural law. The sense in which these laws are discovered, rather than made or freely invented, is the sense that aligns Fuller's theory with the basic natural law idea, the foundationalist idea that laws are drawn from natural sources, rather than being the product of pure will.

The procedural shift

With Fuller's complete secularisation comes the most controversial adjustment to natural law theory: the shift of focus from the substantive to the procedural. What this means is that the validity of individual laws or the legality of the legal system does not depend in any way on an assessment of the justice or other moral qualities of individual laws or the legal system. Without the higher law, there is no absolute standpoint from which to make such assessments. Fuller's strategy is to avoid the problem of the variability of moral codes and conceptions of justice by denying the need to engage natural law theory in this kind of argument. The shift to the procedural is a change of focus to what Fuller regards as crucial: the inner morality of law. What he means is that moral values are written into the very idea of law, in such a way that laws and legal systems can be assessed according to the extent to which they satisfy criteria that are specifically legal and procedural.

What exactly is meant by this idea of 'procedural', rather than substantive justice? What Fuller means by it is that, in all legal systems deserving of the title, the creation and implementation of legal rules are guided and constrained by principles relating to the purpose of these rules. These 'qualities of excellence' include generality and efficiency, clarity and intelligibility. Also, they must be well publicised as guides to action. Laws that are internally inconsistent, applied retrospectively or impossible to comply with are excluded. Taken as a complete set, general fidelity to these principles constitutes observance of the rule of law, which means more than effective coercion authorised by a sovereign power. The rule of law means that the exercise of legal powers is constrained by the requirements of procedural correctness.

Several features of this set of criteria should be emphasised and borne in mind. First, as qualities of legal excellence, they were conceived by Fuller as perfections that legal practice aspires to but rarely attains completely. Second, this implies that fidelity to each of these principles or to the whole set is nearly always going to be a matter of degree. Third, as these principles are conditions for the existence of a legal system, law as such is taken to be inherently moral, in the sense that 'where there is truly law, there is procedural excellence'.

Fuller's rejection of the separation thesis

It should be plain why these procedural criteria indicate a clear-cut rejection of the morality–law separation thesis. If the very existence of a legal system requires the satisfaction of moral criteria, then it is impossible to say what the law is in fact without reference to the way it ought to be. The credibility of Fuller's challenge to positivism hinges on clarifying this claim that the separation thesis is not only undesirable but also actually false, that law may not have any content, that what law is actually includes its positive qualities. Its qualities and defects are not extraneous to the question of whether or not it is law. This, for Fuller, is what the necessary connection between law and morality means. He maintained that the attempt to separate law from morality breaks down with the recognition of law as essentially purposive. Law as a whole – a legal system – has a purpose that makes it what it is. The purpose is to provide a framework of guidance by which people can regulate their own behaviour. Within this framework, each individual law has an essential purpose, for example, to discourage fraud and avoid its harmful consequences. All laws are means to specific ends. The general purpose of law can only be implemented by the acknowledgement and observance of the eight rule of law principles, without which it would be ineffective in promoting its essential purpose and would fail as law.

It should be understood that Fuller – as an advocate of a distinctly secular version of natural law – was not trying to reinstate the traditional outlook that Bentham and Austin had broken down. As we saw in the previous chapter, the integrity of law and morality for common law thinkers like Blackstone was exposed by Bentham as Christian moral sermonising about the virtues of existing law. The necessary connection between law and morality in this context meant that 'if it is law, it must be justified'. The assault on this kind of confusion of law and morality was inspired by the need for clarity, in order to expose and denounce bad laws by the standards of utility, and to campaign for legal reform. The crucial Benthamite point here is that there can be and often are bad laws; their mere legality is not an argument for their moral worth.

Over the course of the following century, this interpretation was upheld by Holmes, Gray, Kelsen, Hart and the Scandinavian realists, all of whom insisted that individual laws are contingently related to morality, in the sense that they can range from the most enlightened to the most reactionary, prejudiced and unjust. The stamp of legal validity guarantees nothing about their moral status. All of these thinkers were opposing what they took to be the natural law idea, whether explicit or residual, that legality means justice. The main reason for this was their belief that every version of natural law theory is essentially Blackstonian in that it encourages the doctrine that all law is good law; that it resists legal reform and has a tendency to consecrate the existing legal order, by conceptually excluding criticism of it. It was also generally recognised, of course, that the natural law slogans inherited from Cicero and St Augustine, to the effect that an unjust law is not law at all, appeared to have the opposite implication. On this interpretation, only good laws are legal. Manifestly unjust 'laws' do not even enjoy the status of legality, regardless of their authoritative source. In this way, 'the necessary connection between law and morality' can mean that legal systems and laws must satisfy a minimum 'morality test'.

Fuller's adoption of the natural law standpoint as the best vehicle for his theory of procedural justice led him to a conclusion distinct from either of these. On the one hand, he rejected outright the notion that mere legality confers moral legitimacy, and denies that natural law implies this. On the other hand, he does not argue that substantive injustice in the content of a law invalidates it as law. What he does argue, in opposition to positivism, is that the violation of or disregard for the basic procedural principles demanded by secular natural law reduces the validity of a legal system in proportion to the extent of these violations.

At the same time, Fuller attempts to turn the tables on positivism by accusing it of degenerating into the kind of formalism that assumes that the law is the law and is there to be obeyed, whatever one may feel about it. This, he argues, is implicit in the separation thesis. The attempt to study law in a coldly factual, scientific manner leads to the acceptance of the authority of law, no matter how unjust. What he is arguing is that the identification of law on strictly factual criteria has the effect of endorsing it as law in such a way that it will, in practice, command moral authority. On these grounds, Fuller follows Rommen, Radbruch and others in holding legal positivism partly responsible for the success of Nazism and its perversion of the legal system.

Fuller also questions the central positivist claim to greater analytic clarity. He denies that the separation thesis, which might have originally been directed against the mystification created by common law moral verbiage, does in fact lead to greater clarity about the nature of law. What it does lead to, he argues, is the command theory, which even the positivist Hart can accept does not reflect the reality of law. Real clarity, he maintains, will only be attained by relinquishing the separation thesis along with the command theory.

What the obsession with trying to describe the law in its pure facticity obscures is the crucial dimension of law, namely, its purposiveness. In eliminating value, the scientific approach is eliminating what is at the centre of law. Stripped of its general and specific purposes, a law or a legal system is not fully intelligible. If the legal analyst deliberately puts these purposes out of play for the sake of scientific accuracy, the picture created will not be one of law the way it actually is, but of the way it would be if legal systems and laws had no essential purpose. This approach treats law as if it were an inert, natural object. For Fuller, it is the result of the inappropriate transfer of positivist methodologies of natural science to the science of law. If a scientific method devised to root out and exclude all traces of teleology is applied to law, the result will be a 'factual' account of legal behaviour that bears little resemblance to the reality of law. Law is essentially a human creation and must be treated as such.

Conclusion

Any assessment of the ongoing dispute between positivists and their natural law critics must take account of the ways in which these doctrines have evolved since the days of the classic theories of Bentham and Austin. The differences between the modern versions of positivism and those of their predecessors are almost as important as their arguments against natural law. Similarly, modern versions of natural law have evolved in response to the valid criticisms made by positivists. What is perhaps most important is to approach cautiously the varying responses to the separation thesis, because it is in their respective interpretations of this thesis that modern legal theorists reveal their most fundamental understanding of the law.

Study questions

General question: Is it possible to have a morally neutral description of law?

Further study questions: Explain and evaluate Hart's criticism of Austin's command theory of law. Is Hart's concept of law more convincing than Austin's? Compare Hart's positivism with Kelsen's pure theory of law. Is the key to the unity of a legal system to be found in Kelsen's basic norm or Hart's rule of recognition? What are the criteria for legal validity? Can the injustice of a law invalidate it *as law*? Is Fuller's theory of natural law more successful than traditional versions in countering the standard positivist criticisms?

Suggestions for further reading

Kelsen (1970) is the main text for his pure theory of law. Some radically different perspectives on Kelsen are available in the collections of Tur and Twining (1986), and in Summers (1971). Useful short commentaries include Harris (1997: ch. 6), Riddall (1991: ch. 10) and Dias (1985: ch. 17).

The basic texts for Hart's critique of the command theory are Austin (1995: Lectures 1, 5 and 6) and Hart (1961: chaps 1–6). Important reactions include Raz (1970: chaps 1–2) and Dworkin (1977b: ch. 2). Useful short commentaries include Lyons (1984: ch. 2) and Riddall (1991: ch. 3). Earlier criticism of the command theory can be found in Gray (1921: 85–8).

Hart's classic work (1961) is fundamental to his theory of law. Among the numerous studies and commentaries on Hart, those that stand out are Lacey (2004) MacCormick (1981) and the essays collected in Hacker and Raz (1977), Gavison (1987) and Summers (1971).

Fuller (1964) is his most famous and important work. Summers (1984) is the best full-length study of Fuller. See also Summers's 'Professor Fuller on Morality and Law', in Summers (1971) and Lyons (1993: ch. 1). For details on the Hart–Fuller debate and the rule of law, see Lyons (1984: 74–87), Harris (1997: ch. 11) and Riddall (1991: ch. 7).

4   Contemporary theories of law

The contemporary period in mainstream legal theory can be dated from the publication in 1961 of Hart's *The Concept of Law*. His successful demolition of Austin's command theory and his own theory of law as a system of rules based on a rule of recognition had two important effects. First, it succeeded immediately in revitalising legal positivism and rescuing it from the inertia into which it had fallen. As a more precise and informative explanation of law, leaving behind the simplicities and explanatory failures of the command theory, it rapidly became the standard model for legal analysis. Second, it created the clearest model to date of the positivist interpretation of law, thus providing the stimulus for new developments in the anti-positivist theories, in particular, that of Dworkin.

Contemporary positivists have focused on a closer analysis of rules, building critically on Hart's theory, which is widely regarded as flawed in detail and incomplete as a description and explanation of law, but basically sound in essentials. The outcome, with the theories of Raz, MacCormick and others, is a more discriminating concept of a legal rule and a more refined general picture of how, for example, Hart's primary and secondary rules interact.

The natural law position today, following Fuller, is predominantly secular, but the central concern remains that of clarifying the nature of legal validity and explaining the relation between morality and the law. The main question is whether the identification of valid laws depends on their social source or their moral content. Raz's positivist 'sources thesis' (1970), for example, according to which the practical reasons for action that are specifically legal can be identified on the basis of social facts alone, without reference to moral argument about their content, is rejected by natural lawyers who regard such moral argument as indispensable and basic to law.

Hard cases and legal positivism

What is of particular importance to contemporary theory is the nature of judicial reasoning and the problem of hard cases, which has become the testing ground for the competing theories of law. It is in this context that the disputes between the positivist models of rules and their critics become most explicit. The problem revolves around the issue of what judges are entitled or obliged to do when faced with a case for which there is no clear judicial precedent, or upon which there appears to be no definite and unambiguous statutory guidance.

Positivist theories of hard cases

Although Austin had little to say about hard cases, he said enough to initiate a tradition of positivist interpretation. It was clear to Austin that in practice – even if the legal system has been thoroughly reformed and purged of the irrational elements in common law – the sovereign could not allow for every eventuality, every case that comes before its courts. For the purpose of cases not covered by posited law, the sovereign delegates powers of discretion to its judges, powers that are only to be used when there are no appropriate general rules to apply to this particular case; which is to say, when the law runs out. The judges are then temporary 'commanders' in their own right; however, they hold their authority only by virtue of appointment by the ultimate commander.

Austin believed that the inevitability of unforeseeable cases arising was due to the inherent vagueness or lack of perfect precision in the wording of the law. The delegation of powers of discretion was unavoidable because laws had what he called 'furry edges'. Therefore, one of the most important functions of a judge is to act as a subordinate deputy legislator to create new law by clarifying these furry edges. These views of Austin on the delegation of judicial discretion were schematic and primitive. He regarded it as a straightforward matter of common sense. Hart, it will be remembered, rejected Austin's command theory in favour of a more sophisticated analysis of legal rules. Hart nevertheless retained, in its essentials, an Austinian approach to judicial reasoning and hard cases.

Hart's approach was more developed and philosophically sophisticated than Austin's, but essentially similar in that he identified an area of discretion created by the incompleteness of existing rules of law. On Hart's conception, the nature of law is such that some degree of discretion is unavoidable, because no matter how well drafted the legislation and how wide-ranging existing precedent in case law, the established rules cannot cover every eventuality. Nearly all rules lack certainty in their range of reference.

On Hart's theory there is usually in hard cases what he calls a 'penumbra of uncertainty' surrounding the application of a rule. This penumbral quality of a rule is explained by the language in which any kind of rules – legal or otherwise – are invariably expressed. Sometimes it is possible to express a rule so precisely as to avoid any ambiguity or vagueness; however, this is often impossible because of the open texture of language.

Hart's standard example is of the use of the word 'vehicle' in a by-law banning vehicles from a public park. There is an undisputed core meaning of the word: it clearly applies to cars and motorcycles; but less clearly to such things as bicycles, pedal cars, roller skates, skateboards or even prams. Unless they are specified by the rule, these cases are left to judicial discretion as to what is to *count* as a vehicle. This analysis can be extended to any major area of law. In contract law, the meaning of 'fraud' has a clear meaning, but there are peripheral contexts in which it is not clear whether a certain kind of action constitutes a deliberate deception and counts as fraud. These peripheral contexts are the areas for judicial discretion. On Hart's conception, then, the law has a core of settled meaning; there are penumbral areas in which the law is not settled. There are 'rules which are determinate enough at the centre to supply standards of correct judicial decision' (Hart 1961: 141–2).

In contrast to legal realists, Hart argues against the idea that the best a lawyer can ever do is to use his knowledge of past legal decisions to guess how a judge will decide a particular case. This, however, is exactly what Hart does accept when the rules become blurred by the vagueness of their language; that is to say, in hard cases. 'When the area of open texture is reached,' he asserts, 'very often all we can profitably offer in answer to the question "What is the law on this matter?", is a guarded prediction of what the courts will do' (ibid.: 143).

This, for Hart, is why it is not always easy or even possible to apply existing law. The indeterminacy of rules makes it inevitable that a certain amount of strong discretionary judgement has to be made in court. It is also, according to Hart, desirable. Without some degree of discretion, it would be a repressively rigid legal system. But while Hart sees this situation as acceptable, others regard it as a gesture of despair in the face of the complexity of the law. Instead of repressive rigidity, they see justice and consistency in complete determinacy.

Between the nightmare and the noble dream: Hartian discretion

In 1977, Hart published an essay in which he responded to Dworkin's growing influence in jurisprudence, reinforcing his own original interpretation of hard cases. In this essay, he depicted Dworkin's defence of complete determinacy and unique right answers as an overreaction to the extreme rule-scepticism of the American legal realists, with Hart's own positivistic account of judicial discretion as the genuinely realistic middle ground. Reviewing the last century of American legal theory, he points to the two extremes of regarding the law either as wildly arbitrary and unpredictable, or as a fully explicable, wholly determinate and certain process.

On the one hand, he maintains, we can see the American 'nightmare view that, in spite of pretensions to the contrary, judges make the law they apply to litigants and are not impartial, objective declarers of existing law' (Hart 1983: 127). In contrast to this surface appearance of impartiality, the judge is in reality a legislator, indistinguishable from a politician. Why is this a nightmare? If it is true, it means that the image of judicial impartiality is a complete fraud. Litigants or defendants are entitled to expect judges to apply the existing law evenhandedly, rather than to have new law made for every occasion.

At the other extreme, argues Hart, we find the utopian noble dream, according to which judges never make new law, that despite superficial appearances to the contrary, judges never determine what the law *shall* be. Judges are confined to saying what they believe the law consisted in before their decision, which is the mere application of it. Dworkin he describes as the latest in the line of these 'noble dreamers', denying, in the face of all the evidence, the reality of judicial discretion. What we need to consider now is whether Dworkin's defence of complete determinacy really does imply this kind of utopian idealisation of the legal process.

Dworkin's theory of law as integrity

The comprehensive theory unfolded by Ronald Dworkin (b. 1931) over the last quarter of the twentieth century owes much to the analysis developed by both Fuller and Hart. Dworkin took over and developed many of Fuller's themes, but the importance of his writings to mainstream Anglo-American legal theory rests largely on the claim that they represent a sophisticated and plausible alternative to Hart's version of legal positivism, succeeding where Fuller failed in providing a concrete exposition of the unity of law and morality, thus undermining the key thesis of legal positivism. He regards all versions of positivism, from Bentham to Kelsen and Hart, as fatally flawed in their assumptions about legal validity. There is nevertheless a degree of convergence between Dworkin and Hartian positivists that had not been possible in the stark confrontation between classical natural law and its positivist enemies.

This is partly because Dworkin's own theory can only loosely be called a theory of natural law. Although it inclines in this direction, he is concerned more with the merits and faults of a historically specific legal system than with general or timeless concepts of law. What does link Dworkin with natural law, however, is his rootedness in the common law tradition and the central claim that the principles of justice that have evolved within this tradition are an essential ingredient of law. This is closely connected with his 'rights thesis', that judges are obliged to recognise and protect pre-existing individual rights. It will also become clear from this account of Dworkin's theory of law that, while it is indebted to many of the insights of philosophical pragmatism and legal realism, especially in its court-centredness and focus on controversial judicial rulings, it rejects the most characteristic of the realist tenets. The result is a strikingly original and independent theory of constructive interpretation or 'law as integrity'. As a complete theory, this emerges gradually from early essays published as *Taking Rights Seriously* (1977b), to the later work, *Law's Empire* (1986).

Rights, principles and policy

The centrepiece of Dworkin's rejection of the positivist concept of law is his distinction between what he identifies as legal rules and legal standards. The assumption he makes explicit from the outset is that the model of law as an elaborate set of rules, whether Austinian or Hartian, expresses only one limited dimension of the law, and this limitation obscures the wider reality of law as a whole. This inclusion of 'standards' of law, in addition to rules, is the keystone of Dworkin's theory because what it amounts to is an attempt to refute, on the grounds of actual legal practice as well as philosophical argument, the defining positivist thesis that law and morality are separate. For Dworkin, as for Fuller, law and morality are inseparably intertwined. Whereas for Fuller, however, the 'inner morality' of law is primarily procedural, for Dworkin, the moral dimension of law is wider and more substantive than this. Law is more than the factual matter of predicting and applying 'black letter' rules as laid down in the past by legislatures and courts; it also comprises intrinsically moral legal standards such as principles of justice, rights and perceptions of good social policy.

Considerations of policy, however, are regarded by Dworkin as subordinate to the principles of justice and the recognition of rights. It is the distinction between rules and *principles* that is crucial to his critique of positivism. The essential point is that a legal rule is something that is either applicable to a given case or it is not. It is an all-or-nothing concept. Principles of justice and fairness, by contrast, have what Dworkin calls the dimension of 'weight'. If a valid rule of law exists, it is normal procedure to apply it automatically. If a legal principle is acknowledged, its weight or seriousness has to be taken into account, possibly to be balanced against other principles, before it is allowed to affect the judicial decision.

Legal validity and interpretation

The purpose behind these distinctions is to show that the positivist theories of legal validity are unrealistic and ultimately incoherent. Although his arguments are aimed equally at past and present versions of positivism, Dworkin concentrates his fire on Hart's account of legal validity in relation to the rule of recognition. What he sees as mistaken in this account is the continued positivist assumption that there must be a single master test for distinguishing legally valid from invalid rules. On Hart's account, the valid rules of law are those that can be traced back to the original rule that authorises the entire structure of law. What Dworkin rejects, then, is the pyramid structure of law that is common to all the leading positivists, whether this originates in the power of the Austinian sovereign, the Kelsenian basic norm or Hart's rule of recognition. What Dworkin is himself asserting is that this image of legal validity does not in fact match the ways in which laws are actually validated in advanced legal systems.

In order to get this match, we have to look in detail at the complexity of arguments that support judicial decisions in controversial cases. The general point, however, is that on Dworkin's alternative to the positivist account of legal validity, judges are under a legal obligation that is imposed, not by hard and fast rules underpinned by a basic norm or rule of recognition, but by 'a constellation of principles' (Dworkin 1977b: 44) as well as rules. This is an obligation to come up with the right answer to the case under consideration, no matter how difficult or controversial. The source of the obligation lies in the past, in the body of judicial and legislative rules, decisions and unwritten principles of the common law. With these raw legal materials to hand, the role of the judge is to aspire to a completely coherent theory of law that will yield a judgement which (1) will provide the best 'fit' with existing legal materials, i.e. with previous rulings and legislation; and (2) will reveal the law in its best possible light, in terms of moral and political soundness, as exemplified by the liberal values of justice, fairness, equality, due process and individual rights. These two aspects of interpretation Dworkin describes as the dimensions of 'best fit' and of 'best light'.

The most illuminating analogy that Dworkin develops at length to justify this approach is a comparison of legal with literary interpretation. As the mouthpiece of the law, the judge is in the position of a creative writer asked to continue an unfinished novel in the vein of the original. 'The complexity of this task models the complexity of deciding a hard case under law as integrity' (Dworkin 1986: 229). The completion of the analogy requires that we imagine a chain of authors each expected to write another chapter. Law is like an ongoing literary narrative, the only difference being that it is open-ended. Each author in this situation would have to interpret what had gone before; the new chapter would have to fit the materials already written. At the same time, however, the author would have to make the novel the best it could be as a novel, integrating plot, image and setting, using substantive aesthetic judgement to accept one interpretation and reject others. The assumption is that there would only be one best way to continue it, rather than several equally good ways. Similarly, the judge has to fit his or her interpretation of previous law to the existing materials, while at the same time making the narrative of law the best it can be, in terms of political morality.

Right answers to questions of law

Must there always be 'right answers' to questions of law? This question, made prominent by Dworkin, is another way of asking about the nature of the discretion exercised by a judge in a hard case. When a case arises, with every appearance of being incompletely dealt with by existing law, one's instinct is to assume that there must be several options left open, more than one way of solving the difficulty. If there were only one way, how could it qualify as a hard case?

One of Dworkin's main endeavours is to show that this is mistaken, and that, contrary to appearances, there must in principle always be one and only one right answer to any hard case, and that this is 'right' both morally and legally. The allowance of alternatives or a range of possible acceptable answers is regarded by Dworkin as the result of a failure to recognise the duty imposed upon the judge to reach a decision that reflects the objective balance of rights in the case. The question here, then, is whether there is one determinate answer to every difficult case in which legal rules or principles or rights are in conflict, seemingly pointing to different but equally persuasive conclusions.

If there were no single decision required by law, then the judge could not decide the case 'according to law'. If more than one outcome is legally possible, then it seems that there are gaps in the law, gaps that must be filled by the judge, whose judicial function is then that of a creative legislator. He or she determines what the 'right' answer in this case 'ought' to be. It would seem that judges are then supplementing their legal knowledge and expertise with their own moral perceptions, that they have a free hand to refer to their own instincts for justice and equity, and so on. It is the freedom or judicial caprice seemingly sanctioned by this view of hard cases that Dworkin is opposing as contrary to the spirit of common law, which requires a degree of principled consistency in its succession of decisions.

Hercules and moral objectivism

Dworkin's advancement of the 'one right answer' thesis is an integral part of his wider defence of moral objectivism against moral scepticism and relativism. This moral objectivism is presupposed by the one right answer thesis and by the rights thesis. The claim that answers to moral problems or conflicts can be 'right' or 'correct', and the related claim that some rights prevail over others, is objectivist in the sense that the standards of morality or justice are taken to be independent of human decision or convention.

It is to illustrate this principle of moral objectivity as a model for legal reasoning that Dworkin introduces the mythical judge Hercules. This is the name he gives to an imaginary judge of unlimited intellectual power, for whom the failings of memory and the pressure of time would be no problem. Without any such impediments, Hercules would find the unique correct answer to every hard legal case, because he would have all the relevant information about the entire history of the rules and principles of the common law, and about the facts and competing claims in the case before him. With these superhuman powers he would not simply follow precedent; he would reason his way to the correct solution by constructing a complete theory of law and what it required for the case in hand. His interpretive reasoning would be guided by the requirement of 'best fit' with all relevant legal precedent, and at the same time by the criterion of 'best light', finding the interpretation that provides the best political reading of past law. Both criteria presuppose moral objectivism, the assumption being that there can only be one morally sound interpretation of precedent. Hercules symbolises legal reasoning at its best because, with maximum knowledge of the law, he can justify his decision by legal precedent and balance the relative weight of the relevant principles and act accordingly, endorsing the rights that are entitled, on the balance of arguments, to prevail. Above all, Hercules will see that he has no discretion to act otherwise.

Dworkin's hard cases

From the many morally controversial cases in English and US law cited by Dworkin, the one he has made pivotal to his argument is the relatively minor one of *Riggs v. Palmer* (New York, 1889). The relevant facts of the case were as follows. Elmer Palmer was a 16-year-old who successfully prevented his grandfather from changing his will, of which he himself was the main bene-ficiary, by murdering him. After serving a prison sentence, there appeared to be no legal obstacle to prevent Palmer from claiming his inheritance. This was challenged in court by relatives (who were minor beneficiaries), but the judge upheld Palmer's claims because the formalities of law in relation to the will had been satisfied. This decision was overturned by a majority decision in the Court of Appeal, depriving Palmer of his inheritance, on the grounds that no one should profit from their own wrongdoing.

It is not difficult to see why Dworkin regarded this case as a striking illus-tration of his concept of law as a complex of rules, principles and policies. The central conflict in the case was between the black-letter legal *rules* of probate relating to the validity of wills and legal inheritance, and the unwritten *principles* of the common law. The case also provides an excellent illustration of the practical implications of the competing theories of law. A number of points should be noted before we examine these.

First, it seems intuitively obvious, given the prevailing moral views on such cases, that anyone who murders for profit thereby forfeits their right to the proceeds. Nobody would suggest that a man convicted for armed robbery should keep the money that he had hidden before serving his sentence. The difference with Palmer, of course, is that he appeared to be legally, if not morally, entitled to it. Second, it should be remembered that two judges did not find it intuitively obvious that he should forfeit the right to inherit, or at least not obvious enough to find against Palmer. One dissenting judge declared that it would be bad social policy to punish someone twice for the same crime. There had also been earlier cases similar enough to *Riggs* v. *Palmer* to be cited as precedent, in which apparently shocking judgements had not been appealed. In *Owens* v. *Owens* (Adams 1992: 138), for example, a widow convicted of being accessory before the fact to the murder of her husband was nevertheless granted entitlement to the legally specified portion of his estate.

Third, many still believe that unworthy claims like these have to be upheld for the sake of legal consistency. If the current state of the law points in an unwelcome direction, it can always be amended for future cases. This might be unfortunate, so the argument goes, but it is necessary for maintaining the credibility of the institution of legal inheritance. Consider now how the advocates of the main theoretical positions might react to and deal with a case such as *Riggs* v. *Palmer*.

(1) *Christian natural law.* It seems unlikely, given their standpoint on the necessary connection between law and morality, that any traditional natural lawyer adhering to the higher law of reason would countenance such a manifest injustice. Good law is derived from the moral precepts of Christianity, rather than a literalistic reading of the law. A decision for Palmer would be contrary to the requirements of right reason. This is not to say that the ruling would be invalid, only that a natural law judge would have been more inclined to apply principles of natural justice.

(2) *Black-letter positivism.* It was probably only those who advocated following the rules of law to the letter who supported the decision in Palmer's favour. This is the narrowest possible interpretation of positivism, according to which judges should apply the rules exactly as they find them, no more and no less, regardless of the consequences. The dissenting judge Gray justified his rejection of the appeal with the opinion that:

> the matter does not lie within the domain of conscience. We are bound by the rigid rules of law, which have been established by the legislature [which] has by its enactments prescribed exactly when and how wills may be made, altered, and revoked, and apparently, as it seems to me, when they have been fully complied with, has left no room for the exercise of an equitable jurisdiction by courts over such matters.
>
> (Adams 1992: 138)

Although this severely literalist approach has a strong following in the courts, it should not be assumed that all positivists accept it.

(3) *Austinian positivism.* One thing that all positivists do accept is that the legal decision on this case must be constrained by the rules governing wills, the validity of which depends upon their having been posited by an authorised body. According to Austin's command theory, judges apply the orders or rules authorised by the sovereign, and in situations that require clarification they act as delegated 'temporary' commanders to resolve ambiguity or vagueness. On the face of it, this seems straightforward; judges stand in for and legislate on behalf of the sovereign when hard cases arise. Austin's own recognition of the problem of cases unanticipated by the drafters of statutes is limited, as we have seen, to the observation that some rules have blurred edges. In a case like *Riggs* v. *Palmer*, however, the rules have run out; there is no relevant rule to apply. This, though, is only the beginning of the problem. Do the 'temporary commanders' make the ruling as they see fit, following their own inclinations, or do they rule in such a way that they believe the sovereign legislature (Parliament, Congress or whatever) would have done with this case in mind? The latter course – which is called 'equitable

construction' – was in fact taken by Judge Earl, who found against Palmer, stating that:

> it was the intention of the lawmakers that the donees in a will should have the property given to them. But it could never have been their intention that a donee who murdered the testator to make the will operative should have any benefit under it.
>
> (Adams 1992: 136)

His reasoning proceeds to justify the reconstruction of the intentions of the lawmaker by imaginary interrogation. This doctrine certainly goes beyond Austinian positivism, but could easily be accommodated by it.

(4) *Hartian positivism.* Despite the greater sophistication of Hart's concept of law and of his approach to the linguistic problems at the root of hard cases, it is doubtful that it takes us much further than Austin. Does the idea of a judge's discretion to bring clarity into the area of the penumbra, where the meaning of the law is indeterminate, provide an answer to a case in which the rules have simply run out? In fact, Hart's response is that it is in cases like these where judges have genuinely free discretion to formulate an appropriate rule and create new law. According to Hart, the 'noble dream' of complete determinacy breaks down in cases like this, leaving judges to their own best devices. What this means is that the discretion they exercise is a freedom to apply their own moral beliefs or values, rather than merely a discretion to interpret the law in their own way. In a case like *Riggs* v. *Palmer*, there is no legal guidance on how to proceed.

(5) *Realism and rule-scepticism.* As we have seen, there is no easily identifiable 'realist' position, and there are many degrees of rule-scepticism. On Hart's account of the rule-sceptic 'nightmare', they see nothing but perpetual *ad hoc* creativity and unreliability in the law. This kind of rule-sceptic would undoubtedly see *Riggs* v. *Palmer* as a dramatic confirmation of the sceptical image of law as a chaos of personal bias and prejudice, in which judges, when backed into a tight corner, do just as they please. The case would indeed have been seen by Hutcheson or Frank as corroboration of their criticism of the false certainties of mechanical jurisprudence. Even these 'extreme' realists, however, were not as one-sided as this. They might also have seen the outcome of this particular case as a vindication of their belief in the ability of the best judges to reason their way intuitively to the just and equitable solution to the most difficult of hard cases. Hutcheson in particular described judges as waiting for the creative flash of inspiration, seeking out the solution from their knowledge of written and unwritten rules and principles of common law.

The important point here is that this kind of solution does not require the 'equitable construction' of the intentions of the original lawmaker. The Aristotelian 'equity', the ability to individualise general principles of justice to a particular case, is in the hands of the judges, not the legislators. Why, after all, should a court appeal to what a legislator or drafter of a constitution, perhaps as long as two or three centuries ago, might or might not have intended in the wording of a statute? Realist reflections such as these in the 1920s and 1930s were an important source of Dworkin's theory of hard cases.

(6) *Dworkin's theory.* Dworkin's treatment of *Riggs* v. *Palmer* as a paradigm case differs radically from all of these interpretations. He took this case as a paradigm because he believed that it brought into sharp focus the shortcomings of every version of positivism. The central point is that, for Dworkin, the rules may have run out but the law has not. Dworkin's argument is that the decision finally reached by the majority of judges in the Court of Appeal was the right one, not only allowed by but also required by law. In other words, the judges were under a duty – in this as in all cases – to find a particular decision in accordance with the objective rights of the parties involved. There was a real solution to be discovered, rather than a workable decision to be taken.

The decisive principle of common law in this case was, as we saw at the outset, the principle that no one should profit from their own wrongdoing. This is why the relevant rules did not prevail. The manner in which this was cited by Judge Earl was, however, more complex than this. The wider context was that:

> all laws, as well as contracts, may be controlled in their operation and effect by general, fundamental maxims of the common law. No one shall be permitted to profit by his own fraud, or to take advantage of his own wrong, or to found any claim upon his own iniquity, or to acquire property by his own crime.
>
> (Adams 1992: 137)

This judge was in no doubt that he could detect the operation of this principle in countless previous rulings in every area of common law. It was to be taken as paramount in this case because he perceived it to be authentically legal, not because it was a worthy moral principle. On the other hand, of course, he believed that unless it were morally sound, it could not have become an embedded feature of the common law. It is this general outlook, binding the moral with the legal, as well as this particular decision that Dworkin is endorsing as an exemplification of the most justified legal practices.

Dworkin, however, does not maintain that such principles drawn from the common law tradition should be treated as absolute. On the contrary, the decision reached in this case was legally sound because it took account of the relevant rules, principles and social policies. As we saw earlier, the status of principles is logically different from that of rules, which either apply or they do not. Principles, by contrast, have the dimension of weight, which means that if they are in conflict with established rules, other principles or good social policy, they have to be balanced against them. Also, the source of their validity is different. Whereas the 'pedigree' of rules is traced back to their enactment, thereby confirming their validity, principles such as 'nobody should profit from their own wrongdoing' have never been enacted or otherwise laid down; they are inferred as the best explanation for existing legal practices.

How far does the outcome of *Riggs* v. *Palmer* support Dworkin's theory of law as integrity? In the first place, it does seem to confirm the proposition that common law moral principles, distinct from legal rules, are themselves an integral part of the law. This in itself, however, is insufficient to support the further claim that a holistic assessment of the case would provide a unique correct answer, according to the lights of political morality. On Dworkin's reading, the judgement of Earl did discover that answer, by applying the criteria of best fit and best light. One of his key comments in this respect was his observation that Gray seemed to have agreed with Earl that the law would be better if it blocked Palmer's inheritance, but did not agree that the law therefore did deny it to him (Dworkin 1986: 36). Faced with conflicting precedents, Earl was looking for the best fit with the past and reading the law in its best possible light, making the best moral sense of it, thereby finding a deeper consistency and making the law speak with one coherent voice.

Others, however, have rejected this interpretation and have even denied that this was the right decision according to law, or that the judges had the legal right to innovate in this manner. On this view, the proper legal procedure was to apply the rules and leave the matter to the legislature. If true, this would imply that Dworkin's criterion of best light is a misconceived intrusion of moral and political values into law and legal reasoning.

Criticisms of Dworkin

The rule–principle distinction

It is central to Dworkin's case against positivism – especially in its Hartian version – that the law is a moral–legal complex of rules and principles. This is the fundamental challenge to the separation thesis. If it is true, there is no morally neutral procedure of legal validation, because it is not possible to abstract the purely factual rules from this complex and identify those that are binding in the sense that they will always prevail in a hard case. The determination of legality always involves the recognition of moral principles. Given this wider and more flexible concept of law, it is possible for Dworkin to argue that while the rules may run out, the law need never do so, that it will always have the principled resources to deal with any question which arises.

There are several plausible responses to the rule–principle distinction. The first is to question the intelligibility of ascribing different logical status to a principle, which according to Dworkin has weight rather than an all-or-nothing quality. What does it mean to say that whereas a rule is either applicable or it is not, a principle can be 'weighed' against another one? In the end, it also either applies or it does not. In the *Riggs* v. *Palmer* example, the principle prohibiting profit from wrongdoing is applied, while in other cases it is not. Indeed, what is the difference between a rule and a principle? It is not a matter of particularity and generality; there can be particular or general expressions of either. It cannot be that a principle can be unwritten or 'understood'; so can a rule. This problem, which has never been satisfactorily clarified by Dworkin, is in the end, though, only a matter for clarification. The implications of the distinction for legal validity are undeniable.

Given that the distinction is accepted as meaningful, one uncompromising line of criticism is to insist that only hard and fast rules laid down by legislation or judicial ruling are genuinely legal, and that the cases which Dworkin highlights, bringing common law principles into play, are examples of dubious legal practice, allowing judicial decisions to be politicised. This has also been said about the case of *Henningsen* (1960), in which substantial damages were awarded against a motor company standing on a valid contract, and about more famous cases deployed by Dworkin, such as *Brown v. Board of Education* (1954), declaring racial segregation in schools to be unconstitutional. With this formalistic approach, saving the predictability and determinacy of existing law at the expense of admitting serious gaps in the law – to be filled by subsequent legislation – judges have to operate within the rules, applying law as they find it. No element of moral or political assessment is required or permitted. On this line of argument, the separation thesis stands intact: the law as we find it (or the sum of the rules as we find them) is one thing, our moral judgement of its merits and defects is another.

Most positivists today, however, accept that something like Dworkin's principles do play a prominent and legitimate part in legal reasoning, while denying that this has the implications Dworkin argues for. It has been argued, for example, that in Hart's account of positivism he understands 'rules' in the wider sense that includes principles, thus bringing them into the system of validation whereby they are traceable back to a rule of recognition. Alternatively, it can be conceded that Hart's account is defective in this respect, that it needs supplementing with principles, but that the resultant legal–moral complex can be subjected to a positivist master test. On this 'inclusive' account, principles as well as rules have ultimately to be validated by the original rule of recognition.

If this much is conceded, however, it might seem that positivism has fatally compromised its position by abandoning the separation thesis, allowing that moral principles are an integral part of the law. What is required, according to 'inclusive' positivists, is a closer examination and rearticulation of the separation thesis, of what is separable from what. According to Neil MacCormick, for example, Dworkin scored a palpable hit in his critique of Hartian positivism's exaggerated attention to rules to the exclusion of principles, but failed to show that the essential tenets of positivism were thereby discredited. MacCormick accepts that law is never value-free; on the contrary – he agrees – in both its rules and principles it *embodies* values, and is always already infused with values. He claims that Dworkin is right to argue that the law cannot be 'hermetically sealed from morals and politics' (MacCormick 1978: 236), but wrong to conclude from this that the law cannot be described in a positivistic manner, independently of evaluative appraisal, or that the rule of recognition criterion for determining the legality of rules should be abandoned.

The real meaning of the separation thesis, for MacCormick, is that one could describe, expound or explain, for example, the South African system of apartheid – rules, principles and all – without thereby morally endorsing or condemning it. The separation thesis, properly understood, requires only the descriptive–normative distinction. This is what moral neutrality means: judgement is suspended for purposes of analysis and description. The laws of England or the USA on sex or race discrimination cannot be explained without reference to moral and political principles, but they can be fully described without moral judgement one way or the other. This, MacCormick argues, is the defensible form of the separation thesis, rather than the claim that the law is intrinsically value-free.

As a modified version of Hart's model of rules, extending it to include Dworkinian principles, this is a plausible alternative to Dworkin's theory of constructive interpretation. MacCormick's further insistence, however, that no positivist has seriously entertained the 'intrinsic' interpretation of the separation thesis, and that this suspension of judgement was what they had in mind all along, is unconvincing. The least that can be said is that the leading defenders of the separation thesis (Bentham, Austin, Holmes, Kelsen) equivocated between the two versions as described by MacCormick. What he implies is that they did not see the issue clearly, and that his explanation is a clarification of what they really meant. There is little doubt, however, that they were proposing more than a method of objective detachment, of refraining from evaluation. The underlying reality of law described from this position – law as an object of legal science – was indeed understood to be 'value-free', a bare pyramid structure of commands, rules or Kelsenian norms, stripped of the moral language of rights and duties. It was this image of law that Dworkin, following Fuller, was challenging.

To use MacCormick's own example (MacCormick 1978: 200–4), the Rent Restriction Act of 1920 would not have been understood by the classical positivists to have no moral implications for the interests of landlords and tenants, but their separation of law and morals would have required not only that they look dispassionately at the content and operation of the Act, but also that they disregard the moral or political principles of fairness, justice and rights governing the introduction of the rules. What they were looking for was the underlying structure of validation of these legal rules, in terms of the authority of the sovereign, the basic norm or whatever. This 'science of law' requires the expulsion of these principles from the domain of law; they are regarded as extraneous factors. Dworkin's response was to argue for their inherent legality, not by virtue of their sources or points of origin, but by virtue of their mere presence in the common law. MacCormick's acceptance of these principles as authentically legal, by virtue of their function in relation to rules, thus indirectly validated by the rule of recognition, aligns him with a developed Hartian positivism against Dworkin while at the same time distinguishing his own position from that of classical positivism.

While Dworkin's assault on the model of rules and his emphasis on the role of principles have received a generally favourable response, and have stimulated refinements and adjustments to the positivist position, it is his own alternative to these models that has attracted the most fundamental criticism.

Dworkin's moral objectivism

Much of the criticism of his theory as a whole is an extension of the wider philosophical disputes about the moral objectivism upon which Dworkin's legal theory rests. If it were true that all moral judgement had an inescapably subjective element (Mackie 1977a), then it would be clear that the one right answer thesis would have to be rejected. Given that Dworkin's concept of law includes moral standards, we would have to conclude that with questions of law there is either more than one possible 'right' answer, or that the very idea of correctness as applied to law is inappropriate. Those critics of Dworkin who do emphatically reject any form of moral objectivism tend to focus their criticism accordingly on the figure of the ideal judge Hercules, who symbolises the possibility of objective judgement. If Hercules can be exposed as a fraud, it is believed, the idea that every hard case has a unique correct answer, and that this answer will be based on the recognition of objective rights, will go down with him.

Arguments from disagreement

The most common criticism of Hercules is that, as a mythical figure embodying the possibility of objectivity about legal problems with a moral dimension, he is inappropriate because the supposition that such a judge is possible in principle presupposes what Dworkin is trying to prove. Sceptical feelings about the role of Hercules are reinforced by the suspicion that the objectivity claimed on his behalf is just another substitute for God as the absolute and omniscient authority and ultimate arbiter of human disagreement. On this reading, the theory of constructive interpretation is no more than a recycling of a discredited legal formalism, declaring that fallible human judges can shed their subjectivity and use the law 'as a whole' to cut through intractable moral problems and conflicts between rights to find the elusive right answer, which in fact does not exist. Those more sympathetic to Dworkin's approach, however, regard this as an exaggeration of the problem of objectivity and a misrepresentation of what it requires. Dworkin himself, it should be remembered, sees objectivity in the assessment of conflicting rights in accordance with existing law not only as a logical possibility, but also as a practical reality, as law working at its best. Hercules – with his unlimited vision – is only the perfected ideal of what is often actually achieved in the courts.

The important criticisms, however, are more specific than this. One of the main types of criticism is that there is too much fundamental disagreement between people, and especially between judges presiding over hard cases, for Dworkin's thesis to be plausible. If there were right answers to moral questions, one would expect more convergence of opinion, at least between rational individuals who have reflected long and hard on the matter. All the more so might we expect such convergence in legal decisions, when the adjudicators are professionals; yet one case after another is inherently controversial, dividing judicial opinion at every level in the system. Surely this is an indication that there cannot be one objective answer?

In this form, the argument from disagreement should not be taken too seriously. The first point is that 'objectivity' does not *mean* convergence of opinion (either of universal or of well-informed opinion); such convergence or consensus is no more than a symptom, and certainly no guarantee of objectivity. Objectivity here means *mind independence*, that the answer is right or wrong independently of any opinion. There is nothing inherently implausible about serious disagreement on difficult moral matters leading the best-informed opinion astray, any more than there is in disputes in the natural sciences in contexts where the point at issue is subject to demonstrable truth. Disagreement in itself, no matter how extensive, proves nothing against a truth-claim. Being right does not mean having the ability to command universal assent. The second point is that the majority is not necessarily right. Two judges on a bench of five can be right, the other three wrong, about the state of the law and what it requires in the instant case. Dissenting judges are often vindicated by a higher court. The frequency of dissent is no indication either way on the question of whether or not there is a right answer to be found.

If the argument from mere disagreement is ineffective, however, others directed more specifically at the nature of judicial reason and at Dworkin's version of objectivism are potentially more damaging. Brian Bix, for example, has argued that there are reasons why it is inevitable – rather than just a matter of fact – that judges would give different judgements if they were to apply Dworkin's criteria. When it is all a matter of interpretation, the criterion of moral soundness ('best light') will vary from one judge to another, according to variations in their political and moral beliefs; as will the criterion of best fit with the relevant legal materials. Furthermore, there is too much flexibility in the application of these two criteria, such that judges are not sufficiently constrained by the requirement of 'best fit'. If applied, Dworkin's theory, supposedly objective, would generate more disagreement than already exists. Dworkin's only defence, he argues, is that his theory is an interpretation of actual judicial practice in its best possible light, but in this case he is prescribing and cannot present the theory as a description of actual practices (Bix 1993: 106–11).

It is doubtful, however, that this criticism does undermine the right answer thesis, or even establish the claim that Dworkin's theory would have this unsettling effect. Dworkin's own understanding of the points at issue here is that he is advocating the interpretive approach to steer it between the undesired alternatives of mechanical jurisprudence and free discretion. The best judicial practices, he believes, adhere to neither of these options. Judges are indeed bound by the constraints of best fit with existing precedent, hence they are not free creators of law; however, at the same time – by virtue of the criterion of best light – they are more free than those who believe that they are mechanically finding law (Dworkin 1986: 234). The question here is whether Dworkin's recommendations, if universally adopted, with every judge constructing a complete theory of law, would be likely to generate more disagreement than exists at present. This question persists through all the significant criticisms of the Dworkinian theory.

MacCormick, who as we saw above accepted the value of Dworkin's critique of Hart's model of rules, develops the argument from disagreement to attack the rights thesis and the one right answer thesis. His argument is that there are no right answers because of the *kind* of disagreement involved in hard cases. Citing Thomas Reid's argument against Hume's subjectivism – that the very presence of genuine disagreement proves that there is always in principle a correct answer to moral questions – MacCormick argues that Reid's mistake here lies in the conflation of two kinds of disagreement, the speculative and the practical. With speculative disagreement, the differences can in principle be resolved because they are wrangles over what is or is not actually the case. With practical disagreement, what it always comes down to is a decision about how best to lead our lives, or how society should be organised. What rights and principles of justice, in the end, do we want to acknowledge?

MacCormick's illustration of this distinction is the principle established in the historic case of *Donoghue v. Stevenson* (1932) (Baker 1991: 90), which changed the course of English law on negligence. The salient facts of the case were that a customer in an ice cream parlour had bought her friend Mrs Donoghue a bottle of ginger beer, the contents of which she had partially consumed before discovering the remains of a decomposed snail. On account of the distress and subsequent illness suffered, she sued the manufacturer Stevenson for compensation. Her first action failed, because the manufacturer was only legally liable to the person with whom he had a contract, the one who had actually purchased it. When the appeal was heard by the House of Lords, however, the decision went in her favour, by a majority of 3–2. The important point established here was that there existed in law 'a general duty of care'. This was expressed by the 'neighbour principle' expounded in Lord Atkin's ruling, according to which every person has a legal duty of care towards his or her neighbour, who is defined as anyone who it might reasonably be foreseen will be affected by that person's acts or omissions, not merely as those with whom one has a contract. This majority ruling was disputed by two judges, whose main arguments rested on the prediction of disastrous implications for the manu-facturing industry.

One question here is whether this principle was already present in English law. Was the prevailing opinion a new departure, or was it a recognition of what was implicitly there? While for most positivists, such landmark rulings quite clearly signal new departures, a Dworkinian interpretation is that positive law on this matter did indeed change in 1932, but that this change was superficial compared with the deeper continuity in terms of its emergence from earlier principles and rulings from which the neighbour principle was inferred. The decision that the Lords reached on this occasion was, legally and morally speaking, the right answer, rather than a deduction from a principle snatched out of thin air. If they had decided any other way, they would have been *wrong*.

MacCormick, however, uses this case to undermine the one right answer thesis. The legal disputes in such cases he sees as distinguishable into both kinds of disagreement, speculative and practical. He concedes to Dworkin that the principle recognised in *Donoghue* may well have been implicit in the law before 1932, by virtue of earlier decisions, and that disputes of this nature do admit of an objectively right answer. Against Dworkin, however, he argues that once such speculative disagreement has been settled, 'we find ourselves beyond that which can be reasoned out'; we are confronted with a choice between what are often equally plausible alternatives. When all speculative disagreement is resolved, the practical question remains: Which right do the courts, speaking for society, prefer to support? In the practical sense, there was no one right answer to which of the equally tenable rights (of the manufacturer's right of contract, or the customer's right to compensation) should be upheld. In the event, a narrow majority endorsed the neighbour principle and significantly changed our way of life. The matter was resolved by mixed considerations of public interest, corrective justice and common sense. The overall point here is that on this interpretation, while it might be true that there is in principle a right answer to the question about fitting precedent, the same cannot be said about the moral soundness of the adjudication between competing rights. Hercules can cope with the first question, but not with the second (MacCormick 1978: 108–15, 251–8).

The best Dworkinian reply to this is not, as MacCormick suggests, the argument that all legal disputes are speculative. The best way is to question MacCormick's Humean premises, which include the supposition that competing conceptions of justice are essentially subjective, in the sense that they must, in the end, simply be a matter of preference. It is not true that, in cases like this, judges can only reach out beyond reason and decide which social policies to endorse. Is it really true that the competing rights here were 'equally tenable'? What was actually happening was that one principle-based right (to compensation) was outweighing the principle behind a rule-based right (of contract). The manufacturer was found to be liable because the outweighed principle was objectively weaker than the one that prevailed. Such claims are not 'objective' in the sense of being value-free. Questions of justice are imbued with value, but they can still be resolved objectively.

Arguments from incommensurability

Two things are said to be commensurable when there is a common standard by which to measure them. Any two trees are commensurable in terms of height. It is meaningful and true to say that a three-yard line is longer than one of eight feet, and a two-mile road is longer than one of three kilometres, because in either case there is a determinate method of conversion from one scale to the other. When two things are incommensurable, lacking a common standard, the one cannot be measured against the other. Only like can be compared with like. The quality of two pieces of music can be compared, but they cannot be compared with the quality of a scientific treatise.

The problem of incommensurability has been raised against Dworkin by a number of critics, including Mackie (1977b), Finnis (George 1992), MacCormick (1978) and Bix (1996). The general thrust of this criticism is that opposing rights cannot be weighed against each other, because there is no common standard by which to measure the respective value of, say, the rights based on contract and the right to compensation. It is a problem of finding a neutral standpoint from which to judge the competing claims. If the situation is such that one of the rights has to give way, then it is a matter of public policy for judge, legislature or society to decide which of the rights is to be preferred. Hard cases cannot be resolved by declaring which right 'scores' higher than another.

Mackie's criticism is that with his rights thesis, Dworkin presupposes a single scale upon which opposing rights-claims can be measured against each other, with one right outweighing another. The idea that a unique right answer can objectively emerge from 'too simple a metric of commensurability on a linear scale' is rejected by Mackie on the grounds that the merits of opposing claims cannot be measured in this manner.

Dworkin's reply to this criticism – that we make such 'best-decision-all-things-considered' arbitrations all the time – has generally been regarded as unsatisfactory. It is difficult to see what distinguishes this from a Hartian positivist interpretation. It is not the best decision Dworkin is looking for; it is the right answer. A better reply here would follow the same course as the reply to the arguments from disagreement. In the same way that there is no need to argue that all legal disputes are speculative, there is no need to argue that all rights are commensurable in the sense of being quantifiable. Rights can have objectively discernible relative weight in terms of principles of justice, without this relative weight being expressible in numerical terms.

Finnis's criticism is quite different. As a natural lawyer, his quarrel is not with Dworkin's moral objectivism. Dismissing the arguments from disagreement and the subjectivist scepticism about correct moral judgements, Finnis argues that Dworkin's mistake is that he has failed to understand the real complexity of the tension between the technical requirements of law for providing the means for unequivocal dispute resolution, and its character as an instrument of justice. This failure, he argues, is reflected in Dworkin's theory of the relation between the dimensions of best fit and best light, which he assumes to be commensurable. According to Finnis, commitment to moral objectivism does not entail the one right answer thesis in law, because looking for one right answer to a hard case is like looking for the single English novel that is both 'the funniest' and 'the best'. Similarly, one answer might provide the best fit, but another answer the soundest morally speaking. In other words, the scales of moral soundness and of fit are incommensurable, a fact that is obscured by Dworkin's assumption that the right answer can always be found on each scale, with Hercules interpreting law in its best light by selecting the morally soundest from the range of those that fit the best. Dworkin's awareness of this problem is apparent from his change of strategy in his later writings. Moving away from the intuitively plausible argument in *Taking Rights Seriously*, that the right answer is the morally soundest with sufficient fit, to the vaguer argument in *Law's Empire*, that it is only a question of striking the right balance, he implicitly admits that the problem is not easily solved.

Conclusion

Within the theoretical framework established by Hart and Dworkin, the most influential interpretations of law in recent years are still essentially rooted in the traditional antagonisms between conflicting perspectives in moral philosophy and radically opposed understandings of the relation between law and morality. In many ways, the contemporary disputes are still seen by some as continuations of the long-standing conflicts between common law thinking and its critics. What has changed, however, is the level of sophistication in the opposed theories and the degree of convergence between them. The exchanges between Dworkin and his Hartian and natural law critics, in particular, are no longer marked by the mutual incomprehension displayed in earlier episodes of these disputes.

Study questions

General question: When judges decide hard cases, should they be understood as applying existing law or as making new law?

Further study questions: Is there always one and only one right answer to questions of law? Explain and critically evaluate either Hart's or Dworkin's theory of hard cases. Critically assess Dworkin's theory of law as integrity. Does Dworkin's criticism of the positivist models of rules succeed in undermining the positivist understanding of law? Which theory of law do the cases of *Riggs v. Palmer* and *Donoghue v. Stevenson* support? Are there morally neutral and legally objective answers to these cases? Is MacCormick's revision of the separation thesis more convincing than the traditional version?

Suggestions for further reading

Recommended general reading on contemporary legal theory, representing a range of views and approaches, are Gavison (1987), George (1996), Raz (1975), Finnis (1980), Lyons (1993) and Posner (1990).

From the extensive literature on hard cases, Hart (1961: ch. VII.1; 1983: ch. 4) and Dworkin (1977b: chaps 1–4) are essential. The revised edition of Hart (1995) contains a postscript in which he replies to Dworkin's criticisms. Useful and important general commentaries include MacCormick (1978: ch. 8), Bix (1993), Cotterell (1989: ch. 6) and Lyons (1984: 87–104).

On Dworkin's theory of law as a whole, the most sympathetic is Guest (1992). An anthology of critical essays (Cohen 1984) includes replies from Dworkin. Discussions of Dworkin can also be found in Mackie (1977b), MacCormick (1982: ch. 7), Posner (1990: ch. 6) and Simmonds (1986: ch. 6).

On contemporary natural law theory, there are valuable collections by Finnis (1991, vols I and II) and George (1992). Other significant works include Finnis (1980), Beyleveld and Brownsword (1986) and Weinreb (1987). On contemporary positivism and the analysis of rules, the main works to read are Raz (1975), Twining and Miers (1976) and George (1996).

For further details and conflicting interpretations of the significance of the case of *Donoghue* v. *Stevenson*, see Baker (1991: 90–5), Halpin (1997: ch. 6), MacCormick (1978) and Fleming (1994: 158–64).

5   Law and modernity

In this chapter we will be looking at some key aspects of the conflict between traditional legal theory and its more radical critics in recent decades. These disputes originate in the wider world of philosophical, cultural and political controversies that flared up in the last quarter of the twentieth century, and can only be understood against that backdrop. Unlike those dealt with in earlier chapters, the most representative and influential of the new theories are deeply confrontational in the sense that their explicit aim is to destabilise and overthrow a traditional approach to legal thinking in its entirety, rather than propose modifications of prevailing images of law. At the same time, it seeks to refocus legal studies on addressing fundamental questions of social justice. Despite this apparent breach with the established traditions, however, it is still the perennial question of justice, what it means and how it relates to law, that stands at the centre of these controversies. Socialist, feminist and race theory critics of law, for example, are concerned with the injustice towards subordinate social classes, repressed women and ethnic minorities, injustices that are argued to be perpetuated by legal institutions and reinforced by legal theory. At the same time, however, much of the criticism aims to undermine the very notion of justice, to expose it as an ideological façade, the function of which is to conceal the essentially oppressive nature of law. This tension – between the urge to broaden the basis of justice and at the same time to denounce justice as a fraud – runs right through the arguments for and against the new criticism.

The roots of modernity and the Enlightenment

To understand this, we have to look at the roots of what is now often disparagingly known as *modernity*. This is a concept with multiple layers of meaning that has become so pervasive today that it is almost impossible to pin down. In cultural terms, 'being modern' can mean anything from being tuned in all the latest fashions to a naïve enthusiasm for the most advanced technology. In a philosophical context its meaning is disputed – as are the related terms 'modern' and 'modernism' – but the sense most relevant here is modernity as a body of thought (ideas, beliefs, values) or way of thinking that took root at the beginning of our 'modern' age, with the changes in mentality that brought about the scientific revolution of the seventeenth century and the political revolutions of the 1780s. Crucial to the contemporary debates is the period of Enlightenment that emerged from and consolidated the age of reason in science, philosophy and politics over the course of the eighteenth century. Much of the philosophy in Europe over the last century has been preoccupied with critically examining the heritage of this period of Enlightenment.

The imagery of light and enlightenment has permeated modern thought so thoroughly, especially with the idea of enlightened thinkers or politicians being the most civilised and morally advanced of their day, that one needs to be constantly aware that the Enlightenment as an intellectual achievement was only established as the result of an immensely complex struggle against ignorance and tyranny, and that it was itself by no means a homogeneous movement, with its leading advocates deeply divided over fundamental issues. It was less the agreement on any particular doctrine than a consensus on more abstract commitments that defined the Enlightenment, such as the belief in the power of the individual human mind to think rationally and arrive at objectively true and reliable conclusions without the assistance of traditional authority. Thus, the mark of enlightenment was described memorably by Immanuel Kant (1724–1804), one of its leading exponents, as humanity emerging from its childhood, as a process of reaching maturity, or the ability to reason independently. This was envisaged less as the abrupt casting away of tradition, more as a process of reaching the kind of maturity that would systematically subject all traditions hitherto received uncritically to the criticism of reason. It was not an enlightened age, declared Kant, but it was an age of enlightenment. Humanity was growing up. The autonomous individual became one of the principal symbols of the age.

Liberal individualism

What was taking shape throughout this period was the philosophy of liberal individualism, with growing demands for freedom of speech and freedom from the arbitrary acts of unjust despots. Universal values, true for every human society, were confidently proclaimed. Truth and reason were presented as the natural enemies of the abuse of sovereign power, an abuse that thrives on lies and irrationality. Above all, reason dictated that a society of free and equal individual citizens be subject to the rule of law, with everyone protected in their individual rights, rather than to the rule of an unchecked sovereign. This revolution in political awareness would not have been possible without the equally dramatic shifts in consciousness that had initiated the scientific revolution in the previous century. At the heart of this enterprise also lay the search for an elusive method to guarantee objective truth. In combination with the dispassionate study of empirical details, the light of reason would eventually illuminate the entire world of nature, society and political morality. With the rapid advances in scientific knowledge, it was natural to believe that the trust in reason would ensure unstoppable progress in every field of inquiry.

Critics of the Enlightenment

These were the main features of the Enlightenment that made it so plausible and attractive to many of the leading philosophers of the day. The prospect was one of complete human emancipation from self-inflicted ignorance and suffering. In recent years it has become fashionable to echo its early critics and caricature it as an age of arrogant certainty coupled with a naïve belief in progress and a quasi-religious worship of Reason as the answer to every problem, ignoring the dark and irrational side of human nature. Many critics have seen it as the beginning of a long hubristic venture, leading ultimately and inevitably to the environmental disasters and dehumanisation associated with advanced technology and globalisation.

Marx and Nietzsche

The two most radical thinkers of the nineteenth century, Karl Marx (1818–83) and Friedrich Nietzsche (1844–1900), were diametrically opposed in their responses to modernity. If Marx represented the internal challenge from the radical wing of the Enlightenment, confronting liberalism with its failure to deliver on its promises of universal emancipation and equality, Nietzsche developed a comprehensive critique of its philosophical underpinnings, aiming to destroy what he saw as the democratisation and decadence of European culture. Both were concerned with exposing ideals as lies and masks for forms of social domination and oppression, but while Marx denounced liberal or bourgeois morality as the hypocritical expression of the interests of a particular social group, Nietzsche represented almost the entire history of morality as a long tale of pitiful self-deception, transforming the experience of human suffering into a magnificent edifice of objective moral values, the truth of which was imagined to be independent of their creators. Whereas it is plausible to interpret Marx and his communist followers as genuine heirs to the Enlightenment, seeking to take it to a higher level, Nietzsche saw in its central ideas, the 'enlightened' philosophers' belief in the universality of values, nothing but the projection of these philosophers' own cultures. Whereas Nietzsche regarded this belief in the objectivity of created values as the pinnacle of human folly, the Marxists never relinquished their belief in objectivity.

Overall, the influence of Marx on the twentieth century's political conflicts has been more visible, but Nietzsche's influence on Western thought and culture as a whole has been more profound and far-reaching. His diagnosis of the nihilistic 'sickness' of modern European civilisation and his prophesy of the crisis that would engulf it in the following century had a formative influence on a number of crucial movements and figures of that century, notably Freud's theory of the unconscious, the development of abstract art and the philosophies of Martin Heidegger (1889–1976) and Michel Foucault (1926–84). The nature of this crisis lies at the centre of all the discussions of the *post*modernist rejection of modernity and Enlightenment.

Nietzsche's perspectivism

The single idea for which Nietzsche has been most celebrated by postmodernists and others is contained in his perspectivism. This should be understood as the opposite pole to the seductive Enlightenment dream of attaining a standpoint from which all truths – metaphysical, scientific and moral – would be visible at a glance. Nietzsche's perspectivism, at first sight, not only rejects this as impossible, but also swings to the other extreme, to the denial of all truths whatsoever. This kind of 'global' scepticism was not new to philosophy – it has always been present as an epistemological overreaction against claims to certain knowledge and can be traced back to the ancient Greeks – but Nietzsche's perspectivist version gave it a novel twist. All truth-claims, whether they relate to everyday perception, scientific theories or moral judgements, are held to be wholly dependent upon the position or perspective of the observer. When they are represented as more than a particular opinion, as representing the 'objective' truth of the matter, they are aspiring to a standpoint that it is logically impossible to occupy. There simply is no outside point of view. One can only look through one's own eyes. Accordingly, no point of view is closer to or further from the object it seeks to represent than any other. All our concepts and elaborate theories of the structure of matter or the requirements of justice are nothing but more or less elaborate and ingenious perspectives provided by interpreters of a world that is not graspable in itself. Every point of view is as good or as 'valid' as any other. In short, there are no truths, only interpretations.

There has always been a tendency to respond to such claims with exasperation, not only because they collide with so many of our intuitions about obvious truths and falsehoods, but also because they are so difficult to refute. There is a standard 'quick' refutation of global scepticism, which involves demonstrating that it involves an immediate contradiction. If there are no truths, then it is not true that there are no truths. Any statement asserting the complete absence of truth is thus self-refuting, because at least one statement must be true. By its own standards, perspectivism is itself only one perspective. Nietzsche's perspectivism, however, has retained its influence over modern philosophy, because those who can see its allure regard such refutations as verbal trickery. Also, it should be noted that on closer analysis Nietzsche's own position was not as extreme as this. He did not in fact reject truth as such, but he has been interpreted by many of his

postmodernist followers as having done so. Nevertheless, however one inter-
prets it, it is Nietzsche's perspectivism that marks him out as the key source of
the postmodernist attacks on the central pillars of Enlightenment rationalism.

The death of God and the will to power

Two prominent themes closely related to Nietzsche's perspectivism are 'the
death of God' and 'the will to power'. The impending crisis of values was
for Nietzsche the threat of cultural nihilism implicit in what he saw as the
illusory rise of reason, science and democracy in Europe, creating a surface
impression of progress towards ever higher levels of prosperity and social
justice. This was an illusion because when reason turns its own critical light
upon itself, it finds itself unsupported. Despite the steadily declining religious belief in an increasingly secular age, people were continuing to think
and act as though God were still there as the basis of reason and thus the
absolute source of all metaphysical and moral truth. It was only a matter of
time before the moral values that were entirely dependent upon the history
of Christianity would be seen as empty. According to Nietzsche's alternative
to traditional metaphysics, all human life is driven by the fundamental urge
that he calls the will to power, not only in the struggle for survival and dominance of nature, or in the explicit power relations between people, but also
in its highest social ideals and cultural aspirations and creations, all of which
are masks for the will to power. Taken together, these ideas about truth,
power and the self-destruction of reason have had an immeasurable impact
on contemporary philosophy.

The postmodernist attack on modernity

Postmodernism, as it emerged in 1960s French philosophy, was in large part
a reaction against its postwar domination by Sartrean existentialism and
Marxism, both of which were regarded as essentially modernist in their
basic assumptions. The reinterpretation of Nietzsche that became the norm
at this time was aimed at putting together a style of analysis capable of
breaking the grip of Enlightenment modernity on philosophy, in order to
initiate a way of thinking that was in turn as radically new as modernity
itself had been at its inception. Every aspect of this old consensus came
under scrutiny, and on all the key values postmodernist philosophy was
asserting the opposite. Almost the defining characteristic of postmodernism
is that it aims at constant disintegration, not in the sense of shattering or
dispersing, but in the sense of dis-integrating apparently seamless unities.
The objective was to take apart the systems and totalities of modernist
philosophies and show how they are constructed, not out of naturally
cohering elements but from either dissonant heterogeneous elements or from
arbitrarily selected elements to the exclusion of anything that does not
cohere. The circle either closes too quickly or it does not close at all. What

they were drawing attention to was the propensity of the knowledge-seeking mind, in its quest for the safety of certainty, to close the general and specific circles of knowledge in such a way that they become impregnable. This is what they mean by the 'closure' inherent in modernity. Hence their main concern was with the breaking up of smooth surfaces, the disruption of false patterns and above all the particularisation of universals. In real life, we experience multiple fragments and loose ends of stories leading nowhere in particular, and to make sense of this experience we impose constructed unities upon these fragments, not least upon our understanding of our own selves. Modernity, according to its critics, does something similar at every theoretical level.

This theme of closure as the principal target of postmodernism opens out into all the other prominent themes. In Jean-François Lyotard's (1924–98) famous formulation, postmodernism is defined as 'an incredulity towards metanarratives' (Lyotard 1984: xxiv), which is to say that it is quite unbelievable that anyone today should have any lingering faith in the greatest of the myths of modernity, the grand-narrative Enlightenment story of humanity's steady progress towards perfection, either in its liberal democratic or communist versions. All grand overarching narratives are regarded with suspicion by postmodernists, and even the micro-narratives by which we live are seen as constantly revisable useful fictions. The closure of the systems of modernity is also seen as being purchased at great cost for those whose histories and experiences are excluded from the closed circle. One of the defining projects of postmodernism is the attempted exposure of the marginalisation and exclusion of those who do not conform with the modernist picture of reason, rationality and justice. Critical attention is thus focused upon what lies beneath the calm surfaces of the false integrities that are subjected to the postmodernist dis-integrative techniques.

Foucault on power and knowledge

Foucault's original and distinctive contribution to postmodernist thought lies in the use he made of Nietzsche's philosophy to undermine the legitimacy of modernity. The most influential dimension of his critique is found in his treatment of power, knowledge and truth. There are several key points to be made about power. The first concerns its location. Foucault regards power as de-centred and scattered throughout society. There is no centre point from which it emanates downwards; there is only a multiplicity of lateral power or force-relations right across the social spectrum. This metaphor contrasts sharply with both the liberal and the Marxist 'modern' views of the location of sovereign power in the state, the central question for them being the legitimacy of this power. The second point about power at first sight contradicts this, because it suggests a central organisation behind the diffusion of power, in that Foucault asserts that power is intrinsically linked with knowledge in such a way that the latter can only be understood as a manifestation of power, which would seem to suggest a central point behind the multiplicity of power–knowledge matrices. All claims to genuine knowledge at any stage in human history are said to be fraudulent, because they are simply the product of the political regime of the day. Thus the claims to objective and universal truths by Enlightenment liberalism are no more than masks for the political power that has successfully replaced the previous power. These two points do not in fact necessarily contradict, if one understands it in the sense that it is through the masking of power that it is diffused throughout society.

Taken together with Foucault's application of the perspectivist denial of truth, this creates the basis for a complete disruption of rational modernist thinking. Science and technology are reduced to power–knowledge complexes, uprooted from any relation to truth or reality. There is no disinterested knowledge, because the very idea of neutral and unbiased scholarship is merely a mask for power, all the more insidious because it represents itself as its opposite.

Derrida and deconstructionism

Jacques Derrida (1930–2004) above all is thought crucial to the emergence of postmodernist critical legal thinking. At the height of his influence in France in the late 1960s he played a central role in taking what was then seen as a philosophical language revolution a stage further. He is most famously associated with the philosophical method of deconstruction, a technique for analysing texts of any sort by taking them apart and revealing the deep instability of meaning in the words in which they are written. Although deconstruction in its very nature is said to resist definition – given the instability of all meaning – it is not intended to extend to any kind of negative critical analysis. It is a specific technique developed and refined by Derrida and his followers for specific purposes. The main purpose is to undo the apparently perfect stability and equilibrium of the concepts and conceptual schemes at the heart of modernity, by 'de-structuring' them and exposing these unnatural constructs as constituting an essentially repressive way of thinking, as an elaborate deception and self-deception on a grand scale. Derrida's central concept to illustrate endemic conceptual instability he calls *différance* (in deliberate contrast to *'différence'*), which has the double meaning of differing and deferring. This is supposed to indicate the impossibility of assigning a fixed meaning to any concept whatsoever. The differences that are found everywhere in a system of linguistic signs, the dissimilarities and oppositions between concepts understood as bearers of fixed meanings, are deficient compared with the *différance* that lies behind them. The concept of *différence* artificially narrows down and freezes the meaning of terms that are inherently unstable into a fixed core that does violence to their real nature, making the term represent something independent of language. The wider concept of *différance* points to the differences in relation to their incessant insecurity and impermanence, which makes them subject to the endless deferrals of meaning implicit in the words and concepts that they differ from.

Derrida's deconstruction of law and justice

In a famous lecture entitled *Force of Law: The Mystical Foundations of Authority*, (Cornell *et al.*, 1992), Derrida's 'deconstructive interrogation' of law and justice was addressed to the perennial tension between established positive law and the timeless standards of justice as exhibited in the debate between legal positivists and natural lawyers. In a highly tendentious and arresting style, Derrida put forward in this lecture a number of reflections on the relation between legitimate authority, enforcement and violence in the law. He proposes a critique of modern legal ideology that involves a desedimentation of the superstructures of law that simultaneously conceal and reveal the interests of the dominant forces in society.

In the course of these reflections, he makes two distinct claims. First, in what he calls 'the ultimate founding moment or origin of law' there is only a *coup de force* that is neither just nor unjust, which cannot be validated by any preceding law. Second, there is no justice in contemporary law without the experience of *aporia*, a sense of paradox or impossible contradiction. The first claim involves the logic of justifying the authority of law. We obey the law, he says, not because it is just but because it has authority. If in our search for justification of this authority, we trace it back to the founding moment of law, 'the discourse comes up against its limit', in which 'a silence is walled up in the violent structure of the founding act'. This is the first sense in which he uses the term 'mystical'.

In the second sense, he discusses the experience of justice as compared to law. In this sense, the experience of justice is so alien to the legal order that it is equivalent to the sensation of a miraculous breach in the order of things, a rending of the fabric of time. What he means is that the deconstructive reading of law reveals the absolute irreconcilability of the smooth running of legal justice and its application of statutes and rules that exhibit the stable and calculable rationality typical of modernity, with the infinite incalculability and other-directedness of genuine justice. This paradox or impossible contradiction lies at the heart of the tension between justice and the law, generating further paradoxes in the experience of the judgement when the judge is aware that the law has to be both conserved and reinvented for each unique case. The judge is also aware that justice always 'cuts and divides', and with genuine justice must undergo an existential ordeal of 'giving oneself up to the impossible decision'. Without this ordeal, the decision can be legal in that it follows the rules, but can never be just.

How plausible is this analysis of justice and the law? The essential points in his argument for the mystical origins of law, on the impossibility of justice existing before or above the founding moment, are similar in structure to the positivist accounts of the origins of law. The standard critical discussions of Kelsen's basic norm and Hart's rule of recognition – to which Derrida briefly refers – have been addressing the same question, some would say with greater acuity. Derrida's description of the founding moment as 'a silence walled up in the violent structure of the founding act' adds little of any substance to Hart's comment on the logical impossibility of validating the fundamental rule of recognition in terms of itself.

In presenting law and justice as necessary antagonists, on the grounds that law in its very nature closes up and congeals the reality of justice into the general rules, norms and values of legality, Derrida contrasts the letter and spirit of the law. In doing so, he highlights the contrast and tension that he claims is buried by judicial language, that is to say the opposition between the general rules and norms of precedent, on the one hand, and the unique particularity of individual cases and decisions by judges, on the other. The aim of deconstruction (real justice) is to recognise and wrest this particularity away from the generality under which the legal cases subsume it.

The internal inconsistencies in this critique are numerous, the most obvious one being the equivocation on the meaning of justice. There are nevertheless features of it that appeal to anyone who has witnessed or experienced the sporadic unpredictability or unfairness of the law. The apparent ease with which the singularity of hard cases can be elided by the application of universal rules is one of the legitimate causes of discontent and disillusion with legal justice. The problems with Derrida's account, however, are numerous. The main problem is that its plausibility is gained by its caricature of 'law and legality' as a justice-dispensing machine, mechanically applying rules and algorithms in the manner rightly criticised by the legal realists in the 1920s. Derrida's assumption is that this mechanical jurisprudence is dictated by the reason and rationality of 'the modern', but this mechanistic approach that he lampoons represents only one narrow line of modern legal thinking. Derrida projects this formalist image of the law onto the entire judiciary, in such a way that his mystical representation of justice as the recognition of the singularity of the individual case gains credibility too easily. Overall, his account must be seen as either too close to the mainstream discussions of the relation between justice and equity in hard cases to constitute a distinctly radical challenge, or as too eccentric to be taken seriously.

Critical Legal Studies

The emergence of Critical Legal Studies (CLS) as a loose-knit movement in the USA and Britain in the late 1970s owed as much to the earlier legal realists as it did to these critical developments in postmodernist philosophy. In large part, it was a conscious and deliberate revival and adaptation of the realist themes of rule-scepticism and indeterminacy to changing social relations and perceptions of justice in the late twentieth century, particularly on questions of sexual and racial equality and justice. The new legal radicalism tended to be more explicitly socialist than the predominantly liberal realists of the 1930s, but most of them had broken clear of the closed dogmas of orthodox Marxism, while still displaying traces of the less orthodox lines of Marxist thought. The critical legal scholars were also well in tune with the assault on modernity, bringing some of the postmodernist methods to bear upon what they saw as the dogmas of mainstream legal theory.

The rule of law

One of the principal virtues of a liberal democracy is widely assumed to be its commitment to the idea of the rule of law. Within the scope of liberalism, there have been several competing versions or models of the rule of law, but what it basically means, in accordance with the long-standing doctrine of the separation of powers, is that politics is kept out of law, so that the legal process resists the political interference of government. It is adherence to the rule of law that is supposed to be the mark that distinguishes contemporary liberal democracies from totalitarian states. It is not merely judicial independence from overt political pressure, however, that constitutes the rule of law. Law is also expected to be independent in the sense that it rises above the special interests of the parties involved in civil or criminal proceedings and makes rulings and adjudications with neutrality and impartiality. That is the hard core of the rule of law, but in addition there are various models relating to the question of how this impartial legal justice should be delivered. There are different views – as we saw in earlier chapters – on the importance of the consistent application of legal rules and the principle of treating like cases alike, on the predictability and reliability of the law, and on the acceptability of judicial discretion. The general point, however, of adhering to one model or another of the rule of law, concerns the issue of legitimation. If the law is systematically haphazard and unfair, it is widely agreed, the state loses its democratic legitimacy.

This essentially political question lies at the heart of the disputes between the critical scholars and mainstream jurisprudence. According to the most radical arguments, the legal process does not have this kind of independence from politics at all. The claims to neutrality, impartiality and objectivity are, in the view of most of the critical scholars, deeply suspect on philosophical as well as political grounds. That is to say, they are conceptually incoherent as well as being empirically implausible. The empirical disputes over this question are essentially trivial. While there are those who will insist that every individual judge always displays these qualities and rises majestically above all trace of interest and bias, there are others who will insist upon the opposite. It seems clear that in most advanced legal systems most judges at least aspire to neutrality and thus to the setting aside of personal preferences – and it is equally clear that not all of them succeed. The more serious question is whether or not, as the radical critics claim, this general appearance of the fairness and neutrality of the law – even when it seems to be operating at its best – is a veil or mask for the kind of partiality that, if established, would completely undermine the claim that judges draw exclusively upon purely legal resources to guide their actions, decisions and rulings. If this claim cannot be upheld, so it is argued, the rule of law is exposed as a pretence, and political legitimacy as little more than a confidence trick.

The critical legal scholars take up a more radical stance than their realist predecessors, whose rule–scepticism was directed in the first place at the early twentieth-century American formalists. Although the new critics have developed the old realist attempts to broaden the awareness of extra-legal factors influencing judicial decisions, these are not seen as sufficiently radical, because they allow for a core of legitimate legal determinacy. More importantly, the realist position on the question of the very possibility of neutrality and objectivity was never consistent or clear, because realism remained within the framework of modernity and liberalism. By contrast, the orthodox Marxist answer to this question was relatively clear. Their explanation is that the judges – trapped within the legal superstructure, which is determined by the base of economic class interest – are either willing or unwitting mouthpieces for the ideology of the ruling class. This approach – however rigid and mechanistic it might have been – did not question the very possibility of reaching objective and just decisions. What was probably decisive for the critical legal scholars' attack on liberal legal determinacy and the rule of law was the Nietzschean postmodernist stance on all problems relating to truth and objectivity. For perspectivism, as we have seen, there simply is no outside standpoint from which to make true and accurate judgements. The values associated with the ideal of the rule of law – neutrality, impartiality, objectivity – are the supposedly naïve and discredited ideals of modernity. From Foucault's perspective, there is no such thing as a disinterested search for truth, or indeed an independent truth standard at all, and all these claims to detachment and a desire for justice can be seen as integral parts of the power–knowledge networks permeating society.

The radical indeterminacy thesis

The critical scholars' arguments for the radical indeterminacy of law stand at the centre of the critical attacks on mainstream legal theory. The precise meaning of this 'radical' indeterminacy is one of the contested issues in this debate. In one sense it is merely an extension of the philosophical controversies in both analytic and postmodern philosophy of language into the area of legal theory. In contemporary philosophy it is generally recognised that a certain degree of indeterminacy is an inescapable feature of any natural language. Vagueness and ambiguity surround any concept, the meaning of which is open to more than one interpretation. Indeterminacy becomes radical when linguistic analysis seems to show that the meaning of virtually any concept or text can be interpreted in a multiplicity of ways. It becomes extreme when it is argued that there are no objective facts about meaning at all, that all meanings are conferred arbitrarily and that any word, sentence or text can be invested with any meaning the interpreter prefers, and no interpretation is superior to any other.

Applied to the language of law, it is easy to see how disruptive the implications of radical indeterminacy would be. If it were true of language as such, all the more so would it be true of the legal language in which statutes are laid down, and the judicial opinions, rulings and decisions declared and written. Any interpretation of what the law requires would be as good as any other. Judges could interpret precedent in any way that suited their personal or political agenda. Critics who support radical indeterminacy in law argue that this is the alarming reality concealed by the rhetoric surrounding the ideal of the rule of law.

One distinction that should be drawn clearly, but is often confused in the CLS writings, is the distinction between indeterminacy and underdetermination. If a judge's decision is *over*determined, it means that there is an excess of reasons or causes for the decision; that there are more legal resources than strictly required. If it is *under*determined, it means that existing law allows for a range of possible outcomes, rather than one or none. The disputes within the mainstream between positivists and Dworkinians over hard cases are focused on the question of whether or not this represents a threat to the authority of law. The point here, though, is that such gaps in the law indicated by underdetermination fall far short of what the critics mean by radical indeterminacy. On this radical view, existing law does not determine any outcome at all. Judicial discretion is total. We can see how extreme and implausible this is by comparing it with the positions defended by the legal realists and by Hart. For the realists Frank and Llewellyn, legal rules were always deeply suspect, but not because they were inherently indeterminate in their meaning. As we saw in an earlier chapter, their scepticism towards rules was moderate rather than nihilistic, in as far as they asserted that the boundaries between judicial discretion and the application of rules was blurred in nearly every area of law, and that they were always open to influence by extra-legal factors. The rules, they were arguing, were usually less than decisive. Hart's 'open texture' argument was more concerned with the meaning of the legal concepts and much more cautiously or 'minimally' sceptical, in that he saw indeterminacy of meaning only at the periphery or penumbra of the core area in which the meanings of the concepts were thoroughly determinate. In their paradigmatic usages, the meanings were entirely fixed. The function of the judge in hard cases was to intervene and authoritatively fix the meaning of any contested terms. In sharp contrast to both of these theories, the radical indeterminacy thesis simply sweeps away this core belief in the fixity of meaning.

The contradictions in liberalism

The point of departure for all the leading CLS critics was the belief that legal and political liberalism had to be confronted and criticised root and branch, rather than in a piecemeal reformist manner, however radical the reforms. Although there was initial uncertainty and disagreement over what they were trying to achieve, a purpose common to many of them was that they should conduct conceptual and historical examinations of prominent legal doctrines, in order to expose the political and social assumptions upon which they were based, to show how these were concealed by liberal ideology, and to reveal their origins as socially specific rather than natural and inevitable. Their main tactic to this effect was to locate and explain what they took to be inconsistencies and contradictions in legal doctrines, contradictions that lay at the heart of liberal modernity and its way of thinking as a whole.

One of the most influential early writings of this nature was Duncan Kennedy's historical analysis of the doctrines underlying legal adjudication (Kennedy 1976). Focusing mainly upon contract law, the analysis was intended to show that beneath the appearance of a coherent ideology rooted in Enlightenment modernity, liberalism is torn apart by inconsistencies and contradictory values and beliefs in such a way that they are always working against each other and preventing the settlement of a genuinely determinate body of law. For Kennedy, this inconsistency is exhibited primarily by the two principal modes in which legal reasoning is expressed: rules and standards. The contrast that he draws out between the clarity and rigidity of rules and the vagueness and flexibility of standards is similar in structure to Dworkin's rule–principle distinction, but while Dworkin was – at around the same time – using this distinction to demonstrate the underlying determinacy of law as the embodiment of both rules and equitable principles and standards, Kennedy was drawing the opposite conclusion, arguing that the difference between rules and standards is expressive of an ineradicable tension driving the law in different directions at once, thus making it radically unstable and stripping it of any unity of purpose or determinacy.

The success of this argument depends partly upon Kennedy's controversial linking of the rule–standard contrast with the wider political and social opposition between individualism and altruism, which he describes as irreconcilable visions of humanity and radically different aspirations for our moral future. The kind of linkage he has in mind is not conceptual but rather a *de facto* historical link, in as far as the legal rule form is congenial to furthering individualist aims, while the looser and vaguer standard is more suitable for communal or altruistic purposes. The advantages of clear-cut rules for the encouragement of business and commerce make it obvious why rules are naturally associated with individualism. Their presence restrains official arbitrariness and provides a degree of certainty. At the same time, however, their predictability makes it easier for the unscrupulous to 'walk the line' of illegality in commercial transactions. Counteracting equitable principles such as 'due care', 'good faith' and 'unconscionability', on the other hand, are standards that are also demanded by the altruistic or

communal side of liberal modernity. The main historical change that
Kennedy identifies in this analysis is the shift in the balance between the two
terms of this opposition. With the passing of the classical individualism of
the nineteenth century, US law (in parallel with other common law systems)
saw the steady expansion of the range and quantum of obligation and
liability to such an extent that it could be called 'the socialisation of our
theory of contract'. With the gradual erosion of formalism in law as a
whole, the two poles in the conflict (individualism and altruism) have faced
each other on increasingly equal terms, creating more awareness of the
fundamental contradiction in the law.

This contradiction Kennedy regards as fatal to the coherence of liberal
theory, because the way that it has evolved has created wide open discretion
for judges who are increasingly aware that 'the presence of elements from
both conceptual poles in nearly any real fact situation' undermines any
attempt to determine the outcome of the case according to what is required
by law. It usually goes unnoticed, he maintains, that this deep tension creates
almost universal discretion behind the façade of judicial predictability and
determinacy. The reality is an internal struggle between conflicting impera-
tives to apply rules in the true spirit of individualism or to appeal to
standards in the communal spirit of equity, both ostensibly within the frame
of liberal individualism. Accordingly, most areas of law in the liberal era
should be understood in these terms.

Criticisms of Kennedy and CLS

Kennedy's arguments stimulated a long-running debate that raised many
questions central to the dispute between CLS and mainstream legal theory.
They drew out criticisms from other CLS writers, from positivists, natural
lawyers and Dworkinians, too numerous to cover here. The most obvious
one concerns the correlation of rules with individualism, and standards with
altruism. If this is shown to be suspect, by producing counterexamples (that
there are rigid rules, for example, protecting consumer interests), the argument clearly collapses. It was widely and wrongly assumed, however, that
Kennedy intended this linkage as a conceptual one, rather than a contingent
one of 'general tendency'. As such, it remains plausible, for the reasons
initially given in his contrasts between the functions of rules and standards.

There are, however, more fundamental criticisms. Even if these modes of
legal argument are that closely linked to the heart of the modern political
struggle between individualist and communalist values, why should this lead
to radical indeterminacy? Is it, to put it bluntly, such a bad thing that these
values are in perpetual collision within the operation of the legal justice
system? One can concede the plausibility of the deconstruction of the myth
of judicial unanimity on such issues, without accepting the claim that this
leads to complete incoherence in the liberal understanding of legality. One
of the strongest positivist criticisms developed by Coleman and Leiter

(Marmor 1997: 203–79) challenges Kennedy's assertion that the oppositions he has described are typical of a liberal legal system rather than an inevitable feature of the human condition as such, and therefore of any conceivable legal system. According to this criticism, there is a balance to be struck between the pressures of individualism and altruism, the protection of privacy and the interests of the public, selfishness and sacrifice, and so on, and that it is the ability to strike this balance that makes us human. Furthermore, Kennedy traces the history of the evolving values of liberalism and modernity, which as a history of pragmatic compromise and moral progress is of the very essence of liberalism, rather than fatal to its coherence, as he maintains. Finally, many critics reject the use made by Kennedy and CLS generally of the term 'contradiction' to capture this idea of the tension between conceptual polar opposites. The term is used to suggest and heighten the sense of logical absurdity and literal incoherence, but it is only properly employed in logic to indicate a formal contradiction. It is only a contradiction in the formal sense to assert a proposition while at the same time denying it.

A more general criticism of all the leading CLS writings is that they set up too easy a target in order to demolish it more effectively. Too many of them take as the paradigm of liberal law the rule-fetishism that had been effectively demolished by their legal realist forebears, and to which very few contemporary mainstream theories subscribe. Even with the acknowledgement of the operation of standards in conflict with rules, the assumption is that there is no general awareness in mainstream theory of the complexity of the problems relating to the application of rules, when the truth of the matter is that these have been discussed extensively in the context of justice versus equity throughout the modern period. In particular, many of the early CLS writings ignored Dworkin's critique of rule-based positivism. Dworkin, however, soon became one of the main targets of their criticism.

CLS criticisms of Dworkin

Most of the CLS evaluations of Dworkin take the view that he was to be commended for pushing legal theory in a radically egalitarian direction, but criticised for the ultimately contradictory nature of this enterprise, which failed because he had a defective understanding of the sense in which law is thoroughly political. Although Dworkin is usually criticised from the right for his allegedly dangerous politicisation of the law, these critics from the left take issue with his conception of the rule of law as being set up to ensure that power remains within the hands of a political and judicial élite, to the exclusion of more democratic political participation.

There are two important lines of criticism of Dworkin. The first, argued by Hunt and Hutchinson (Hunt 1992), applies postmodernist critiques, especially those of Foucault, to Dworkin's overcentralised conception of power. His rights thesis is said to presuppose a legitimately all-powerful liberal state legislating and adjudicating competing rights, creating and protecting sovereign individuals within supposedly power-free zones, as if the state were the only source of power. In the light of Foucault's analysis of the diffusion and decentralisation of power, the reality of the situation is that these 'free' zones are shot through with relations of oppressive power, in the family, the workplace and society at large. Dworkin is said to ignore corporate economic power, male–female power relations and other forms of oppression, because he is preoccupied with the kind of legal rights to which they are impervious. This is an important line of criticism, but it should be noted that these criticisms have a tendency to downplay or interpret negatively the progressive side of liberal legislation protecting tenants, the rights in employment and property for women, the introduction of a national minimum wage, and so on, all of which Dworkin, among other liberals, strongly approves of.

The second line of criticism by Altman (Hunt 1992) is addressed directly to Dworkin's theory of law as integrity as a more expansive version of the traditional liberal conception of the rule of law. The main charge is that Dworkin's conception of the rule of law, as judicial adherence to the law conceptualised as a whole, is a naïve distortion of real legal practices in the modern world. According to Altman, the real situation is that the courts enforce settled law that is in fact the outcome of a political power struggle beyond the courts, and that this does not match Dworkin's ideal of a political community thrashing out competing principles and conceptions of fairness and justice. It is also said to be dubious as an ideal to which law and politics should aspire, because Dworkin's 'law as integrity' would be completely undermined by his own political pluralism. Either ideal realised consistently would destroy the other.

There are two problems with this critique. First, it seems clear that contemporary democratic politics displays both features as described by Altman, on the one hand, a complex of sectarian interest power struggles, on the other hand, campaigns for the recognition of genuine rights both within mainstream politics and from pressure groups. In fact, it is difficult to see how there could be one without the other. Second, the criticism follows the usual CLS pattern of demanding the kind of perfect consistency in a liberal theory that it does not adhere to itself, expecting an unequivocal commitment to one of the poles in a conceptual opposition, rather than a recognition of the inevitable ongoing tension between them.

Justice modern and postmodern

If the case for radical indeterminacy as argued by the critical legal scholars and others were established beyond doubt, it would certainly add strength to the argument that the courts are the agents of systematic injustice. If determinacy requires observance of the rule of law in the sense that it reaches a certain minimum level of predictability and reliability, that it is accessible and its content well advertised, that like cases are treated alike, then its failure to attain this standard in itself constitutes structural injustice and facilitates the judicial operation of personal prejudice and political bias. This minimum standard was the main point of Fuller's natural law criteria for the existence of a just legal system. It has never been clear, however, that the radical critics' case should rest upon the argument for raging indeterminacy. It is also entirely plausible that the body of law as a whole in any given system at a particular phase of its development can operate discrimination and bias, and effect the same kind of marginalisation and oppression, without appearing to violate any of these procedural principles. This is indeed one line of radical feminist criticism – that under the liberal rule of law, many individual laws, such as those governing marriage and divorce, ownership of property, rape and other offences against the person, may be substantively unjust without any hint of indeterminacy, and with the current state of the law plausibly represented as 'natural', so that determinate outcomes of legal decisions will only reinforce the injustice that reflects the male-dominated moral consensus of the day.

This ambivalence about the value of determinacy raises an important question about the relation of the new radicalism to traditional natural law theory. Given the justice-centred tradition of natural law, why do the new critics not simply merge with this tradition, confronting the specific injustices embodied in positive law with the independent standards of universal justice? One answer, of course, is that some of them do. Belief in natural human rights has had a continuing impact on critical race theory in particular, since the civil rights movement of the 1960s, and on campaigns for specific legal rights by liberal feminists. Others, however, are more sceptical of the idea of universal justice. Despite its premodern origins in Aristotle and Aquinas, natural law today is too closely tied up with modernity and liberalism, and with the natural rights proclaimed by the Enlightenment. The concepts of nature and reason as the foundational source of justice are thoroughly suspect to anyone influenced by postmodernism, and the idea that there is a standard of justice that transcends particular societies and cultures is seen as hopelessly abstract and non-situated. The last issue that we need to consider at this point, then, is the overall credibility of the relativist and perspectivist thinking that has brought about this scepticism towards the idea of universal justice.

Perspectivism and truth

The relativisation of all absolutes implicit in Nietzsche's perspectivism took hold of the philosophical imagination in Europe in the latter half of the twentieth century. Its main attraction in legal studies as elsewhere lies in its potential for the kind of critical analysis that exposes as fraudulent various theories and doctrines which do actually disguise specific vested interests as a natural and inevitable way of seeing things. First encounters with this mode of criticism (and the deconstructive techniques that it engendered) are often experienced as a liberation. It has to be acknowledged, though, that perspectivism is a double-edged sword, not merely because its criticism can be turned upon the critic, exposing his or her own nefarious hidden agendas, but also because it levels down every angle or viewpoint to the same standing. Applied to the interpretation of history, for example, it serves the creditable purpose of undermining the false official histories of political powers that seek to manipulate the past in order to control the present. At the same time, however, it has the unwelcome implication that if there is no historical truth, only a multiplicity of perspectives masking various ideologies, it levels out all interpretations and raises problems relating to notorious 'histories' such as Holocaust-denial, which are elevated to the same status as the meticulously documented demonstrations of the real extent of the Holocaust, which are subject to methodological constraints and the systematic weighing of evidence. Deconstructionism in particular has been extensively criticised on these grounds.

Within the arguments for universal perspectivism there is nearly always an illicit move from the discovery that many claims to objectivity and justice are false, to the conclusion that all perspectives must be false and that there can be no objectivity and hence no impartiality or disinterested pursuit of justice. It always has to be remembered that this conclusion does not follow. Critical examination of the premises of Aristotle's defence of slavery as natural, or the modern pseudo-scientific theories of natural female and racial inferiority, exposes these theories as false; it does not show that there can be no objective truth on these matters. Assumptions such as these may well be built into the Western way of thinking, but this should prompt relentless rational criticism, aimed at revealing the true picture, rather than a nihilistic assault on the concept of truth. It is insufficient to deconstruct these theories and unmask the will to power behind them, showing how they are rooted in specific social circumstances, and it is misleading to direct this criticism indiscriminately at every theory of law and justice.

Universal perspectivism has often been criticised as self-defeating. On this reasoning, in order to show that some views lay false claim to objectivity, one already assumes that one view is truly objective. Without this assumption, the charge of falsity would not make sense. It has to be said that this criticism has never convinced universal perspectivists. Atheists might argue that there is nothing but an array of false images of God, but it would not count as a valid argument for the existence of God to assert that atheists thereby commit themselves to a true image of God. It is the same with the denial of all absolutes or all truths. Other criticisms highlight the excessive use of optical and spatial imagery in Nietzsche's often inconsistent accounts of perspectivism, and argue that the case is made only by illicitly reducing all forms of knowledge and understanding to inexplicable switches of perception and literal changes of standpoint. It has to be accepted that there are no conclusive refutations of universal perspectivism, but it can be rendered less persuasive by focusing on the contrasts between concrete instances of justice and injustice.

Study Questions for Part I

General question: What difference has postmodernism made to legal theory?

Further study questions: What is the significance of the Enlightenment for critical theories of law? Do the arguments for radical indeterminacy undermine the entire range of liberal theories of law? Compare the rule scepticism of the legal realists with the radical indeterminacy of the critical legal scholars. How does Foucault's concept of power affect our understanding of law? Compare Derrida's concepts of justice and equity with those of Dworkin and the legal realists. Critically assess Kennedy's critique of the contradictions in liberalism. Can perspectivism be applied usefully and consistently to legal theory?

Suggestions for further reading

Recommended general reading on the critical theories are Morrison (1997) and Davies (1994). The best introductory books on postmodernism generally are the selections in Bertens and Natoli (eds) (2002) and the articles in the Cahoone anthology (1996). One of the most influential texts is Lyotard (1984). For the relevance of postmodernism to legal theory, see Stacy (2001) and the article by Douzinas in Connor (2004).

From the numerous commentaries on Foucault, Gabardi (2001) and Owen (1994) are recommended. Gutting's (1994) *The Cambridge Companion to Foucault* is also very useful. On Derrida's philosophy, see Royle (2003), Davies (1994: ch. 7.3), Murdoch (1992: ch. 7) and Culler's article in Sturrock (1979). Derrida's article on justice is included in Cornell, Rosenfeld and Carlson (1992), which also contains discussions by others of Derrida on deconstructionism and justice.

The best general books on CLS include Fitzpatrick and Hunt (1987) and Kelman (1987). Important general articles include Kennedy (1976), reprinted in Patterson (2003), and Altman (1986), reprinted in Adams (1992). Hunt (1992) is a collection of critical essays on Dworkin. For critical discussions of the radical indeterminacy thesis, see the essays in Marmor (1997) by Coleman and Leiter. For discussions of impartiality and the rule of law, see the essays in Dyzenhaus (1999) and Montefiore (1975).

On Nietzsche, truth and perspectivism, see Clark (1990), Robinson (1999), Hunt (1991) and Owen (1994). For an excellent overview of truth and perspectivism in general, see Campbell (2001). The best short introductions to 'continental philosophy' are Critchley (2001) and Solomon (1988). On the meaning of the Enlightenment, see the selections from Kant *et al.* in Schmidt (1996), and for defences of the values of the Enlightenment against postmodernism, see Wolin (2004), Porter (2000) and Porter (2003).

Part II
The reach of the law

6 Authority and obligation

When we switch our attention from the nature of law to the reach of the law, the first question is whether we have good reason to accept that the law has any proper authority at all. Why should we obey it? To a certain extent, the answer is implicit in the analysis of the 'nature of law' question. If law is held to be morally authoritative by definition, it will seem that an obligation to obey flows simply from the recognition of law as law. If the definition of law excludes this moral authority, the source of obligation must be sought elsewhere. The question about authority, however, is not as straightforward as this. What we are asking about is the kind of connection to be found between the authority of rulers to lay down laws and the legal and moral duty of the ruled to obey them. It is often asserted that there is a *prima facie* general duty of obligation to obey the law. What this means is that in the absence of special reasons that might justify a specific exemption, the acknowledgement of the law's authority leads to the acceptance of the duty of obedience. How it might lead to this, however, is a matter for debate. It may be for reasons quite independent of the authoritative status of the law. The special reasons for suspending this presumption, furthermore, suggesting that there are limits to the general duty, must arise from considerations powerful enough to override the standard reasons for compliance.

Common reasons for obeying the law

On the assumption that there are sound moral reasons for not breaking contracts, committing frauds or acts of violence, does the unlawfulness of wrongful acts provide an additional reason to conform? This is the question. If sound moral judgement were a sufficient guide to action, legal obligation would simply be a reinforcement of moral obligation. The law would be no more than a system of coercion to prevent or discourage people from acting harmfully. One obvious reason in addition to moral obligation is the instinct of self-preservation, the fear of sanctions. This is not the point. The question is whether the fact of legality as such creates an obligation beyond the moral obligation that might already be felt. Do we have to respect the law as law?

One fairly common belief is that the obligation is self-evident, because the law is, by definition, 'what you have to do'. The law is the law and it is there to be obeyed. The theoretical expression of this reason is the claim that the obligation is derived conceptually, that the obligation to obey is written into the very idea of legitimate authority. This is a *conceptual* justification. To say that 'X is a law' just means that X has to be obeyed. Disobedience is wrong by definition and the sanctions of the law are automatically justified. It should be stressed that on this argument the obligation is derived solely from the legality, not from the content of the law.

Another common belief is that the law has to be obeyed because its authority is essential for the continuation of civilised society. The emphasis here is on the dangerous social effects of any relaxation in the general obligation to obey. This argument is rooted in the utilitarian tradition, which today is more commonly termed *consequentialist*. This is a broader term that includes theories which reject the specific standard of utility but retain the basic principle that all actions are to be judged in terms of their effects, rather than, for example, their inherent goodness or badness. In the same way that Bentham in his critique of common law judged the merits of individual laws by reference to their overall utility, contemporary consequentialists justify a general obligation to obey the law by referring to the good and bad effects on society as a whole of obedience and disobedience. Given that general disobedience would have dangerous consequences, this approach establishes at least a *prima facie* duty of obedience, but leaves open the question as to whether this duty can be overridden in specific circumstances in which the effects of the injustice perpetuated by an unjust law outweighs the negative effects of disobedience.

A third type of justification is *contractual*, according to which the obligation arises from an agreement – either explicit or unspoken – already reached between the rulers and the ruled. The commitment on this line of reasoning is to obey the law, not for the sake of what might happen in the event of widespread disobedience, but as an expression of what is already due. The state has the right to expect obedience because consent has already been implicitly given. This justification is also open to refutation, depending on whether or not the rulers have honoured their side of the contract.

Obligation and legal theory

It is vital to understand that there is no simple correspondence between the major theories of law and these theories of obligation. It is a common mistake to divide natural lawyers from positivists by imagining that while the former urge us to disobey unjust laws, the latter insist that a bad law is still a law that has to be obeyed. In fact, the problem of how the nature of law relates to the source of obligation to obey is one of the most complex and paradox-ridden areas in contemporary jurisprudence. We can open up this area by observing that the mere statement or exposition of what the law actually expects and demands of those subject to its jurisdiction in no way begins to answer the question about their obligation to obey these laws. The fact that there are sanctions to enforce the law does not create an obligation, it means only that we can be obliged to conform (Hart 1961: 80–1).

The central problem derives from the deep ambiguity in the terms 'authority' and 'authorisation'. Both positivism and natural law have been unclear about the relation between obligation and the authority of the law. Positivists have frequently been interpreted as arguing that any law that is valid according to purely technical criteria automatically creates alongside its legality a general obligation to obey. On the other hand, many positivists have seen the identification of the appropriate formal criteria for determining legal validity as having no direct bearing on the source of legal obligation. On this reading, the traceability of a law to a rule of recognition or a basic norm authenticates its status as law, but although this stamp of legality confers authority on the agencies of the law to coerce citizens into conformity, this does not settle the question of whether this authorised coercion should be obeyed. For those positivists who are also utilitarians, the obligation to obey is usually derived from criteria drawn from consequentialist arguments about the likely outcome of specific acts of disobedience or a general rejection of the authority of the law.

Within the natural law camp, the conceptual link between authority and obedience has been more prominent, but the implications overall are equally ambiguous. Some of the traditional Christian theories, in arguing that law is by definition morally authoritative, seem to build the obligation to obey into the concept of law. On the other hand, the stipulation that only just laws are truly legal has led many to conclude that it is only the body of just laws that can by definition lay claim to obedience. Rules or commands that are posited as law cannot, merely by virtue of being the authentic issue of a legitimate sovereign, make this conceptual claim. Most of the great natural lawyers nevertheless concede that any body of rules or commands authorised by a sovereign, irrespective of the degree of justice it exhibits, does constitute a system of positive law that lays serious claim to obedience. What they deny is that those laws that are not sanctioned by the higher law can be justified on the conceptual argument. When faced with laws that are manifestly unjust – such as laws that are detrimental to human welfare, or calculated to benefit only the ruler – the influential response of Aquinas was to argue that obedience could only be justified on consequentialist grounds. Although they are not truly lawful, there might yet be an obligation to obey unjust laws, if it was clear that the community would suffer greater harm from the rebellion than from the continuation of the tyranny. Nevertheless, Aquinas discusses at length the conditions under which abuse of power may release subjects from their obligation to obey, and the arguments for the justifiability of civil disobedience. It is important to note also that he regarded laws that directly contravene God's law, such as the worship of false idols, as laws that 'must in no circumstance be obeyed' (Aquinas 1948: 134–85).

Social contract theory

Apart from the conceptual and consequential arguments, the other main source of theories of obligation is the idea of a contract between rulers and ruled. On this account, we are obliged to obey, not by virtue of the meaning of 'law', nor by the bad consequences of breaking it, but because by living in society we have already in some sense placed ourselves under such an obligation. By far the most important and influential contract philosopher in recent times is John Rawls (1921–2002), whose writings have had their main impact on political and moral theory. Since the 1950s, Rawls has been developing a systematic liberal theory of substantive justice, based on radically egalitarian premises. In his major work *A Theory of Justice* (Rawls 1972), he established the main lines of argument for the renewal of social contract theory. What his theory of justice contained was an original and distinctively modern theory of obligation that was aimed at avoiding the weaknesses of traditional contract theory. His project in this respect can only be fully appreciated with a clear idea of the background.

The idea of an original contract

The idea that obedience to the law can be justified by reference to a prior agreement, contract or covenant between rulers and ruled is an ancient one. It was expressed by Socrates and Plato, by medieval theologians and by early modern philosophers from Hobbes to Kant. The essential feature of the traditional idea is that the justification looks backwards in time to find the source of obligation. We are obliged to obey the law, not primarily because of its intrinsic qualities as law, nor because of the good or bad effects of lawbreaking, but because of a prior agreement to do so.

The most vivid example of the contract argument is found in Plato's account of Socrates' response to his sentence of death in the dialogue *Crito*. To the frustration of his supporters, Socrates argued that he must accept the verdict of the court, because although unjust, it was *lawful*. This is the outcome of an imaginary dialogue with 'the laws' of Athens, in which Socrates admits that he would have no answer to their accusations if they saw him trying to escape the process of law. The arguments attributed to the laws – all of which Socrates endorses – include several aspects of the contract theory. The crucial types of argument in these passages can be classified as follows. The citizen must obey the laws in everything, because (1) general obedience is the condition for the existence of society, and without it there would be anarchy; (2) the citizen owes the state everything, including his or her life; (3) the citizen has agreed, both explicitly and implicitly, by virtue of receiving benefits from the state and choosing not to emigrate, to obey all the laws; (4) the citizen has the opportunity to persuade the state, through legitimate lobbying, to change the laws, but not the right to disobey them.

The conclusion towards which Socrates' arguments lead overall is that the obligation to obey the law is virtually unconditional. The only hint of a condition is the implication in the 'freedom to persuade' argument that it must be the kind of society which allows such criticism. The most important point concerning the idea of the contract is that 'the laws' argue that it was never their agreement that all their decisions would be just. The agreement was made and consent given to submit to the authority of the law on the basis of the benefits conferred on every citizen, who is free to take advantage of all the institutions created by law. On Socrates' account, there is no talk in the contract of fairness or justice.

Classical contract theory

The great age of social contract theory in Europe was the socially and politically turbulent seventeenth century, the outcome of which had great significance for the shape of the contemporary world. For many centuries before this, medieval theologians had sought justifications in the idea of the original contract both for the political power of the day and for rebellion against it. The practical problem that inspired the development of the theory was that of justifying the removal of tyrants. In the course of the arguments to this effect, they also laid down the terms under which an acceptable and effective monarch does rule. The answer, briefly, was that monarchs rule by virtue of the consent of the subjects, who have voluntarily subordinated themselves to the ruler in return for the ruler observing certain constraints on the exercise of power.

The situation in the early modern period was such that the leading political thinkers were deeply affected by the constitutional conflicts that culminated in the revolution of 1688, establishing the settlement that brought more or less permanent political stability to England. This century as a whole saw the transition from the accession in 1603 of James I – himself an intellectual defender of the divine right of kings and critic of social contract theory – to the establishment in 1688 of a monarchy firmly subjected to democratic constraint. The interim saw a succession of civil wars, the execution of a king and a period of military dictatorship. The leading English contractarian thinkers, Thomas Hobbes (1588–1679) and John Locke (1632–1704), were both motivated primarily by urgent political purposes. Hobbes, forced temporarily into exile in Paris by the English Civil War, inclined towards strong government without too much concern for its political colour. Locke, on the other hand, also suffering exile as a result of the repressive government of James II, was more interested in limiting the power of government.

The versions of the social contract elaborated by Hobbes and Locke, each based on radically different premises, have been and remain enormously influential in the modern world. What they proposed – Hobbes in *Leviathan*, Locke in the *Second Treatise on Civil Government*, which was largely a reply to Hobbes – were diametrically opposed accounts of political obligation, based on conflicting views of human nature as it exists, or would exist without law or the other structures of civil society.

In both cases, their contract theories rest upon their understanding of *the state of nature*, which is the state presumed to have existed prior to the creation of any laws. For Hobbes, this was a state of permanent war of all against all, in which there are 'no arts, no letters, no society; and which is worst of all, continual fear and danger of violent death' (Hobbes 1962: 143). Locke had a more benign view of the state of nature, but still saw in it enough danger to bring about the existence of law, the main purpose of which was the peaceful settlement of disputes (Locke 1924: bk 2, ch. 3).

It was the manner of the transition from the state of nature to civil society with which the contract theories were concerned. For Hobbes, the source of our present obligation to obey the law is the agreement that first brought it into being, a contract that was made when the majority of people invested authority in a few people or one person who was powerful enough to suppress the warlike state of nature and keep the peace. This original contract involved a trade of their natural liberty for security and protection. For as long as those invested with the power can enforce the rule of law, the contract is binding.

Locke's interpretation of what the contract consisted in was a direct challenge to the absolutism of Hobbes. For the latter, the contract was valid even under extreme duress, rather in the manner that a military surrender is valid, despite the obvious duress. For Locke, it was a strictly conditional trade by those who voluntarily became subjects, granting the sovereign or sovereign body the right to rule on condition that he, she or they administer justice efficiently, as well as simply enforcing the peace. For Hobbes – the initiator in England of the command-positivist tradition – the will of the sovereign is absolute. For Locke, the sovereign is constrained by the democratic rule of law. If the sovereign's side of this bargain is not kept, the contract is void and rebellion is justified.

Weaknesses and criticisms of contract theory

Hobbes and Locke, in common with all contract theorists up to their time, wrote as if the contract between sovereign and citizens had actually taken place at some definite point in the distant historical past. From their point of view, this was a reasonable assumption. Given their theories about the social and political hierarchies in which they found themselves, and their respective interpretations of the free and equal state of nature, it stood to reason that there must have been a point in time at which this freedom and equality of status were negotiated away, in order to escape from the dangers of the state of nature. It was a question of establishing what this negotiation, this original agreement at the point of transition to political society, must have involved. So the main assumption was that the contract was a real event, rather than some kind of metaphor or convenient myth to underwrite obligation.

Given that the contract was a real event, and that this was necessary for it to be binding, the next question that arises is how it continued to create an obligation for all the subsequent generations. If their forefathers had signed away their freedom and equality, why and how should this affect their own position? Was there still an obligation to obey the sovereign? The answers to this question have varied. For medieval thinkers, the obligation is renewed by the reaffirmation of the contract with the succession of every monarch. This was implausible, to say the least. It could hardly be argued that the formal endorsement of a *fait accompli* was a free agreement carrying such significance. Hobbes's answer was not clearly formulated, but suggested a continuing obligation by virtue of the same arguments that had been persuasive at the time of the original contract. Hobbes's contract, it should be remembered, did not require free consent. For Locke, on the other hand, such consent was central; his answer to the question of continuing obligation was based on the claim that contemporary consent is *tacit* as opposed to the actual consent given at the time of the original contract.

The nature of social contract theory changed substantially in the period leading up to the American and French Revolutions. David Hume accepted the contract as a real event accounting for the origin of obligation, but denied that it could continue to operate as such a justification in the present. In particular, he poured scorn upon Locke's defence of tacit consent, likening it to the plight of a press-ganged sailor expected to accept the authority of the ship's master. For Hume, contemporary obligation has to be justified on the basis of actual benefits to be derived from a state that is generally obeyed.

The important breakthrough came with Kant's (1724–1804) relinquishment of the assumption that the social contract must be understood as an actual, literal, historical contract between sovereign and subjects. For Kant, the contract was indeed the source of obligation, but it was to be understood not as something that had happened in the past, but as 'an idea of reason' that exercised its influence in the present. The Kantian contract is hypothetical rather than real. It is what rational people *would agree to* if they found themselves in such circumstances as described by the traditional theory. For Kant, it is rational to assume that such a contract between subjects and sovereign does exist.

One major type of criticism that should be mentioned in conclusion here is the charge of logical incoherence. It has frequently been argued that the very idea of a social contract as a literal historical event, brought into being between free subjects and a designated sovereign, is self-contradictory. In order for such an agreement to be reached, it is argued, there must already have been in existence the kind of institutions, the recognition of which depends on a prior agreement to respect them. What this suggests is that the original contract would be trying to create an authority that is itself needed to create it. An extension of this criticism is that the concept of a contract is a legal one, which by definition cannot be applied in a prelegal situation. A further extension of it is the argument that in a genuinely presocial state of nature, the individuals seeking a sovereign would not even have the appropriate language for appointing one and formulating the agreement.

While these criticisms show that the traditional versions of contract theory were making simplistic assumptions about the origins of political power and legal systems, they are not entirely convincing. They seem to depend on the more modern belief that the idea of a presocial state is a myth; however, even if this is so, there is nothing mythical about the creation of political authority and law. It is not clear why the transition from a prelegal society to a legal one would require a contract in this very literal legalistic sense; or that it would not have the linguistic resources to innovate in this way.

Even if these criticisms are not as damaging as they sound, however, the fate of literal social contract theory was sealed largely by the rise of utilitarianism from the late eighteenth century. For utilitarians, the source of obligation was essentially forward-looking or consequentialist; the justification for general obedience is future-oriented rather than rooted in a past agreement. The idea of a binding contract was seen as an anachronism. It was not until the second half of the twentieth century that this largely discredited idea was seriously revived.

Rawls: the original position

With this historical background in mind, we can now return to the contemporary revival of contract theory by John Rawls. One of his main explicit purposes was to promote a coherent alternative to utilitarianism as a general moral theory as well as a theory of obligation. The overall aim was to construct a theory of substantive justice rooted in the contract tradition. Rawls maintains that his own contract theory leads to principles of justice that would not be endorsed by utilitarianism. Within the social contract tradition, this firm linking of the contract to principles of justice owes more to Locke and to Kant than to Hobbes.

On this new interpretation, the idea of a real historical contract is completely defunct. As we have seen, there were early hints that a hypothetical contract could operate as the ground of obligation, and that this only became explicit in Kant's philosophy. Even in Kant, however, the notion was rather sketchy, and Rawls's project was to develop a complete exposition of this theme.

With the proposal that the contract is hypothetical, it becomes irrelevant whether such an agreement had any historic reality. It is more appropriate to understand it in a 'let us imagine ...' sense. Imagine a scenario in which a number of people are called upon to make the kind of agreement necessary to escape from the state of nature and establishing civil society. Assuming that they are rational individuals in the sense that they are all concerned with striking the best possible bargain for themselves, what would be the content of the contract they would freely consent to?

In this imaginary situation, which Rawls refers to as 'the original position' or 'the initial situation', the parties to the contract would be required to reflect on the principles of justice to be adopted by the society in which they subsequently have to live. The contract would then involve the endorsement, in advance, of these principles, to which they would subsequently be committed. The crucial feature of this imagined position is that when choosing the principles that would govern a just society, each subject would be 'veiled' from all knowledge of the place he or she is to occupy in that society. They would have no knowledge of their natural endowment of intelligence or practical ability; or of whether they would be male or female, black or white, rich or poor, healthy or disabled, intelligent or disadvantaged. What is concealed is anything that might give them a head start or a handicap. They would not even have foreknowledge of their own personality traits and inclinations, whether acquisitive or unambitious, adventurous or cautious. This is Rawls's 'veil of ignorance', one of the most famous metaphors in contemporary philosophy.

This original position, despite its intended similarity to the presocial 'state of nature' of classical contract theory, is quite different in as far as its subjects are not real reasoning people, deciding on the nature of the bargain to be struck with a sovereign. Rawls's 'parties' to the contract are theoretical constructs, individuals stripped of all knowledge of themselves. In important respects they are not presocial; they understand everything of the basic workings of society except their own nature and their own position in it. What they are deciding is what it would be rational to accept as a principle of justice if they did not know how they personally were going to be affected by it. As such, the veil of ignorance, and the original position that it qualifies, are essentially a device for the elimination of unconscious bias and prejudice.

Rawls describes his theory of justice as 'justice as fairness'. What this means is that given the 'blind' starting point from which the principles of justice would be agreed, that of the original position, no one has an unfair advantage through inside knowledge of how the arrangements chosen will affect them. Justice is fairness in the sense that it is chosen in the dark, so to speak.

What is actually chosen by the parties in the original position is a conception of justice, which embodies a set of principles of justice. These will determine the nature of the constitution and a legislature to enact laws, a legal system to administer it, and so on. The important point is the nature of the principles upon which all the other arrangements will rest. Rawls argues that the rationality of self-interest of those who do not know which way their luck is going to turn will inevitably guide them towards principles that safeguard the interests of everyone in society with as much equality as is practically realisable. This leads him to two basic principles of justice, whereby everyone would have the right to equal basic liberties and socio-economic inequalities would be arranged for the benefit of the least advantaged, with 'all offices and positions open to all under conditions of fair equality and opportunity' (Rawls 1972: 302).

These principles are certainly not self-evident, and Rawls does not make any such claim for them. They are what rational self-interest, veiled by ignorance, would demand. The truth of the matter, of course, is that such principles would be rejected by many in the real world. What Rawls does claim is that in modern democracies they are already widely accepted, and that those who do not can perhaps be persuaded by philosophical reflection The important point is that the reasoning is not based on considerations of utility or a concern for the general welfare, but on straightforward self-interest in the original position.

Criticisms of these basic features of Rawls's theory of justice have come from many different angles. Some critics have regarded the veil of ignorance as an elaborate way of expressing the commonplace observation that justice is objective and neutral, or that it achieves the same result as other less complex devices for adopting the position of the disinterested observer, such as the imaginary visitor from Mars. Others regard all these visions of impartiality as a sham, and Rawls's version of it as merely a projection of his own sense of justice. Others again have argued that on Rawls's own terms, the impartiality of the veil and rational self-interest would not lead to these two principles of justice. The basic assumptions behind the 'maxi–min' idea – that it would be in the rational interests of all to arrange inequalities for the maximum benefit of the least advantaged – has been subjected to extensive analysis and criticism. Robert Nozick (1938–2002) in particular has argued (Nozick 1974) that Rawls's egalitarianism is not justice at all, that it is a sophisticated piece of trickery to justify excessive intervention by a non-legitimate state, for the redistribution of the wealth and property legitimately held by those who have acquired it rightfully to those who have no right to it. For Nozick, only a minimal 'nightwatchman' state, protecting negative rights and regulating legal transactions, is justified. The Rawlsian contract, from this point of view, justifies systematic injustice.

On balance, however, Rawls's theory of justice and later theories influenced by it still stand up well against many of these criticisms. Although Nozick's rival libertarian interpretation of justice and rights has been influential, it is widely regarded not only as too extreme in its anti-welfare implications, but also as being basically flawed in its uncritical assumptions about the rightfulness of the acquisition of property holdings.

Rawls on duty and obligation

Throughout Rawls's analysis of the duty to obey the law (Rawls 1972: ch. 6), his reference point is that of the parties in the original position, the arguments that would prevail, the conditions they would insist upon and the social arrangements they would reject. For example, when he argues that consenting to unjust arrangements amounts to an extorted promise that is void *ab initio*, and hence that such consent does not create a natural obligation, his justification for this argument is that the parties in the original position, rationally aware of their own interests, would insist on these conditions. The original position, then, is the contractual source of the obligation.

From this position, Rawls argues, it would be relatively easy to establish 'a natural duty of justice' to support institutions that are in fact demonstrably just, in that they show no favour or discrimination. If they are consistent with the two principles of justice – or if they come as close as possible to satisfying them as circumstances allow – the parties to the contract would agree to accepting the duty to obey, because each individually would expect to flourish under such arrangements. This natural duty, he argues, would be endorsed in preference to a principle of utility, because the latter is based not on rational self-interest, but on a calculation of what would be best for the aggregate welfare of all the citizens.

The more important question for Rawls is that of whether there can be a duty to comply with an unjust law, or with unjust social arrangements. From the outset, Rawls rejects the idea that the duty to obey can be restricted to perfectly just laws and institutions. This, he says, is as mistaken as regarding the legal validity of a law as a sufficient reason for obeying it. Clearly, in the case of an unjust law, the natural duty of justice does not apply. What the proper attitude depends on, according to Rawls, is the arguments that would be persuasive from behind the veil. He anticipates the objection that nobody in this initial position in which they are still 'free and equal' would contemplate endorsing a situation in which they will be expected to obey clearly unjust laws, an endorsement that would be contrary to their own interests.

It is this voluntary relinquishment of complete freedom from a duty to obey unjust laws that Rawls seeks to explain. In so doing, he argues that the parties to the original contract would reason, with the benefit of their knowledge of the way society works, that all social arrangements being fallible and imperfect, it is better to consent to one fallible procedure that is bound to produce some injustice than to make no agreement at all. The important distinction for Rawls in this context is between a 'nearly just' society and constitution and a clearly unjust society and constitution. The conclusion he is seeking is that there is a certain amount of injustice in the specific form of unjust laws that we have to put up with and recognise as binding, so long as the basic structure of society is reasonably just. His argument is that this conclusion is warranted by reference to the considerations that would be persuasive in the original position; the parties would recognise the inevitability of a certain amount of injustice. As fully rational agents, they would know that it would be in their own interests to curtail their expectations of perfect justice.

As Rawls realises, the real problem lies in distinguishing between circumstances in which we are bound to comply with unjust or unreasonable laws, and circumstances that involve a degree of injustice that is entirely unacceptable. His central argument is that the duty to obey depends on the degree of seriousness of the injustice. We are only obligated to regard unjust laws as binding within certain limits to what would be acceptable to the parties in the original position. It is to establish the nature of these limits that Rawls's analysis turns to the question of how and when civil disobedience can be justified.

Injustice and civil disobedience

The central question in any discussion of civil disobedience concerns the point at which it becomes morally permissible – or even obligatory – to resist the authority of unjust laws or institutions. It should be noted immediately that it is never a question of legal permissibility: civil disobedience is illegal by definition and only reaches the political agenda when it is widely held that certain laws are wrong.

Definition of civil disobedience

A provisional definition of civil disobedience is that it means 'deliberate principled lawbreaking'. This makes it clear why it cannot be a legal activity, such as a campaign of demonstration against laws perceived to be unjust; its very purpose is to challenge these laws with defiantly illegal actions. One of the difficulties in defining it more precisely lies in the fact that its meaning has evolved by convention. Henry David Thoreau (1817–62) is thought to have been the first to use the term – in 1848 – in an essay justifying his principled refusal to pay tax to finance the US war against Mexico. The same term has since been used in many different contexts, the most famous of which have been the strategy of passive resistance employed by Gandhi against British rule in India and the civil rights movement in the 1950s–1960s in the USA.

In each of these cases, there is an emphasis on civil disobedience as essentially a non-violent strategy of resistance. So, in addition to the illegal activity being based on principle, it must also avoid violence. Non-violence is usually stipulated as part of the definition of civil disobedience in order to distinguish it from other forms of resistance to injustice, such as direct action, rebellion or revolution. This does not necessarily mean that violence is always wrong; what it does mean is that if the action is violent, it cannot count as civil disobedience. It should be noted, however, that this condition is not universally accepted (Bedau 1991: 130–44).

A number of other stipulations are conventionally associated with the definition of civil disobedience. It must be used only in the last resort, when all other legal methods to change the law have been explored and exhausted. It must be undertaken openly, which is to say that it must be an act of open defiance with the intention of publicising the injustice, rather than quiet non-compliance. Furthermore, those engaged in it should be prepared to submit to prosecution and punishment, rather than attempting to evade the process of law. Finally, it is usually stipulated that principled disobedience to one unjust law should be accompanied by scrupulous obedience to the law as a whole.

The initial definition from which we started was that of civil disobedience as 'deliberate principled lawbreaking'. This 'principled' feature distinguishes it from (1) common criminal or civil lawbreaking for personal convenience or personal gain; and (2) opposing injustice to oneself for the sole purpose of asserting or defending one's own rights. In the sense intended, 'principled' means that it is motivated by a selfless concern with opposing injustice. It has often been objected that the exclusion of the second of these is an unfair condition. If an injustice is generalised, then those participating in organised disobedience are likely to be affected by it themselves. Principled activity and the defence of one's own rights should not be seen as inconsistent. A striking example would be the refusal to fight in what was widely held to be an unjust war. A second complication here, with the insistence on selfless motivation, is that the appeal to conscience on every issue of moral significance is thought by critics of civil disobedience to display another kind of self-centredness: a refusal to accept that the consciences of others must be respected and weighed against your own.

Justification of civil disobedience

On the question of the justification of civil disobedience, there are two polarised positions of unqualified approval and complete rejection.

First, those who argue that active disobedience to unjust laws is always a matter of personal moral decision according to conscience are arguing that conscience always overrides any general obligation to obey the law. This in effect means that there is no obligation at all, because it implies that, in the case of just laws, the obligation derived from conscience would be sufficient.

The most renowned advocate of this position was Thoreau, who had little time for the idea that the law is owed any respect:

> Must the citizen even for a moment, or in the least degree, resign his conscience to the legislator? Why has every man a conscience then? I think we should be men first, and subjects afterward. It is not desirable to cultivate a respect for the law, so much as for the right. The only obligation which I have the right to assume, is to do what at any time I think is right.
>
> (Thoreau 1983: 387)

The appeal of this statement rests on the plausible assumption that one always has the right to resist outright injustice. Read more carefully, however, what it amounts to is a thoroughgoing individualism on all questions of moral seriousness, the implications of which are anarchic.

Second, those at the opposite end of the spectrum maintain that civil disobedience is never in any circumstances justified. From this point of view, the 'general' *prima facie* obligation to obey the law means general in the sense of 'universal' or 'exceptionless', rather than 'generally speaking' or 'in most circumstances'. This position includes Socrates' *Crito* position, allowing criticism and persuasion but completely outlawing principled disobedience. It also includes Bentham's famous dictum, urging legal reformers to 'obey punctually, censure freely'. The view that civil disobedience is always wrong is usually confined to the context of liberal democracies or other forms of government under which some freedom of expression and criticism is possible.

Between these two polarised positions, many philosophers, including Rawls and Dworkin, have sought to develop a qualified defence of civil disobedience in carefully defined circumstances. What they are defending is the moral legitimacy of a certain kind of principled lawbreaking, overriding the *prima facie* obligation to obey the law.

Rawls on civil disobedience

Rawls's approach to civil disobedience flows directly from his contractual theory of obligation. Bluntly speaking, when the state breaks its side of the hypothetical contract, the obligation to obey is abrogated. Civil disobedience is then justified in carefully specified circumstances. What this means for Rawls is that a situation exists whereby the parties in the original position would find it irrational to agree with the disallowal or suppression of basic liberties or the equality of opportunity for any group in which they might find themselves when the veil of ignorance is lifted.

What Rawls explicitly assumes from the outset is that civil disobedience is only appropriate and feasible in a democratic society, a society that is – at least in principle – committed to the values of liberty and equality. In non-democratic societies, other forms of opposition and resistance are appropriate; however, this is not what Rawls is concerned with. Civil disobedience is taken up by citizens who regard the system as in the main a just one. A precondition for justifying it, he believes, is that those resorting to it accept that the system is a 'nearly just' one. Although it goes outside of the law to make its protest, civil disobedience stays within the limits of what Rawls calls 'fidelity to law, albeit at the outer limits of it'. That is to say, they accept the moral legitimacy of the law as a whole; this acceptance is evidenced by their willingness to accept the legal consequence of their actions.

Rawls is arguing, then, that there is a general duty of obedience and that civil disobedience can be justified in a contemporary democratic society. As we have seen, he argues not only that there is a natural duty to obey just laws, but also a duty to obey them – within certain limits – when they are unjust. If the society is 'well-ordered and nearly just', accepting the democratic principles of equality and mutual respect, there are many injustices that have to be accepted. It is only when an injustice becomes grave enough that civil disobedience is justified.

What he means is something like this. In any large society, there will inevitably be many grievances, real and imagined, about the distribution of wealth, undeserved privileges, miscarriages of justice or the state of the law on many different issues. Some examples of these will be serious, while some will be relatively minor injustices. Most of them are more appropriately dealt with within the channels of the democratic political process. Relatively few of them justify civil disobedience.

In some cases, though, he accepts civil disobedience to be justified. How then does Rawls define it?

> I shall begin by defining civil disobedience as a public, non-violent, conscientious yet political act contrary to law usually done with the aim of bringing about a change in the law or policies of the government. By acting in this way, one addresses the sense of justice of the majority of the community and declares that in one's considered opinion the principles of social co-operation among free and equal men are not being respected.
>
> (Rawls 1972: 364)

Rawls is conscious of the restricted nature of this definition, which excludes many other types of principled disobedience. He adds that he does 'not at all mean to say that only this form of dissent is ever justified in a democratic state'. What he seeks to emphasise is the distinctiveness of this form of dissent, as opposed to, say, conscientious refusal.

What he means by calling it a political act is that (1) it is addressed to 'the majority that holds political power'; and (2) that it is an act 'guided and justified by political principles, that is, by the principles of justice' (ibid.: 365). What it always involves is an appeal by this dramatically public action to the commonly shared conception of justice in the society. When it is justified, Rawls sees civil disobedience as playing an important part in the democratic process, by highlighting the failure of society to live up to its own principles. So by its very nature, he argues, civil disobedience is a public act rather than a covert or secretive one. It is a form of public speech, and as such it needs a public forum. And for the same reason it is non-violent: as a form of speech, it is principally a form of communication. As violence, it negates itself as communication.

There are three presumptions that, according to Rawls, circumscribe the limits of justifiable civil disobedience. The first of these is the most important, identifying those types of injustice that are the appropriate objects for this kind of protest. What he argues here is that 'it seems reasonable, other things being equal', to limit it to instances of 'substantial and clear injustice' (ibid.: 372). For this reason, he says, civil disobedience should be restricted to protesting against serious infringements of (1) the principle of liberty; and (2) the principle of fair equality of opportunity. Both of these he describes as guaranteeing the basic liberties: the rights to vote, to hold office, to own property, and so on. Having included these clearly identifiable injustices in the category of wrongs that are rightfully opposed by civil disobedience, he proceeds to exclude socioeconomic injustices as suitable cases for civil disobedience on the grounds that they are much more difficult to ascertain. There is so much conflict of rational opinion as to whether and to what extent the existence of socioeconomic inequalities constitutes an injustice, that civil disobedience would become too difficult to justify. Thus, apparently unfair tax laws, he says, unless they are clearly designed to attack a basic equal liberty (for example, a tax on a religious group or an ethnic minority) are best left to the political process.

Rawls's second presumption is that, for civil disobedience to be justified, legal means of redress have been tried, to no avail. Attempts to have discriminatory laws repealed have failed, so civil disobedience should normally only be taken up in the last resort. He accepts that this is not always the case and that sometimes the matter is too urgent to spend years on legal campaigns.

The third and last condition is more confused than the first two. The natural duty of justice, he says, may require a certain restraint. If one minority is justified in disobedience, then any other minority in relevantly similar circumstances is likewise justified. So many groups with an equally sound case might take up civil disobedience and cause a complete breakdown of the law. There is an upper limit on the public forum to handle all these complaints. It does seem odd that Rawls can contemplate such a scenario, with so many minorities being deprived of basic rights, and still call it a nearly just, well-ordered society.

Criticisms of Rawls

Criticisms of Rawls's general approach to obligation and civil disobedience have come from every direction. Clearly, those who reject contract theory based on rational self-interest will also reject these implications of it. A standard consequentialist justification of principled lawbreaking in pursuit of civil rights will be based, not on an appeal to an implicit rational contract, but to a comparison with the consequences of continued acquiescence. What releases them from the general duty of obedience is an outweighing of the consequences of submitting to unjust laws by the positive consequences of defying them.

Criticism also comes from those who reject the justification of civil disobedience unconditionally, on the grounds that the obligation is universal in a democracy, where it is possible to change unjust laws through more conventional political channels. On this kind of conceptual argument, 'principled lawbreaking' is a contradiction in terms if the law is by definition morally authoritative, even in its unjust manifestations. The implausibility of this criticism is highlighted by any consideration of the claim to have established an automatic link between the existence of a proper legal authority and the obligation to obey. It is quite clear that we can accept the democratic authority of a government without submitting to such an unconditional obligation. People can and do recognise the political legitimacy of governments, while quietly disregarding not only the laws that do not suit them, but also the ones they think irrational or unfair.

Others have criticised Rawls on his own terms, suggesting that there is something arbitrary about his narrow confinement of legitimate civil disobedience to the special case of the civil rights of minorities. It seems obvious to many critics that there are other serious moral issues that might equally merit principled lawbreaking – issues relating to environmental dangers, unjust wars or unjust taxes – which are held to be wrongs or injustices that would not be countenanced in the original position. There is also felt to be something excessive about his justification of unjust laws that fall short of the threshold at which they create systematic structural inequality, on the assumption that rational agents – veiled from knowledge of whether they would be the victims – would regard such a high threshold of toleration of such injustices as 'the best possible world'. The objection here is either that this is not what we would agree to from behind the veil, any more than we would agree to extreme inequalities; or if it does imply this, then there is something radically wrong with the veil as a metaphor for justice.

If this last criticism is justified, however, it means in effect that there is no general *prima facie* obligation to obey the law, beyond the moral obligation that is there already. If at the first sign of injustice or unfairness the duty to obey disappears, it means that there is no special reason to respect the authority of the law. Another interpretation is that 'respect for the law' is just one reason to weigh against other reasons, enjoying no special status.

Conclusion

In contemporary legal theory, the relation between the idea of law and the meaning of its authority is still very unclear. As we saw at the outset of this chapter, any serious examination of the link between a valid authorised law and the duty of obedience leads into a conceptual quagmire. One thing that Rawls and his critics have done in recent years is to bring more structure into the debate on the origins of obligation and the conditions under which it might be suspended. One point upon which a degree of consensus is perhaps emerging is the recognition that there are limits to the authority of the law, and that the obligation to obey is not unconditional.

Study questions

General question: Do you agree that there is a general duty to obey the law? If so, what is its source?

Further study questions: What are the problems with the traditional social contract theories? Explain and critically evaluate Rawls's 'hypothetical contract' theory. Does it solve all the traditional problems of contract theory? Does he show that there is a natural duty of obligation to obey the law? What is civil disobedience? Is it compatible with the general obligation to obey? Does Rawls's 'original position' provide a sound basis for determining the justifiability of civil disobedience? If not, is there a better justification for civil disobedience?

Suggestions for further reading

Among the general books and chapters on political and legal obligation, the most noteworthy are Greenawalt (1987), Horton (1992), Pateman (1979), Beran (1987), Smith (1976) and Flathman (1973).

Important chapters and articles to consult include Raz (1979: 266–75; 1986: ch. 4), Lacey (1988: chs 4 and 6), Soper's article and the subsequent discussion in Gavison (1987). Useful shorter comments can also be found in Lyons (1984: ch. 7), Bix (1996: ch. 16) and Harris (1980: ch. 16).

For Aquinas's writings on obligation, see Aquinas (1948). On the history of contract theory, see in particular Jean Hampton (1986; 1997: ch. 2). There is also an excellent anthology by Lessnoff (1990), containing key selections from Hobbes, Locke, Kant, Rawls and others. The essential passages on contract theory can be found in Hobbes (1962: chs 6, 11–21) and Locke (1924: sections 1–6, 47–55, 123–41). Abridgements of these and of Hume's criticism of contract theory are reprinted in Cottingham (1996: part IX).

The essential reading from Rawls's *Theory of Justice* (1972) is Chapter 6. Important critical discussions of Rawls's theory as a whole include Nozick (1974: ch. 7) and Barry (1973). Daniels (1975) is a collection of critical essays.

On civil disobedience, the most valuable collections are both edited by Bedau (1969, 1991), including Plato's *Crito* and influential essays by Thoreau, Martin Luther King, Rawls and Raz. See also Singer (1973), Greenawalt (1987: chaps 3–4), Leiser (1973: ch. 12) and Kipnis (1977: section 4). There are useful shorter comments by Riddall (1991: ch. 15) and Singer (1993: ch. 11).

7   Legal and moral rights

Rights we take for granted today include a maze of political, civil, legal and human rights so complex and deep-rooted that the idea of rights being indispensable to moral and legal discourse seems to be part of the fabric of social life. We have rights in property and rights created by contract. Everyone has the right to a fair trial and access to civil and criminal justice. We have rights as citizens and as consumers. The basic rights to 'life, liberty and security' are protected by the European Convention and the 1998 Human Rights Act. At a more mundane level, everyone has the right to voice an opinion and to express dissent. We regularly claim the right to know or the right to reply. Controversy on these matters usually relates to the genuineness of each of these rights, or the extent to which they should be allowed. Nevertheless, in the debates that have raged around the subject of rights in recent years, there is one particular issue that, logically speaking, precedes all the others. This is the question of whether we can meaningfully say that there actually are any rights at all, human or otherwise. While the rights theories of Dworkin, Rawls and Nozick begin from the assumption that there are indeed rights to theorise about, others are more sceptical.

So do rights really exist or are they phantoms? Sceptics argue that all our talk of rights is nothing but rhetoric and bluster, designed to draw public attention to specific moral claims. There are two extremes here. At the realist end of the spectrum, we find writers such as Norberto Bobbio declaring that the problems about rights are not philosophical at all, that the real problem is 'to find the surest method for guaranteeing rights and preventing their continuing violation' (Bobbio 1990: 12). From this eminently practical point of view, the existence of rights and meaningfulness of rights-claims is presupposed. At the sceptical end of the spectrum, we hear Alasdair MacIntyre comparing belief in rights with belief in witches and unicorns, claiming that 'every attempt to give good reasons for believing that there *are* such rights has failed' (MacIntyre 1981: 67). From this standpoint, there are no rights to be guaranteed. What we will be examining in this chapter is the philosophical support for each of these positions.

A more cautious scepticism than the outright denial of rights as such is expressed by those who regard it as meaningful only to talk of legal rights.

On this view, the background to any right properly so-called must be that of legal definition and sanction. Without this background, the language of rights as used to explain moral relations between people is at best metaphorical, and at worst meaningless. This denial of the intelligibility of moral rights is of course contested vigorously by those who regard legal rights as merely the codification of pre-existing human rights, which some philosophers describe as natural. As we shall see, this dispute is not easily resolved.

An equally prominent theme here is the most general consequence of taking a realist view of rights. If there are indeed rights to be recognised, the bearing this has on the matter of the law's authority is immediate and problematic. To what extent is the state compelled to accept individual or collective rights as an effective constraint on the implementation of public policy through the criminal and civil law? What limiting effects do they have on the reach of the law? This will be taken up in the next chapter in the specific context of personal privacy, but the problem here is more general. It is a question, philosophically speaking, about how rights stand in relation to utility. What are we committed to when we accept that there really are rights? Does it mean merely that they should always be respected in the sense of being taken into account in every calculation of the common good? Or does it mean more than this, that rights can on no account be overridden by utility?

This points to the closely related problem of identifying 'basic' rights, those supposed to be guaranteed as a bare minimum. Are these the ones that should be defended unconditionally against utility or convenience? If so, which among the vast numbers of rights claimed today should qualify as basic? Does being basic mean that they are to be regarded as absolute, in the sense that there are no imaginable circumstances in which they might reasonably be suspended or overridden? The problem at the heart of the rights-utility conflict is that of determining the extent to which legislators have a free hand in deciding what is to be included, allowing in pragmatic concerns about resources and practicability; and the sense in which these choices are pressed upon them by the intrinsic nature of the rights in question.

Overall, the question of how rights and legality are to be understood is the paramount one. A great deal of the rights analysis in twentieth-century legal theory has focused exclusively on legal rights, independently of the question of how they relate to rights in general. The most important single influence on this development was the analysis initiated by Wesley Hohfeld (1880–1919), who was inspired by the closely connected aims of legal realism and analytical jurisprudence. What Hohfeld sought was an analysis that would clarify the real structure of legal relations between people, expressed in terms of rights and duties as they actually exist and are operated in the courts. The twin objectives were conceptual clarity and a faithful reflection of legal reality. To this purpose, Hohfeld stipulated a deliberately rigid eight-term structure, consisting of four pairs of conceptual opposites and correlatives, through which all rights-related legal phenomena should be viewed. This structure has been revised and reworded in various ways by others, but this was how Hohfeld originally presented it:

Jural Opposites	{right	privilege	power	immunity
	{no-right	duty	disability	liability
Jural Correlatives	{right	privilege	power	immunity
	{duty	no-right	liability	disability

Source: Hohfeld (1919: 36)

The main purpose of this method was to dispel the confusion created by indiscriminate use of the word 'right' when something else (a privilege, a power, an immunity) was meant. Each word commonly used to designate a right is given its real meaning in terms of what it is not and what it implies as a correlative. Thus, a right, as opposed to a 'no-right', held by X, always corresponds to a duty in Y, instead of the privilege that would be had if X had no-right. X's privilege in doing something, as opposed to a duty, implies that Y merely has no-right against X, rather than the duty that would be created by X's right. If X has a legal power, as opposed to a disability, Y has a liability instead of the immunity that would be had if X was legally disabled. If X has a legal immunity, as opposed to a liability, then Y has a disability against X, rather than a power.

The general point of Hohfeld's analysis was that it is wrong to talk about rights when what we are seeking to indicate is a different kind of legal relation, with very different practical implications. It is only correct to speak of a right in the strict sense when there is a correlative duty. This is known as the correlativity thesis. There are several points to be grasped for present purposes. First, this schema was only intended to apply to the classification of legal rights. It has no direct implications for non-legal rights. Second, it does not imply that there are only legal rights. Third, Hohfeld did not mean that there are no rights at all, either legal or moral. The purpose was only to sharpen up talk about legal rights, to lay the foundations for more accurate and useful analysis. Hohfeld's main thesis was that the only legal rights in the full sense of the word are those with correlative duties. The Hohfeldian terminology will not be used in this chapter, but the reader should bear in mind the restriction of the use of the term 'right' to indicate a claim to which there must be a correlative duty.

Rights and rights-scepticism

In everyday language, most people have little doubt about what a right is. It is something about which they are entitled to protest if they are deprived of it, or it is withheld without justification. Consider now exactly what it means to assert, for example, that you have the right to the repayment of a loan. Clearly you would like it repaid, but is this all? Beyond the expression of a desire, there is an insistence with all rights-claims that you 'ought' to have certain things or be free to perform certain actions.

A right is usually understood to mean more than a standard moral claim, but when we move beyond this, the interpretation becomes controversial. If the right to the repayment of the loan is a genuine one, it may be argued, it is not merely a morally reasonable or worthy claim, the merits of which are to be evaluated against others, such as the use of the money for other purposes; it is something that you can demand as an entitlement, something to which you can lay claim. What you are laying claim to is in a sense already yours; it is not something that you merely ought to have. If you do have the right, you are in possession of a distinctive moral force or power to insist upon receiving it.

This is one popular interpretation of what a right means. It is a particular kind of strong moral claim. There is another interpretation, however, of how rights go beyond standard moral claims, which is inconsistent with it. According to this line of thought, rights are not held by people as a kind of natural property, they are granted or ascribed to people with a guarantee of protection. One does not merely have a moral case for the right to recover a loan; the right can, if necessary, be enforced. What we are talking about here is actual force rather than moral force. This is what makes a right a right; it can be insisted upon with the backing of the sanctions of law. What this means in effect is that for rights to be more than standard moral claims – which is to say, to exist as distinctive rights at all – they must be legal rights. This in turn implies that there are only legal rights.

A historical point of some significance is that the idea of a singular right ('a' right, rather than 'right' or 'the' right) held by individuals dates only from the early seventeenth century. The concept of an individual right as something held against other individuals or against the world was virtually unknown to the Greeks or Romans, or to medieval Europe (Finnis 1980: 205–10). Second, the idea of the reality of such a right was steadily eroded over the period between the French and American Revolutions and the Second World War.

A central philosophical problem, then, concerns the ontological status of a right. If it is taken to be an 'entity' of some sort, can we give a coherent account of what kind of entity is involved when we speak of someone having a right, for example, to compensation for an injury? It is clearly not an entity in the sense of an ascertainable object such as a physical attribute like weight, or a mental faculty like memory. The mere existence of either of these can be demonstrated. How does one demonstrate the existence of a right? If it is anything, it would seem, it is not a natural, observable phenomenon.

On the face of it, the most promising interpretation is that it is a moral power. Leaving aside for a moment the question of legal enforcement, which may or may not be available, the belief of an injured person that he has a right to compensation is a belief that he has a power that other people do not, a power to insist upon it. This would be a power that could be used to exert pressure on the party or parties alleged to owe compensation. This kind of analysis of rights as moral powers has been the target of a prominent strain of thought in European philosophy since Bentham, i.e. rights-scepticism. From the standpoint of this scepticism, a right is not seen as a natural entity of any kind, nor does it exist in another mysterious moral domain. It simply has no existence, and beliefs to the contrary are explained in various ways, ranging from dishonourable political motives to belief in the supernatural.

Bentham's attack on rights

Bentham was in the forefront of the attack on the theories of natural law and the social contract, both of which were associated with the idea of natural rights as natural powers. His own writings displayed a general unfriendliness to the idea that rights could pre-exist their legal codification. There were two reasons for this, one political, the other philosophical. Bentham was developing the doctrine of utility at the same time as the revolutionary movements in America and France were asserting the rights of man, under the influence of the doctrine of natural rights, especially as expressed by Locke and Rousseau. It is against the background of the Jacobin Terror in France that Bentham's intemperate and apparently eccentric outburst against the idea of 'the rights of man' should be understood. As far as Bentham was concerned, the only way in which it is appropriate to speak of rights is in acknowledgement of those codified in law. In short, there are only legal rights, no moral or natural rights, any talk of which is confusing and dangerous political rhetoric.

As a thoroughgoing empiricist, Bentham regarded all rights, including those codified in law, as at best 'fictitious entities' and at worst imaginary conjurings. *Legal* rights, then, along with the legal concepts of duty and obligation, and most of the language of the common law, he regarded as 'legal fictions'. These legal concepts, however, can be interpreted by Bentham's method of paraphrasis. A sentence containing the word 'right' can be rewritten and translated as a legal duty. Thus, 'X has a property right' can be translated into a sentence of equivalent meaning: 'Y has a duty to refrain from appropriating or trespassing on X's property'. But a 'duty' is also a fictitious legal entity. This in turn can be translated into the language of coercion: 'If Y appropriates or trespasses on X's land, then Y will be liable to a certain punishment'. Every legal term can be traced back in this manner to the pleasure–pain calculus of utilitarian social welfare. The threat of punishment is a perceptible and tangible, hard empirical reality. Bentham believed that all legal terms could be explicated by this method of paraphrasis.

The important contrast that Bentham draws is between these 'translatable' fictitious entities, which do have a meaning to be uncovered, and non-legal rights, which are not translatable at all. If they cannot be thus rendered into the language of coercion, we have to accept that they are literally unintelligible, or just plain nonsense. 'Natural rights is simple nonsense; natural and imprescriptible rights, rhetorical nonsense, nonsense upon stilts' (Bentham 1987: 53).

Bentham regarded talk of natural and imprescriptible rights as 'terrorist language' and as so much 'bawling upon paper'. A natural right, which cannot be translated into a corresponding duty-sentence, is a self-contradiction. It is as nonsensical as the term 'cold heat'. There are no rights in nature. Natural rights are conjurings of the imagination. Talk of the 'Rights of Man' is 'a preposterous fraud', because it cannot be rendered into concrete meaningful terms.

Bentham's main substantial point which is of lasting importance is his argument that the legal rights which are actually recognised should be those that, having had their claims considered on their merits, are freely ascribed by government and are thereafter permanently on probation. If they turn out to be contrary to utility, it is self-evident that they should be suspended forthwith. It is worth noting at this point that while this may be self-evident to a utilitarian, if this is what legal rights amount to, then they are not rights in any deeper sense at all – *they are merely licences.*

Elimination of rights

As indicated earlier, there has been a general trend in modern jurisprudence towards the complete elimination or negation of the concept of a right; however, what exactly does it mean to 'eliminate' rights as a concept? Broadly speaking, it means that those who use the popular terminology of rights are labouring under the delusion that their language has objective reference, that there is something at some level of reality corresponding to the words they are using.

This ultimate conclusion applies as much to a legal right (and duty) as it does to a moral or natural right. It was expressed concisely by the Scandinavian realist Karl Olivecrona (Olivecrona 1971) in his assessment of the legal meaning of rights and duties. Rights are chimeras or imaginary entities 'interposed between the operative facts and their legal effects'. What this means is that in the situation in which we assume a right and a correlative duty to be created in law, such as the drawing up and signing of a contract, and the contract taking effect, the only reality is the complex of facts surrounding the contract and the actual consequences in law, all of which can be described in empirical terms. The idea that a right is created somewhere in this process is at best a metaphor or expressive abbreviation for a complex of facts. Between the two terms, the operative facts and the legal effects, which do have objects of reference, there is a universal tendency to conjure up the concepts of right and duty, which have no such objective reference. They are simply unreal figments of the imagination, as unreal as ghosts or hobgoblins. The same can be said, *a fortiori*, about the prelegal moral institution of promise making.

The rooting out of the idea that the concept of a right has objective reference was rather like a process of exorcism. The ghostly object to be laid to rest was the moral power assumed by natural law theory. This was the power assumed to be held in the prelegal state of nature, the power to which the term natural 'right' refers. This concept continued to hold sway in theories such as the willpower theory of the early positivist Savigny (1779–1861), in which important features of natural law were retained, such as the continued recognition of an independent but accessible spiritual realm of reality in which rights existed. The denial of the existence of this spiritual realm was an essential theme in the working through of the philosophical recognition of the implications of the advance of the physical sciences.

The same sceptical line of thought was developed by Oliver Wendell Holmes:

> Nowhere is the confusion between legal and moral ideas more manifest than in the law of contract. Among other things, here again the so-called primary rights and duties are invested with a mystic significance beyond what can be assigned and explained. *The duty to keep a contract at common law means a prediction that you must pay damages if you do not keep it – and nothing else.*
>
> (Adams 1992: 93)

What Holmes recommends is that for heuristic purposes one takes up the point of view of 'the bad man', who only wants to know what the courts will make him do. A legal duty means no more to a bad man than that 'if he does certain things he will be subjected to disagreeable consequences by way of imprisonment or compulsory payment of money' (Adams 1992: 93).

In Holmes's vivid metaphor, the legal analyst needs to follow the example of the bad man who applies 'cynical acid' to the legal concepts he encounters. In the case of legal rights and duties, the application of cynical acid strips down the ideas of such things to their real legal consequences. In reality, Holmes insists, all rights-claims come down to no more than prophecies of the ways in which the courts will decide concrete cases. If the courts ignore them, they are not in any meaningful sense 'rights'.

Response to rights-scepticism

In the light of these sceptical arguments against the very existence of the rights that are dealt with as a matter of course in contemporary litigation, in the criminal courts and in the European Court of Human Rights, what should the proper response be? Most people today believe that they do have equal rights, that they have procedural and substantive legal rights, that typically rights are universal, and that it is often possible to enforce them in the courts. Should we conclude that all these people are deluded and that their belief in rights is analogous to, and no more justified than, belief in the supernatural?

Rights-sceptics may answer these questions in one of two ways. The first is that the denial of the reality of rights does not have any practical implications of this nature. Statutory 'rights' will continue to be claimed and enforced, regardless of what we call them, and in the struggles for civil rights campaigners against governments that practise genocide, torture or the suppression of civil liberties will no doubt continue to use the phrase 'human rights' without embarrassment. This type of answer suggests that the ontological issue is purely philosophical, that the denial of rights as 'entities' has no practical implications.

The second type of answer is quite different, and more fraught with ambiguity. On this kind of argument, rights-scepticism does affect the practical realities of the claims to legal and moral rights, but not in the sense of dispensing with rights altogether. The implication is that with this theoretical enlightenment, the status of 'rights' changes, that they are to be understood not as objective entities which are owned or held by every individual, which is precisely what has been disproved by the sceptical arguments, but rather as claims to our moral attention, claims that can have greater or less moral worth. None of these claims can be properly construed as an entitlement. This line of argument suggests a discriminating critique of any declarations of human rights that proceed on the assumption that they are merely declaring or endorsing rights that already exist. It is this assumption that the various versions of rights-scepticism are denying. The important point here is that this approach affects the content of any such declarations of rights. It is this second kind of interpretation of the implications of rights-scepticism to which the defence of the reality of rights must be addressed. First, however, we have to consider what is involved in the reassertion of this reality against the kinds of scepticism as outlined in the last section.

It is often asked how it can be true that there are human rights when they are routinely abused and almost universally ignored. This kind of scepticism is quite easily refuted. Widespread abuse or even universal neglect of rights does not count as an argument against their existence, any more than the failure to develop physics would have shown that there are no such things as electrons. Furthermore, just as the doctrine of natural law was only ever developed to counteract cultural relativism, it is only because people and their governments often act as if there were no human rights that the existence of such rights was ever asserted. The classical natural rights doctrines of the early modern period were developed mainly in resistance to the absolutist governments that almost completely ignored such rights. The later modern movements for women's rights and the rights of ethnic minorities started from a position of almost complete neglect.

More importantly, the insistence that rights are real must confront the reductivist and eliminativist arguments that deny their reality. The overall argument against reductivism – the claim that there are only legal rights – is that it is incoherent. If it is conceded that legal rights exist, then there must also be prelegal rights. Rights cannot suddenly spring into existence with the wave of a legal wand. Statutory recognition of a right only provides legal backing for what already exists, for example, a slave's right to be free. The legal emancipation does not suddenly create the right to be free, it merely acknowledges it and provides a sanction to prevent the continuation of slavery.

One reductivist reply to this is that it is merely one interest among others, with no special claim to our attention, which pre-exists the legal right. A law transforms an interest into a protected interest, which is all a legal right is. It exists in the sense that it is tangible, by virtue of its real effects. The realist argument, however, is stronger than this. If rights are suddenly created as legal entitlements, and this is on the grounds that there are interests that need to be given legal protection, then the legal rights are merely licences that can be revoked at the first sign of difficulty. On this conception, legal rights have no deep foundation. In other words, legal rights are not rights at all and reductivism is incoherent, because if prelegal rights are denied, then legal rights must also be denied. Reductivists can in turn reply that this would make all rights absolute or unconditional, which is absurd. They could never be overridden by other considerations or conflicting rights. We will see later how this objection can be countered.

The response to eliminative rights-scepticism – the claim that there are no rights of any kind, moral or legal – is more difficult. In what sense, we are asking, is the rights-theorist asserting or reasserting that rights do exist, when faced with the claim that there are no entities whatsoever corresponding to the concepts of legal and moral rights? Does it have to be reasserted that rights are things that exist in a 'spiritual' realm? Do they have to assume again that rights are magical or supernatural 'powers'? Are rights moral powers after all? Is a legal right a mysterious power held by the right-holder in addition to the observable facts about the legal process?

The argument against eliminative rights-scepticism that there are rights, both within the law and beyond it, would be implausible if it rested solely on the fact that it is widely believed that there are ways in which people should or should not be treated, solely by virtue of certain qualities they possess, such as reason or consciousness. The fact that it is widely believed that there are UFOs does not mean that UFOs have a certain kind of existence. The fact that in the nineteenth century virtually no one believed that women had the right to vote does not show that they had no such right. What the claim that there are rights means is that people who have rights have a stronger than standard moral claim, and that there is a *prima facie* case for their prevailing over moral claims that do not embody rights.

The irreducibility of rights

A central question, then, is whether there is any more to a right than that which can be expressed in moral or legal language that makes no reference to rights. Are rights reducible to needs, desert or utility, or does the entitlement implicit in a right give you a stronger claim than this? Consider again the case of *Donoghue v. Stevenson* (1932) (see Chapter 4), which established the general duty of care in English law. The question here relates to the nature of the claim made by the plaintiff who had suffered illness as a result of a defective product due to a manufacturer's negligence. Did she deserve or need compensation? Possibly. Is the right reducible to these deserts or needs? Did it enhance the overall utility of everyone concerned? This was not really the point. The Law Lords eventually determined that she did have a right to compensation, despite arguments that there was no clear precedent in English law and that the case would open a floodgate of litigation.

One argument against this decision – that it would make the manufacturer of a defective axle liable after a train crash – was a consequentialist argument against the recognition of this right. The claim to compensation that the plaintiff had was more than a standard moral argument based on desert, need or utility. Many people deserve compensation, but are not awarded it. Mrs Donoghue had brought the case and taken it to appeal because she believed that she was morally entitled and must be legally entitled, despite legal advice that she was not. What does this entitlement mean? Legally speaking, it might be simply that the law will back your claim. If you have a 'title' to it, the law *should* back your claim. Legally speaking, an entitlement is more than a desert or a need. The decision to recognise the right to recover for, say, emotional damages may originate in the recognition of desert or need, but it becomes more than this, and irreducible to it. A legal right to X means that you already have X; you are trying to claim what is already yours. If you merely deserve compensation, you are making out a case for being given what is not yet yours as of right.

Morally speaking, Mrs Donoghue's belief that she was entitled to compensation is also irreducible to the belief that she deserved it. It might include this belief, but it states something more. Once the moral right is recognised, there is no alternative but to hand it over. If it were merely desert, one might argue that there are more deserving claims. If it were merely need, it might be argued that there were others in greater need. Given that it is a right, she can demand it in a way that others cannot.

Absolute rights

It is very commonly argued against rights-based moralities that, for a right to have any force at all, it must be regarded as absolute. Rights must be either subordinate to utility or they must be held to be completely inviolable. Either way, they are absolute and unyielding, or there is no way of stopping them dissolving into utility. Jonathan Glover, for example (1977: 83{-}4) argues that anything short of a defence of absolute rights, falling back on a theory of *prima facie* rights, is indistinguishable from his own utilitarian position.

There are essentially two rights-based positions on this. Either they take the middle course advocated in Dworkin's rights thesis, according to which rights that are less than absolute nevertheless have a quality which enables them to prevail more often than not over non-rights considerations (i.e. they can 'trump' them), or they can take the line that absolute status means in practice that they can 'virtually never' be violated.

A standard argument to the effect that no rights, however apparently basic, can be absolute, proceeds from an imagined 'ticking bomb' scenario in which one is forced to choose between violating the rights of one individual and allowing the deaths of millions. If the only way to prevent a nuclear attack is to torture the person who knows the whereabouts of the bomb, in such a case it is said to be self-evident that nobody has the absolute right not to be tortured. If such a right is less than absolute, the argument continues, then all the more so are all the other 'basic' rights, for each of which possible exceptions can be imagined. There are many faults with this argument, but the most relevant one for present purposes is that it highlights rather than detracting from the absolute status of these rights. The extremity of the examples required to undermine them only illustrates their intrinsically absolute status.

This is what Finnis means (1980: 223–6) when he defends absolute rights against utilitarians, for whom only utility is absolute. When we say that the right not to have one's life taken as a means to an end, or the right not to be condemned on false charges is absolute or exceptionless, what we mean is that even the violation of rights in these extreme circumstances is absolutely wrong. It may be a lesser evil, but it is still an evil. Anybody who commits it is not exonerated. The value of absolute rights-talk, for Finnis, is that it keeps the idea of justice in the foreground and undercuts the persuasiveness of pure consequentialism.

Rights versus utility

The concept of a right is intimately connected with the concept of justice. If the modern natural lawyers are right to regard justice as a necessary feature of the law, the consequence of this is that the concept of a moral right is equally indispensable. On Dworkin's thesis, it is not optional for the courts to take rights into account in their deliberations; on his reading of the meaning of law, they are legally required to do so. The demand for justice relating to any particular situation is translatable into an insistence on the recognition of all the genuine and justifiable rights relevant to that situation. The point of identifying and defending any specific right is to raise an obstacle against arguments from utility, whether this means the general welfare or overall aggregate of benefit, or merely more effective government.

Bentham on utility and rights

For Benthamite utilitarianism, the above line of argument is complete nonsense. From Bentham's point of view, it was by definition false to argue that it was morally defensible to raise obstacles against social utility. A rational legal system as he imagined it would withhold or suspend the status of legal right from any interest that did obstruct the general welfare in this way. The common law system, with its entrenched principles protecting traditional privileges, was abhorred by Bentham precisely because it did not balance real interests in the cause of the general social good. In Bentham's rational legal system, any codified right that turned out to obstruct the general good would be revoked.

The important point to stress against Bentham, though, is that legal rights – properly understood – as much as moral rights, *must* operate to some extent as obstacles to utility. If there were no presumption at all in favour of rights prevailing over other interests, thus diminishing to some extent 'the general good', they would not in any effective sense be rights at all. They would merely be protected interests, protected only for as long as they do not become inconvenient. Rights only become important when they are likely to be denied, that is, precisely when they are inconvenient and unwelcome to the majority, especially when the majority in a democratic society is faced with the accusation that withholding minority rights constitutes an injustice. Defending them in these circumstances is one of the things Dworkin means by taking rights seriously.

J.S. Mill on utility and rights

Although the Benthamite doctrine was highly influential, it did not prevail unchallenged. John Stuart Mill's (1806–73) discomfort with the utilitarian tradition was manifested in his rejection of Bentham's pleasure–pain calculus and his attempt to reintroduce the non-legal notion of a moral right. What he was attempting here was the modification and completion of the utilitarian doctrine by arguing that it was compatible with moral rights and justice. Mill's attitude to rights differed sharply from that of Bentham, but his ultimate conclusion was not entirely dissimilar. Mill was more aware than Bentham of the dangers inherent in unchecked majority rule. With some prescience, he saw the main source of injustice in modern industrial democracies in the growing suppression of the rights of individuals and minorities, for the sake of the greater good of the majority, rather than in the oppression of the masses by small governing circles. At the same time, however, he was defending his own version of utilitarianism. One of Mill's main theoretical objectives was to reconcile the requirements of utility with the demands of liberty, justice and rights, to demonstrate their deeper compatibility.

Mill's strategy to effect this reconciliation was not to argue directly against the anti-utilitarian theories of rights and justice, but to absorb them by representing them as distorted versions of the doctrine of utility. Kant, and Kantian theories of rights in particular, were interpreted as justifications of individual rights ultimately rooted in instrumental conceptions of the social good. The central thrust of the Kantian approach was a *non*-instrumental attitude to human rights, which are recognised in Kant's famous maxim that individuals are always to be treated as ends in themselves, never solely as a means. From Mill's point of view, the only thing that can be treated as an end in itself is utility, or the general happiness. On his interpretation of Kant, which attempts to neutralise his influence on moral and legal theory, the justification of treating individuals as ends lies ultimately in the value of this kind of policy for society.

This is a projection of Mill's own solution to the problem of rights and utility, on to Kant and other respect-centred theories of rights derived from him. The justification in these theories really does end with the individual rights-holder, which is held to be the value in itself. Rights are respected for their own sake. Mill's solution, as outlined in his celebrated defence of liberty (Mill 1972a), was to argue that the cultivation of respect for individual rights and liberty, as exemplified by the right to freedom of speech, freedom of worship, the right to pursue one's own lifestyle and so on, has a strengthening rather than a weakening effect on the health of society, and the repression of individual difference and creativity has a devitalising effect that will ultimately lead to its destruction. What he is arguing is that legal and moral respect for individual rights and liberty is ultimately utilitarian, that such respect does serve the interests of society as a whole.

As a matter of historical fact, this claim may or may not be true. But can respect for individual rights be supported by this kind of appeal to utility? One reason this is not a popular theory of rights a century later is that it has become increasingly obvious that short-term utility is more persuasive than the long term. In the short term, the suppression of individual rights makes government more effective; the uncomfortable truth is that democratic freedoms do not always coincide with the interests of the majority, or with raising the aggregate welfare of society. It is much more conducive to efficiency to suppress dissent. The interests of utility, it seems, do conflict with a general respect for individual rights. Mill's is one of the more serious utilitarian attempts to accommodate a theory of rights, but ultimately, in making rights contingent upon utility, it does not essentially differ from Bentham's negative view of rights. With Mill's assumption that rights and utility are compatible and complementary, there is no room for the defence of rights for their own sake, in cases where they are contrary to the dictates of utility.

Dworkin's theory of rights

In modern thinking in philosophy of law, there is agreement between most utilitarians and their critics that there is no deep compatibility between the doctrine of utility and the concept of a right. From the utilitarian point of view, it seems that the unacceptable price of conceding reality to any kind of prelegal moral right is the acceptance of it as an absolute, as an unconditional barrier to social welfare or public policy.

Dworkin's rights thesis offers a perspective that avoids this dilemma. As we saw in an earlier chapter, Dworkin argues that the law consists of a combination of rules, principles and policies, all of which are and should be employed by judges in reaching decisions. They are all genuine components of the law, rather than external moral standards that can be made use of in an *ad hoc* manner to resolve particular hard cases. Along with the established rules of law and the principles or maxims of common law, then, we find an established practice of applying policies as determined by experience of the social consequences of various types of judicial decision. It is against this utilitarian background that Dworkin's defence of the rights thesis is unfolded.

The presence of rights that are both moral and legal in Dworkin's broad sense can, he insists, be deduced from the general sweep of judicial decisions on complex cases, the only explanation for which is often the supposition of the existence of various kinds of rights implicitly recognised by the law, and embodied in common law principles. Finding the right decision – the just and equitable one – is a matter of weighing these moral-legal principles against considerations of good social policy, neither of which automatically prevails against the other. It is in his metaphor of 'rights as trumps' that Dworkin's non-absolutist alternative to utilitarianism becomes apparent. A right, properly understood, is like a trump card that defeats competing considerations. 'Rights are best understood as trumps over some background justification for political decisions that states a goal for the community as a whole' (Dworkin 1977b). To say that such a goal is 'trumped' by a right does not mean that any right is absolute, that it can never be defeated. It will always be possible that there will be cards of a higher value to be played. A right can be outweighed by other rights, or by particularly pressing considerations of policy.

The right to free speech, for example, should in most circumstances be protected, even when it is not conducive to the general welfare. This does not make the right unconditional or absolute. It does not mean that the freedom of speech is unlimited. The basic condition is that, in order for a right to have any effect as a right, it must have some real power to override consideration of the goals of the community; it must have some power to cause inconvenience. As a trump card, this right can itself be defeated. It can be outweighed or overridden by another competing right. The right to free speech is sometimes opposed by the right to the protection of one's reputation, which is supported by the laws of libel and slander. But this competing right is itself a trump card to be played against the general good. When the general good is cited as a reason for overriding a right, it must be determined whether or not a competing right is involved. If the right to freedom of expression runs to making inflammatory speeches, the protection of the right is removed because it is trumped by the rights of the individuals or groups who are threatened by this abuse of free speech. What the rights thesis does mean is that there is a strong presumption in favour of the right prevailing. This, for Dworkin, is what it means to take rights seriously.

Criticisms of Dworkin's theory of rights are too numerous and diverse to explain here. The most obvious line of criticism comes from the utilitarian and openly rights-sceptical perspectives at which it is aimed. The most serious and persistent criticism, however, is that Dworkin's thinking is itself confined within the narrow space of utilitarian calculation, to such an extent that his 'rights' are no more real as obstacles to the tyranny of the collective than Bentham's equality of interests. The main thrust of this criticism is the suggestion that, in the first place, the mere presumption in favour of rights is not strong enough to establish the kind of firm protection needed, and, second, this failure is due to the lack of grounding of his rights in a source independent of utility. In short, it is just too close to utilitarianism for comfort. While there is certainly some truth in these criticisms, given that Dworkin's rights are always defended within the context of acceptable policy, against which they are weighed, it is quite false to claim that the only alternative to absolute rights is no rights at all. The problem of establishing the threshold at which pre-existing rights can be outweighed by arguments from public policy is a much larger one than that faced by Dworkin. Second, the rights defended by Dworkin are rooted in the standards of justice established by common law, which are usually understood to have been implemented despite the demands of utility, not because of it.

The Human Rights Act (1998) and the case of the conjoined twins

The Human Rights Act UK (1998) (HRA), which came into force in 2000, has in its first few years already made an enormous practical impact upon English law. It has been woven into case law in such detail that it is now becoming a fundamental point of reference. Described by many as a constitutional landmark, the HRA is applied every day not only in such areas as family law and mental health law, but has also featured prominently in campaigns for legal reform, such as the attempt to legalise assisted suicide, and now places principles of human rights at the centre of the process of judicial review, through which the decisions of public officials and bodies can be scrutinised and challenged. This enactment was the outcome of the decision in 1997 by the British Government to incorporate the 1950 European Convention into English law. This in turn had been strongly influenced by the United Nations Declaration of Human Rights (UNDHR) in 1948. The result of incorporation is an Act that protects 'basic' human rights and liberties such as the rights to life, liberty and security, the right not to be subjected to torture or degrading treatment, the right to a fair trial and to freedom of thought and expression.

While it obviously does not settle any of the philosophical questions about the status of human rights as moral phenomena, the application of the HRA does add force to the Dworkinian argument that rights that are less than absolute can be defended against rights-scepticism. Predictions by its critics and opponents in the 1990s that it would open a floodgate of trivial and dubious litigation have been confounded. This is largely because of the unwarranted assumption that individual rights and liberties would be treated by the courts as absolutes, automatically endorsing them and over-riding wider group interests. This has manifestly not happened and is unlikely to in the foreseeable future. One of the reasons that it will not is that the Act is rooted in the internationalism of the late 1940s, when the drafting of the UNDHR drew as much upon Eastern communitarian values as those of Western individualism. The principles embodied in the HRA are open to continuous interpretation. The only article to have been authoritatively declared 'absolute' is the one prohibiting torture and degrading treatment. This is absolute in the sense that no exceptions will be made and no excuses heard. All verified instances of it will be declared unlawful. For each of the other articles, it seems, the rights can be balanced against factors relating to the public good.

One striking example of the problem of absolutes in relation to the HRA is provided by the first case that was heard after it came into force, the case of the conjoined twins, Jodie and Mary (*Re A (Children) Conjoined Twins: Medical Treatment (No.1)*, 2000). The case concerned two baby girls who were joined at birth in such a way that an operation to separate them would give Jodie an estimated 70 per cent chance of survival, with a serious chance of severe disability, but at the same time certainly kill Mary. Given that Mary's brain was not fully developed, that her vital organs had failed soon after birth and that she had thus become entirely dependent upon her stronger sister's heart and lungs, the only one who had any prospect of continued life was Jodie. The crucial point was that without surgical inter-vention both would certainly die within six months.

When the Court of Appeal was called upon to rule in advance on whether the operation would be lawful, the judges were facing several complex questions of family and criminal law. The important points in this context were that, first, the best interests of each child had to be taken into account, second, that the killing of one to save another had never been admissible as a defence under English law, and, third, that under the HRA each child had the right to life. The judges were not unanimous on the reasoning behind the judgement, but they were unanimous in declaring the operation lawful and in the ruling given by Lord Justice Ward he declared that, although the killing of Mary would in law be 'intentional', given the certain consequences of the act, the interests of Mary had to be balanced against those of Jodie, and that although each equally had the right to life and the comparative quality of their lives was irrelevant, neither had the right to live at the expense of another. The crucial point was that while the Court recognised the universal human right to life, regardless of the quality of such life, it did not accept that this right was absolute. In a case such as this, the right of one has to give way to that of another.

The subsequent outcome of the operation was entirely successful. Mary died immediately, but Jodie lived and flourished, without any disability. It is important to note that this outcome does not vindicate the morality of the decision, but those who criticised it on the assumption that it had exposed the hollowness of the HRA almost as soon as it had come into force misunderstood the status of these rights. The claim that the right to life can in extreme circumstances be overridden does not imply that there is no right to life at all. On the contrary, it requires circumstances as extreme as these to be overridden. If Jodie's life had not been in imminent danger, the operation would not have been lawful. As we will see in Chapter 10, this ruling has potentially far-reaching implications for criminal law.

Conclusion

Despite the shift in recent decades in favour of recognising legal and moral universal rights in so many areas, there is no sign of a consensus emerging. In the current debates, the twin issues of the rights–utility conflict and the assertion or denial of absolute or basic rights remain central. These are still linked to the fundamental question of whether it is meaningful to speak of rights at all. The sceptical challenge, although it is often obscured by disputes between realists, is still prominent in philosophical and political debate. The more radical versions of rights-scepticism will be dealt with in a later chapter. For now, it is enough to note that the contemporary analysis and comparison of substantive theories of rights and justice constructed and developed by Rawls, Dworkin, Nozick and others, which differ radically in their respective emphasis on the types of rights to be regarded as genuine and fundamental, need to proceed from an understanding of how they offer distinctive responses to the sceptical challenge.

Study questions

General question: What is a right? What does it mean to claim that you have a right to something?

Further study questions: How does a legal right differ from a moral right? What does it mean to say that there is no such thing as a right? Does this apply equally to moral rights and legal rights? Critically examine the claim that a right is nothing more than the legal power to enforce one's interests. How might rights-scepticism be refuted? Are there any absolute rights? Do absolute rights have to be exceptionless? Is the recognition of rights compatible with utilitarianism? Does Dworkin's rights thesis resolve the conflict between rights and utility?

Suggestions for further reading

The classic texts for the major contemporary theories of rights are Rawls (1972), Dworkin (1977b) and Nozick (1974). Anthologies of critical essays have been edited by Daniels (1975) on Rawls, Cohen (1984) on Dworkin, and Paul (1981) on Nozick. For critical discussion of Dworkin's rights thesis, see especially MacCormick (1982: ch. 7).

Waldron (1984) contains a collection of key articles by leading rights theorists, including Dworkin, Raz, Hart, Gewirth, Lyons and Scanlon. Stewart (1983) is another valuable collection, with notable contributions from MacCormick, Alan White and others. Among the general introductions to legal and moral rights, the most accessible are Jones (1994), Simmonds (1986), Stoljar (1984), Perry (1998) and Brenda Almond's article in Singer (1991: ch. 22). There are useful chapters in Oderberg (2000: ch. 2), Harris (1980: ch. 14) and Riddall (1991: ch. 8). More advanced studies are found in Finnis (1980), Thomson (1990), MacCormick (1982), Raz (1994: ch. 12) and Halpin (1997).

On rights-scepticism, Waldron (1987) contains the relevant text of Bentham, with a critical reply. Other key texts are Holmes (1897), Olivecrona (1971) and Hagerstrom (1953). On rights and utility, the most useful is Frey's (1985) collection of essays. See also Lyons's 'Utility and Rights', in Waldron (1984). For commentaries on Hohfeld, see Halpin (1997: ch. 2), Thomson (1990: ch. 1) and Harris (1980: ch. 7).

8 Liberty, privacy and tolerance

Only in recent times has the debate about tolerance and respect for diversity become a prominent feature of democratic societies. What is often not realised is the extent to which toleration of the right to deviate from social norms relating to personal codes of morality is at odds with the principles of democracy as majority rule. The issue at the heart of the debate about 'the enforcement of morals' is that of drawing the line between the moral and the immoral in personal behaviour. Are individuals the best judges of their own interests, or does the state, acting on behalf of society, have the right to set limits on what it regards as morally acceptable? Although the question of a right to privacy is a much wider one, the emphasis here is on sexual and sex-related practices and lifestyle. Until the 1950s, it was widely assumed that the state did have the right to criminalise homosexuality, prostitution, pornography, abortions and many other related practices. Rapid social changes over the following decades have brought about extensive revisions in the law governing this area, but it has not been a one-way process of liberalisation. On most of these matters, there is an ongoing conflict between the rights of the individual and the rights of society.

Liberalisation and the Wolfenden Report

The debate was initiated in 1957, when the Wolfenden Committee made two recommendations to the government: (1) that private prostitution should remain legal and public soliciting be outlawed; and (2) that male homosexual acts in private between consenting adults over the age of 21 should be legalised. What was of particular importance was the Wolfenden view of the function of the criminal law, which was stated with exceptional clarity as follows:

> The function of the criminal law, as we see it, is to preserve public order and decency, to protect the citizen from what is offensive or injurious, and to provide safeguards against exploitation and corruption of others ... particularly the specially vulnerable, the young, weak and inexperienced.... It is not, in our view, the function of the law to intervene in the

private lives of citizens, or to seek to enforce any particular pattern of behaviour.... There must remain a realm of private morality which is, in brief and crude terms, not the law's business.

(Wolfenden 1957: cmnd 247, para. 13)

In short, Wolfenden was advocating a new spirit of tolerance. Any private individual activities that presented no threat to other citizens, or to the maintenance of public order and decency, should remain beyond the reach of the criminal law. It should be noted that the emphasis of the recommendations was firmly on the private sphere; there were no liberal implications for the publication or public display of pornography, or any other kind of public behaviour that might be found offensive. Also, the spirit of the report was morally neutral, in that it passed no judgement on what was taking place in private. It simply declared that it was none of the law's business. It was this spirit of liberalism that also guided the subsequent legislation.

Superficially, perhaps, this sounds like a straightforward story of reasonableness and tolerance prevailing over outdated repressive and moralistic attitudes. When we look more closely, however, we find that the relation between the criminal law and private morality is far from simple. What exactly, for example, does 'private' mean in this context? Does it mean 'out of public view', or does it mean that it is the individual's own business? Are privacy and publicness really separable? What does 'harm' or 'giving offence' or 'causing distress' mean? These ambiguities have to be resolved.

J.S. Mill and liberty

The findings of the Wolfenden Committee were clearly based on Mill's classic essay *On Liberty* (1972a). In one of the most influential statements in modern political and legal philosophy, Mill had declared that:

the sole end for which mankind is warranted, individually or collectively, in interfering with the liberty of action of any of their number, is *self-protection*. The only purpose for which power can be rightfully exercised over any member of a civilised community, against his will, is *to prevent harm to others*. His own good, either physical or moral, is not sufficient warrant.

(Mill 1972a: 78)

This is sometimes known as the 'harm principle', or more accurately as the 'no-harm principle'.

According to this principle, there is no justification for the use of the law (i.e. 'mankind collectively') against citizens for any purpose other than the prevention of harm to other citizens. The law is limited in its function to the 'self-defence' of society, and is legitimately employed if an individual's action is threatening society in some way. The second point Mill is making is that the law should also be limited to protecting people against others, not against themselves. These two points are easy to conflate, under the heading of a single 'no-harm' principle, but they need to be kept distinct. According to the first point, if there is no threat to others, there is no justification for legal intervention. According to the second point, if the action is only a threat to the agent, there is no such justification. The first point is an argument against legal moralism, or the enforcement of moral norms regardless of whether there is any danger. The second point is an argument against paternalism, or the interference in a person's freedom of action, when it is ostensibly for that person's own good.

One crucial exception to this principle should be noted. It applies neither to children nor to people vulnerable by virtue of mental defect or disorder such that their autonomy is seriously in doubt. In these cases, legal intervention for their own good is regarded by Mill as legitimate. Otherwise, for everyone of sufficiently mature years and sound mind, their own private behaviour – no matter how dangerous or self-destructive – is their own business.

It requires some effort of imagination to realise how bold a principle this was in Victorian England. The received wisdom about the purpose of law was that, while it included the prevention of harm to society, it was also for the protection of the moral and physical welfare of individuals affected by it, and for the general upholding of the Christian moral order. Mill's 'no-harm' principle, in both its anti-moralist and anti-paternalist aspects, was a radical challenge to the belief that the law was the proper arbiter of matters concerning morality, whether public or private. Furthermore, the temptation to regard the principle as a liberal platitude in the contemporary world, reflecting modern legal practice, vanishes with any serious attempt to think through the consequences of fully applying it. It would, for example, allow the unrestricted sale and use of heroin by adults.

The problems, of course, as Mill realised, only begin with the statement of the 'no-harm' principle. It was no less problematic than the supposedly 'very simple principle' behind his interpretation of the utilitarian philosophy, the principle of the greatest happiness for the greatest number. What he was interested in with the liberty question was establishing the 'no-harm' principle as a first base, so to speak, for theoretical negotiation. The idea was that, once accepted as basically true, the principle could be seen as establishing a dividing line, a cut-off point between the areas legitimately under the control of the individual, and the areas properly belonging to law and society. Once this distinction was accepted, it would only be a matter of thrashing out the details and defining the limits as appropriate to any particular society. The real difficulty, however, lay in having it accepted as a basic truth that there are areas in which the law should not intrude.

Mill's essay as a whole is an eloquent defence of the value to society of the recognition of the unconditional liberty of the individual in matters of conscience, expression and lifestyle. His defence of freedom of speech and liberty of action is a significant milestone in the development of democratic theory, but the most important feature of *On Liberty* concerns his claim about lifestyle that the greatest danger to the life of the individual in modern society lies in the increasing tendency towards a moral tyranny by the majority, threatening the complete elimination of private moral choices by individuals:

> And it is not difficult to show, by abundant instances, that to extend the bounds of what may be called moral police, until it encroaches on the most unquestionably legitimate liberty of the individual, is one of the most universal of all human propensities.
>
> (Mill 1972a: 216)

Mill believed – as we saw in the context of rights – that this propensity, always a danger, was actually growing rather than receding with the development of democracy and the realisation of the principle of majority rule. The idea of moral policing involved the suppression of eccentricity and peculiarity of taste, which Mill described as a latter-day Calvinism, shaping individuals in a manner reminiscent of the cutting of trees into the figures of animals.

The main point about moral policing, for Mill, is that it involves the invasion of the private space of individuals. In his examples, this space includes such forms of deviance from social norms as were widely regarded as morally degenerate – gambling, fornicating, drunkenness, uncleanliness – but it also includes any kind of behaviour that is eccentric or different in any way from that of the crowd. What Mill was condemning and resisting was the growing tendency of society and the state to seek to control every aspect of the lives of individual citizens, to enforce norms of social behaviour for their own sake, or because they believed them to be desirable and dressed these desires up as moral laws, irrespective of whether the non-conformity was actually dangerous or harmful to others.

The area in which the law should not intrude, then, is abstractly defined as the area of individual privacy, the area consisting of those actions that are of sole concern to the individual. Mill anticipated some of the problems and criticisms relating to the distinction between the private and the public. The most common objection to the idea that there is any real privacy in moral matters is the 'no man is an island' objection. Mill acknowledges the argument that there are virtually no seriously self-destructive actions that are a matter of indifference to others, to friends, family, and so on. The network of social relations is such that there are repercussions and reverberations. He concedes that nothing is truly private in this sense (ibid.: 210–11); however, his reply to this objection is that it only warrants interference by the law if it leads to any breach of duty, such as the non-payment of debts. A related objection is that bad behaviour, while it may have no direct effect on others, is 'injurious by example', which may damage by corrupting or misleading others (ibid.: 211). Mill's response to this is to distinguish what he terms the merely contingent or constructive injury to society from definite damage to another or to the public. If there is no such definite damage or real risk of such, his contention is that 'the inconvenience is one which society can afford to bear, for the sake of the greater good of human freedom' (ibid.: 213).

A closely connected yet distinct set of problems relates to the *kind* of harm, damage or injury under discussion. If – according to the 'no-harm' principle – legal intervention is only justified when the issue is one of harm to others, what kind of harm are we talking about? Is it restricted to real tangible damage of the type that can be measured, or does 'giving offence' or 'causing distress' count as harm? Mill's treatment of this question is vague and inadequate; it will, as we shall soon see, become one of the most important questions in the modern debates on legal moralism.

A most important general feature of Mill's defence of the liberty of the individual in matters of private morality is that it is rooted, not in a general theory of rights, but in the doctrine of utility. He is not arguing that there are individual rights which create an inconvenience for society, but which must be tolerated out of respect for these rights. What he is in fact arguing is an empirical historical thesis about the conditions of a healthy society. It is, he insists, in the long-term interests of society as a whole to encourage the flourishing of the individual. Society should refrain from using the law to repress either criticism or non-conformity, because individual freedom of expression and lifestyle, and the conflict that these engender, are the real sources of dynamic development in any society. Without them, society withers and dies. This is a utilitarian argument, because he is basing the claims to liberty on the general welfare. Society strengthens itself when it gives ground to the individual.

Devlin's critique of the Wolfenden Report

There was little doubt about the intentions of the authors of the Wolfenden Report when it was published in 1957. They had been commissioned by the government to investigate the state of the law on the two issues of prostitution and homosexuality. Their recommendations were that both were to be permissible in private, with public soliciting subject to prosecution. In their view, Mill's 'no-harm' principle was paramount. Private consensual activities between adults that did not directly harm anybody else should be beyond the reach of the criminal law. There was a great deal less certainty in the reactions to the report. The government accepted the proposals on prostitution and rejected the proposal on homosexuality, which was to remain illegal until 1967.

More interesting was the response by Patrick Devlin, a senior judge who had given evidence in favour of legal reform. Although he was not opposed to legalisation, he delivered a lecture in 1958 in which he attacked the thinking behind the findings of the Wolfenden Report. In this lecture, which was the opening shot in what was to become a very long debate, Devlin argued forcefully against the Wolfenden interpretation of how the law should be used against behaviour regarded as immoral. This apparent contradiction between his support for legalisation and his rejection of the liberal thinking behind it is explained by his recommendation that there should be tolerance of unconventional sexual practices solely on humane grounds, without the state conceding any rights.

Devlin bluntly rejected the assertion of Wolfenden that there is a realm of private morality and immorality that is not the law's business. As Devlin saw it, 'there can be no theoretical limits to legislation against immorality' (1965: 14). Accordingly, he also rejected the separation of morality into a private and public sphere, a distinction that he regarded as no more intelligible than 'carving up the highway into public and private areas' (ibid.: 1965: 16). What this amounted to was a complete rejection of Mill's 'no-harm' principle, according to which the harmfulness of an action is a necessary condition for using the law against it. If there are no limits to the reach of the law, and hence no recognition of privacy, it cannot be conceded that there is an area of activity – however apparently harmless to the public – that the law cannot touch.

Devlin's argument for this strong and provocative conclusion is developed in three stages, and takes its point of departure from the fundamental principles of English law as it currently existed. First, he argues that the function of law is to enforce morality – 'the moral order' – as well as to promote public order and the smooth running of society. That is to say, the real function of law is wider and includes the one advocated by the authors of the Wolfenden Report. Second, he argues that this is how it should be, that it would be dangerous to relinquish such a fundamental principle, because a serious offence against morality constitutes an attack on society, which should retain the right to use the law to protect its own interests. Third, he argues that the law should be used sparingly and with maximum toleration to enforce morality.

At an early stage in the lecture, Devlin accepts that the authority of the law can no longer depend on Christian doctrine, because in contemporary society the civil right to disbelieve is beyond dispute. In the search for a secular alternative, however, he insists that society must retain the right to pass moral judgement, to approve or condemn from the standpoint of a clear-cut distinction between good and evil. It is precisely this right that he accuses the Wolfenden authors of undermining. What they were saying, he reminds us, is that although we retain the right to disapprove, we should relinquish the right to enforce this disapproval. Once an area of privacy in matters of morality and immorality is conceded, Devlin argues, the right to approve or to condemn has been implicitly given up. Without such a right, even a murderer will only be apprehended and punished for purposes of public order; the immorality of such offences will be irrelevant because we will have relinquished our right even to find the act morally repellent.

How do legislators tune in to this collective moral judgement? How do they know they are not speaking for themselves and a relatively small group of like-minded people? Devlin is on very difficult ground here, and his forthright answer is highly controversial. Legislators are to refer to the standard of 'the right-minded man', 'the man in the Clapham omnibus', or the conclusion that 'any twelve men or women drawn at random' would be expected to reach unanimously. It is the mass of experience embodied in 'the morality of common sense'. Most importantly, he distinguishes the reasonableness of these people from their rationality. The reasonable man 'is not expected to reason about anything and his judgement may be largely a matter of feeling' (Devlin 1965: 15). One problem here is that the assumption of unanimity in this context can scarcely make sense, given that we are talking about matters on which there is an unknown but presumably sizeable number standing out against the supposed consensus. Deeper problems, as we shall see, arise from the explicit abandonment of rationality in favour of feeling as the basis of moral judgements.

In the course of reaffirming the wider function of the criminal law, Devlin makes two telling points about the consequences of adopting the narrower Wolfenden conception of this function, as derived from Mill's 'no-harm' principle. First, it would overturn the established principle that consent by the victim is no defence in English law to any form of assault or murder. Such offences with consent can be committed without any threat or harm to the wider community. The reason a victim may not either consent beforehand or forgive afterwards is that a criminal assault is an offence, not merely against an individual, but against society. Second, if there is to be consistency, many other specific acts would have to be allowed:

> Euthanasia or the killing of another at his own request, suicide, attempted suicide and suicide pacts, duelling, abortion, incest between brother and sister, are all acts which can be done in private and without offence to others and need not involve the corruption or exploitation of others.
>
> (ibid.: 7)

His argument here is that if consent between prostitutes and their clients, and between adult homosexuals, is made the basis of their legality, then consistency will demand that all of these other acts are legalised as well.

Devlin's main concern in this lecture was to argue for the continuing right of society to pass moral judgement on the behaviour of its citizens, and the right to use the law to enforce this judgement. His central argument for these rights is by his own description a conceptual one, which can be established *a priori*. In short, the argument is that a society is entitled to pass judgement on any of the activities (public or private) of the individuals of which it is composed, because a society is, by definition, a community of political and moral ideas. This is what makes a society more than an aggregate of individuals living on the same territory. Being thus defined as a community of common ideas or beliefs, it follows that those who are out of step with these beliefs are threatening the continued existence of society:

> Society means a community of ideas; without shared ideas on politics, morals and ethics, no society can exist.... if men and women try to create a society in which there is no fundamental agreement about good and evil, they will fail; if, having based it on common agreement, the agreement goes, society will disintegrate.
>
> (ibid.: 10)

For Devlin, then, passing moral judgement and enforcing it with the sanctions of law is analogous to political judgement and suppression of sedition and rebellion; both are justified by the right of society to protect itself. This is his central argument for legal moralism, for the use of the law for the enforcement of moral norms. One point that should be noted is that this argument seeks to establish a conclusion diametrically opposed to that of Mill. Where Mill argued that there was an empirical link between a healthy and enduring society and allowance of maximum freedom to individuals in choice of moral principles and lifestyle, Devlin argues that it is a necessary truth that, without individual conformity with the consensus, society will collapse. He softens the authoritarian tone of his argument with his urging of legal restraint in the prosecution of immorality, but this makes no essential difference. The most he is conceding is that there is sometimes a case for tolerating moral 'depravity'; he is equally clear that this tolerance can be withdrawn whenever society feels sufficiently threatened.

Devlin's setting of the limits of such tolerance brings us back to the instinctive moral reactions of 'the reasonable man'. At which point can this reasonable tolerance of offensive behaviour be withdrawn? Devlin's central argument here is that, while toleration should be stretched well beyond the point at which most people feel moderate dislike and disgust, the limit is reached when the acts in question are perceived to represent a real danger to society. He argues that what must be present to justify depriving individuals of freedom of choice is a genuine and deeply felt 'intolerance, indignation and disgust'. Comparing sexual offences with cruelty to animals and sadism, he argues that the limits cannot be set by rational argument, but must depend on feelings of real abhorrence (ibid.: 17). This is the most notorious of Devlin's arguments, but it should be remembered that what he is actually arguing for here is maximum toleration. He is not, as is frequently assumed, arguing that anything that makes people sick should be criminalised. It is nevertheless a vague and highly subjective standard that he is proposing, which opens the door to the perpetuation of popular prejudice as the guiding force behind the use of the criminal law.

Hart's reply to Devlin

In 1963, H.L.A. Hart published the text of three lectures as *Law, Liberty and Morality*, in which he developed a qualified defence of Mill's liberalism, supporting the recommendations of the Wolfenden Commission and countering Devlin's critique of both. His main purpose was to clarify the issues at stake, and in so doing to argue that the use of the criminal law to enforce morals was deeply misguided. Much more in step than Devlin with the liberalising spirit of the early 1960s, Hart set out to undermine moral conservatism and to defend the Wolfenden contention that there is an area of private behaviour that should be no business of the criminal law.

Mindful at the outset of the vulnerability of Mill's libertarian position to a criticism of its dangerous implications, Hart took care to distinguish between coercion for the sake of enforcing society's moral norms, and coercion for the agent's own good. According to the version of liberalism that Hart was developing in these lectures, it is only the latter form of state coercion that is to some extent defensible. Society does have the right to prevent its members from harming themselves as much as from harming others, but it does not have the right to enforce conformity with collective moral standards. The particular example he has in mind here is the prohibition of the sale and use of hard drugs, which is justified on paternalistic grounds. In the name of liberty, Mill had opposed any state interference into such activities, but Hart sets a new limit to the 'no-harm' principle, which is in fact a more literal interpretation of this phrase. What he argues is that the proper reach of the criminal law stops at the point of tangible harm as such – to self or others – whereas for Mill it stops only at the point of harm to others. What Hart endorses in Mill is his defence of the right to follow one's own lifestyle; what he rejects is his insistence that this right has no internal limits.

With this modified version of Mill's defence of individual liberty to hand, Hart was able to confront Devlin's arguments on more solid ground. One of his main complaints about Devlin's case against liberty is that he blurs the distinction between paternalist law and what Hart now labels 'legal moralism'. This is the distinction between laws for the protection of people against themselves and laws that merely seek to enforce moral standards. It is easy to see how this distinction can be blurred and the issue confused. If behaviour deemed to be immoral is widely regarded as by definition harmful and self-destructive, laws prohibiting it will be seen as paternalistic and defensible. With this distinction now drawn clearly, however, it becomes a question of whether – as Devlin argues – society does in fact have the right to condemn actions as inherently immoral and to punish them solely as such, irrespective of their effects on others.

The question of whether society has such a right is a normative one. For Hart, employing Bentham's distinction, it is a question of critical rather than positive morality, and of normative rather than descriptive jurisprudence. It is not a question of determining whether this right already exists in common law; it is a moral question behind the campaign for legislative amendment to the law. Hart argues that there is a strong and unwarranted presumption in Devlin and other legal conservatives that the current state of the law is justified, by virtue of its natural evolution. Hart argues that if society is indeed, as Devlin believes, a community of political and moral ideas, it is a contingent matter whether these ideas will stand up to critical moral scrutiny. Devlin in particular wrongly assumes that any society has the automatic right to protect itself when its morals are threatened, regardless of how defective or misguided these might be. In the past, the moral conventions of the day have justified slavery and the persecution of witches. Hart questions Devlin's assumption, even to the point of denying that a morally defective society is automatically justified in preserving its own existence, if it is grossly unjust in substance or if the steps taken to preserve it are abhorrent. If society does have the right to pass moral judgements on its citizens and to use the law to enforce these judgements, it is not by virtue of Devlin's conceptual argument from the positive morality of that society.

Perhaps the most important of Hart's criticisms is the distinction, which he dwells on only briefly, between the core morality of a society and its sexual morals. This is in fact the crucial point, because the limitations of the English language have always produced a tendency to conflate these two senses of morality and immorality. In the core sense of the word, 'immoral' simply means 'wrong'; the core morality as enforced by virtually any legal system worthy of the name includes all the central prohibitions against violence, theft and other anti-social behaviour. In the more specific sense of the word, 'immoral' refers to deviations from conventional norms governing sexual and sex-related matters. Hart's criticism of Devlin is that his implicit merging of these two senses of the words establishes an underlying assumption, quite unwarranted, that:

> all morality – sexual morality together with the morality that forbids acts injurious to others such as killing, stealing and dishonesty – forms a single seamless web, so that those who deviate from any part are likely or perhaps bound to deviate from the whole.
>
> (Hart 1963: 50–1)

When we are dealing with moral 'crimes', which do not actually affect or harm anyone else, the implication of this 'seamless web' assumption is that if these private offences are allowed to proliferate without threat or sanction by the law, then the core morality of society will also suffer.

This assumption that morality constitutes a seamless whole, with every aspect meshing together to form a unified model of personal integrity, is also related to Hart's distinction between what he sees as extreme and moderate versions of legal moralism. The extreme version he attributes to James Fitzjames Stephen, the nineteenth-century judge who had published a critique of Mill's *On Liberty* from a utilitarian standpoint, emphatically rejecting Mill's proposal for an area of privacy. Stephen's arguments for the punishment of all forms of 'vice' rested on his claim that it was the function of the criminal law to punish wrongdoing as such, regardless of whether it had any harmful effects. Stephen rejected Mill's 'no-harm' principle because it would remove this essential part of the function of the criminal law, the duty to condemn vice. One of Stephen's main arguments for punishing purely 'moral' offences was based on the practice of judicial sentencing in a case that actually does involve harm. In such cases, he argued, judges invariably take into account not only the degree of harm or damage, but also the odiousness of the crime and its perpetrator. Variations in sentence reflect malice, responsibility and degree of temptation, over and above the actual nature and extent of the injury caused. Moral judgement and condemnation are inescapable. The implication is that the 'surfeit' part of the sentence is purely to reflect the moral revulsion felt by the judge, speaking for society; the conclusion is that the prosecution of vice solely because it is immoral is a function and duty of the law quite independently of whether any harm has been caused (Stephen 1874).

This argument is clearly invalid, because it trades on different senses of immorality and moral revulsion. What is condemned in a case of, say, aggravated burglary is quite different from what is condemned in unconventional sexual activity. Also, the immoral 'component' of the crime would not be punishable in isolation from the criminal act. Hart's refutation of the argument is less important than his use of it to draw a contrast with what he sees as Devlin's moderate version of legal moralism. The extreme thesis is that the state's right to punish wrongdoing is derived solely from its wrongness and excitement of public revulsion. The moderate thesis is that the state's right to punish wrongdoing is derived from its social dangers, that if it is allowed to go unpunished the society whose morals it is flouting will, by definition, begin to fall apart.

Hart's rejection of this supposedly moderate social disintegration thesis is based largely on his observation that it is expressed by Devlin as a conceptual truth, based on his definition of society as a community of ideas and moral values. If this were the case, any permitted deviation from these ideas and values would constitute not so much a threat as a *de facto* disintegration of this society or body of values. Apart from Hart's criticisms, already noted, that it is wrong to assume that every society is worth defending or that any measures taken to defend it are justified, he argues that the assumption in the first place that a society is simply identical with every aspect of its positive morality is highly dubious. There is no reason to suppose that societies cannot evolve morally, allowing more personal liberty and diversity of values, without losing the core morality that sustains them or without losing their essential identity.

Dworkin's critique of Devlin

Defending liberalism and toleration from a different angle, Dworkin's arguments against Devlin focused on the question of the foundations of the moral judgements made by or on behalf of the community as a whole (Dworkin 1977b: ch. 10; 1989). Against Devlin's feeling-centred ethics, Dworkin argued that the minimal requirement for even granting an opinion the status of 'moral position' or 'moral principle' is that it is based on reasons and satisfies demands for consistency. The important feature of the argument is his contention that some 'reasons' must be discounted if the moral case for legal intervention is to be taken seriously. To be excluded are prejudices posturing as judgements, personal emotional reactions, false propositions of fact and parroting the beliefs of others. If genuine reasons are produced, and they can be shown to be applied consistently, then there will at least be a moral case to be answered. Devlin's attempt to show that the legislator is obliged to act on behalf of the deeply held moral beliefs of the majority is undermined by his identification of 'the reasonable man' as the barometer for public opinion, because there is nothing reasonable about the criteria of 'intolerance, indignation and disgust'. These are precisely the kind of reasons that are ruled out in any other context for determining a sound moral judgement, so they should be ruled out in the context of personal morals as well. The mere fact of a moral consensus, if it is not based on reasons that will stand up to scrutiny, does not for Dworkin make it morally legitimate.

One common objection to Dworkin's argument is that it would also disqualify vast numbers of ordinary moral judgements on acts of gratuitous cruelty, which an average jury member will condemn primarily on the basis of angry indignation and disgust. Many statutes embody prohibitions originally based on this kind of popular revulsion. This is a mistaken objection, because most people in this position, jury members or legislators, would be able to give non-prejudiced reasons to support the emotional reaction, to explain why such acts should not be allowed.

The other key feature of Dworkin's critique of Devlin is his rejection of the democratic majoritarian argument for the right of a community to impose the moral views of one section – even if it is a very large majority – on the rest of the community. Drawing an analogy between 'the ethical environment' and the economic environment, he argues that just as the majority does not have the right to gather all economic resources to itself and leave the rest to starve, it does not have the right to dominate the ethical environment in such a way that the minority is completely deprived of the right to make its own impact on this environment. The majority in turn has no rights solely by virtue of being the majority; its rights to mould the ethical environment exist only in proportion to its numbers. This is defended by Dworkin as a democratic principle that works against and in tension with the democratic principle of majority rule.

Conclusion

Forty years on from the Hart–Devlin debate, various social factors in both Britain and the USA might seem to have changed the original issues beyond recognition. While one can say that there has been a decisive shift of opinion towards tolerance in private matters of sexuality, such that it is difficult to imagine the 1960s legislation being reversed, the controversy about the state of the law on these and related matters, and the rights of the community to enforce its moral norms, has continued to evolve in ways not countenanced by the early protagonists. Nevertheless, the wrangle between Devlin and his critics created the framework in which the political and philosophical differences have continued.

Study questions

General question: To what extent, if any, should the criminal law be used to regulate private behaviour that does not conform with the moral norms of society?

Further study questions: Was the Wolfenden Report correct in its insistence that 'there must remain a realm of private morality which is, in brief and crude terms, not the law's business'? Do Mill's arguments in defence of liberty show that there is never any justification for laws that are aimed at protecting people from themselves? Is Devlin right to insist that there can be no theoretical limits to the authority of the state over the individual? Is Hart's defence of paternalism consistent with his criticism of Devlin's legal moralism? Is Dworkin right in claiming that Devlin does not have 'a moral position'?

Suggestions for further reading

The basic texts for the issue of the enforcement of morals are Mill (1972a), Stephen (1874), the Report of the Wolfenden Committee (1957), Devlin (1965) and Hart (1963). Other important contributions include Dworkin (1977b: ch. 10 and 1989), Basil Mitchell (1970) and Hughes's 'Morals and the Criminal Law', in Summers (1968).

Of the collections of relevant material, Wasserstrom (1971) is the established text. Kipnis (1977: section 2) contains several important items. The discussion in Gavison (1987: part III) of toleration and the harm principle is particularly useful. The articles collected in Dworkin, G. (1994) address this and a wider range of issues relating to liberty. Other useful commentaries and critical surveys of the Hart–Devlin debate and related issues can be found in Leiser (1973) and (1981), Lyons (1984: 178–93), Golding (1975: ch. 3), Feinberg (1973: chs 1–3), Dias (1985: ch. 6), Harris (1980: ch. 10) and Riddall (1991: ch. 14). For a close analysis of the problems of harm and distress, see Thomson (1990: chs 9–10). For specialist books on Mill's defence of liberty, see Ten (1980), Gray (1996) and Gray and Smith (1991).

9 Modernity and the reach of the law

The questions and problems relating to authority, rights and liberty as we have encountered them over the last three chapters arise from differing interpretations of the proper reach and limits of the law in the modern world. For the radical critics who conceptualise and attack 'modernity' as a whole, however, the real problem lies in the complete absence of justification or grounding to give the law and its declared rights any authority at all. From this point of view, any attempt within the theoretical framework of modernity to define the reach and limits of the law in terms of authority and rights is no more than an exercise in power. In this chapter, we will be looking at the themes that have been most prominent in the radical writings in recent decades and how they relate to the origins of modernity, and we will be considering the responses in defence of mainstream jurisprudence and its philosophical basis.

The liberal concept of the individual

Right at the centre of these debates, we find the concept of the individual. The very purpose of modern liberalism at its inception was to affirm the value of the human individual against the despotisms of the premodern world and to make the protection of its interests paramount. The important point concerns the way in which the individual has been conceptualised. The specifically liberal conception took shape in the classic accounts of the social contract and the state of nature in the seventeenth century, and was later given a more complete formulation in the following century in Kant's moral and political philosophy. According to the modern contract theories, the assumption had to be made that the contracting parties were free and equal, fully conscious and rational agents. Similarly, the emerging theories of natural rights were based on the assumption that it was the autonomous, reasoning individual who was the bearer of natural rights. In more recent times, the defence of the liberty of the individual against the state in all matters of private morality presupposes sufficient autonomy and rationality to make reasoned decisions on one's own behalf. The ideal that took hold of the Enlightenment imagination, then, was of the individual with more or less perfect self-control, equal in standing to any other, able to make responsible judgements and act upon them without reference to authority, consenting to obey laws that he himself has (at least in theory) rationally affirmed. The fundamental moral right that flows from this is the universal right to be treated as an end in oneself, and the fundamental duty is to treat others with reciprocal respect. What was radically new about this was that the only ground for it was the reason possessed in equal measure by every individual.

Critiques of the liberal concept of the individual

This liberal conception of the individual has come under fire from many different directions, both from within and without what is usually seen as 'modernity'. The most influential critique – that this conception was both abstract and skewed to favour one type of individual – came from Western democracy's most trenchant critic, Karl Marx, and was developed not only by the ideology of Soviet Marxism, but also by a wide range of critical social theories in the West. Critiques of liberal individualism, however, are by no means confined to the political left. Communitarians of all political colours reject the basis of individualism, on the grounds that it destroys the communal ties that are fundamental to a cohesive society. Radical feminists who reject the traditional liberal attempts to extend the recognition of equality of basic political and civil rights to women tend to do so because they regard the liberal conception of the individual as inherently distorted and deeply biased towards masculinity. Critical race theorists have also developed critiques of the liberal conception as carrying cultural assumptions specific to the white societies of modern Europe and North America, thus facilitating the exclusion of black African slaves from the category of humanity. Postmodernists from various points on the political spectrum generally regard the liberal concept of the individual as the cornerstone of the 'grand narrative' of the progressive liberation promised by modernity, and thus as eminent a candidate for deconstruction as can be imagined. As an invention or a 'construct' that comes to seem natural, as the only way in which to conceptualise a human being, the liberal conception can supposedly be unmasked as a complete fiction and thus as a very poor foundation or grounding for human rights.

We can see how this scepticism gains a firm foothold by considering the problems surrounding the concept of the human individual. When liberals speak of the value and autonomy of the individual, who exactly is it they are talking about, and what is it individuated *from*? The fundamental point that has to be remembered through all the philosophical debate is that what the analysis always has to come back to is the flesh-and-blood human beings of both sexes and all races and creeds, thinking, feeling, acting and generally experiencing the world in an infinite variety of ways. So which of these individuals are they talking about? Clearly, what is at least consciously intended today is that 'the' individual refers to none of these in particular, nor to one particular type, but to each and every living human individual. 'The individual' is the human individual in the abstract, the outcome of deliberately setting aside idiosyncrasies and abstracting the characteristics common to all of them. In other words, it refers to the essential humanity in each individual, the qualities whereby each is a member of the species.

Liberal humanism and the individual

When the philosophers of the Enlightenment and the French Revolution's Declaration of the Rights of Man were articulating their humanistic defences of the freedom and equality of 'Man' (as opposed to 'men' and/or 'women'), it was this essential being who was conceptualised as being in possession of reason and universal natural rights. At the same time as creating a liberating and at the time shocking vision of fundamental human equality, confronting the old social hierarchies with the demand for their own dissolution, they were launching what would soon be criticised as an abstract humanism, divorced from the reality not only of society as a whole but also of any of the real individuals that comprised it. In truth, the concept of the individual was arrived at by abstracting from a limited range of real individuals, not from the full spectrum of humanity. The idealised conception of Man nevertheless took root as the inspiration for the continuing political struggles for liberal democracy. The political value of proclaiming basic rights to be natural and universal is too obvious to require explanation, and the idealised nature of the concepts deployed to justify such proclamations is not necessarily a fatal defect. The point was that however defective its actual manifestation might appear in retrospect, the principle of universality had been established. The proclaimed rights were at least potentially open to all.

The point of the postmodernist attacks on this humanism of the early modern period is to draw out what they see as the repressive character of the specifically modern version of humanism. This is based on their perception of the distinction between the theoretical 'subject' of the liberal conception of the individual and the really existing empirical self. The idea of individual subjective selves with the right of ownership over their own minds and bodies was in fact a philosophical creation of the seventeenth century, quite unknown to premodern thought, as critics of modernity are never slow to point out. What these postmodern critics emphasise is the artificiality of this newly created 'individual subject' and the way in which it was immediately passed off as part of a natural state of affairs, as the only way it could be. The essence of the political revolution at this time was the transfer of power from the old hierarchy to this sovereign individual, who became the source of legal authority and the bearer of fundamental rights, which were now portentously declared to be universal, when it was plain for all to see that they were born out of a historically specific political struggle, and natural, when these rights along with their fictitious 'owner' were manifestly artificial constructs.

The contextualisation of universal rights

The key word in the line of criticism of Enlightenment humanism and universal rights that has persisted throughout the modern period is 'context'. Taking words or actions out of context and thereby distorting their meaning is one of the most familiar features of everyday disputes and verbal skulduggery. Keeping or placing them within context is generally seen as a precondition of understanding. It is not so much, though, merely a question of placing them within their proper context as *weaving* them in. This is the etymological root of the word. Linguistic context is often interpreted as analogous to a closely woven fabric. The insistence upon the contextualisation of anything – words, ideas, theories – can be understood as the demand that they be woven into any 'fabric' or background to which they are said to apply. This is the main thrust of the type of criticism of universalism and natural rights that complains of their lack of context-sensitivity. From this point of view, the proclamation of universal rights is not merely worthless but positively dangerous if the rights are not rooted in the specific historical and cultural context to which they are supposed to apply. In its postmodernist versions, this idea of contextualisation is expressed in terms of positionality, embeddedness or situatedness, all of which emphasise the particularity of the social conditions at any point in history. The general idea here is that one cannot rise above history and impose moral truths upon society from a universalist standpoint outside of it.

This contextualist strain of criticism has a complex modern history in political and legal thought. It is associated as much with progressive as conservative and reactionary thought. Although the most famous instance of it is Edmund Burke's (1729–97) attack on the natural rights of the French Revolution, its influence has pervaded the critiques of the Enlightenment up to the present day. It has been particularly strong in English jurisprudence and was a motivating force in the 1990s resistance to the campaign for a Bill of Rights and the passing of the UK 1998 Human Rights Act, which was thought by many to be alien to the tradition of English common law. This was one of Burke's original complaints, and it has been echoed ever since.

The idea behind this resistance depends upon an organicist conception of society. In opposition to the dominant mechanistic paradigm of modern scientific thought, the analogy between society and a living organism assumes that a society is composed of mutually dependent elements, which, taken together, grow naturally and spontaneously, rather than through any conscious overall design. This natural evolution involves the gradual transformation of custom into law and the emergence of *de facto* rights and duties. Laws or rights that have thus emerged from the ground of local custom are felt to be solidly rooted in the indigenous social and legal culture.

It follows that if laws or rights that have no pedigrees within that culture are abruptly introduced from outside, they will not take root and will probably be violently rejected. This was the essence of Burke's critique of natural rights universalism. Laws that are claimed to embody universal rights, derived solely from reason (which in its Enlightenment sense is by definition ahistorical), are precisely the kind of alien rights that can only be imposed by force. If a right is natural and universal, it emanates from nowhere in particular and therefore does not belong anywhere in particular. It might be added that universal rights can be seen to suffer from the same defect as rigidly applied general legal rules, which do not take into account the uniqueness of every set of facts in each unrepeatable case. Genuine rights – if such are possible – have to be such that they are adaptable to local diversity and can be genuinely instantiated.

This kind of response to the universalism of modern natural rights has always had a very wide appeal, not least because of the natural suspicion that such universalism is intrinsically linked with an arrogant cultural imperialism, as the Western liberal democracies expand their influence throughout the world and impose their own standards of justice and rights on cultures that have not evolved through the same channels of 'enlightenment'. The dispute between the cultural relativism that this criticism embraces, and the moral objectivism of those who believe that there are trans-cultural moral standards to be defended, is in its twentieth-century form a heritage of Western colonialism and long predates the contemporary disputes between the modern and postmodern. There are many dimensions to this general moral question, but it is not resolved by simplistically declaring each culture to be as morally sound as any other. It should be remembered that one of the main implications of a strict adherence to the principles of cultural relativism, and to the kind of organicist theory of society that supports it, is that in the case of extremes it becomes impossible to criticise societies that have deeply embedded traditions of slavery and other racist institutions that are anathema to the standpoint of universal natural rights. Even with less extreme injustices, strict cultural relativism also deadens criticism if the standpoint of natural justice is ruled out.

Abstractness and irrelevance

The criticism that is often thought to strike at the heart of modern natural rights is that they are 'abstract' in the sense that they are merely formal. Connected with this is the complaint that charters and bills of universal rights are irrelevant to the real needs of actual concrete individuals, especially those who are living in conditions of severe deprivation. What is the good of guaranteeing the right to liberty under the rule of law to somebody dying of starvation? What is the practical value of the right to life for the victims of ethnic cleansing? To the people in such situations, all the rights proclaimed over the last few centuries are nothing but empty documents.

This kind of criticism is well founded, but we have to be clear what it is a criticism of. The gap between the vision of a just society governed by Kantian principles of mutual respect for the dignity of every individual, and the reality that often falls a long way short of such a vision, certainly provides grounds for moral and political criticism or even condemnation of the existing institutions that create or allow this gap. The confusion sets in, however, when this criticism is translated into a wholesale rejection of rights on the grounds that they are empty because they are merely formal. This is based on a misunderstanding of what 'formal' means. This will become clear in the light of the following critical theories.

Marx and Marxism

Many of the doctrines of Marxism that evolved with the political conflicts of the twentieth century are relevant to the disputes between radical and mainstream jurisprudence. As a general theory of law, it can be seen from one angle as a radical and somewhat narrower version of the command theory developed by English positivism, as it strips away the moral rhetoric to reveal the mechanics of political power, and reduces legal doctrines to expressions of the interests of the ruling class. As such, the law is regarded as one of the main arenas of class struggle. As a wider theory of history, Marxism depicts social development as a morally progressive spiralling upward ascent. Marx himself saw history as an epic 'human journey' from the natural primitive communism of early hunter–gatherers, through a succession of civilisations, empires, wars and revolutions, towards the final goal of a complete realisation of human potential in a 'return' to the original communist state, built upon the experience and knowledge acquired along the way. The belief that in the modern world the human race was about to enter the last phase of struggle towards this collective destiny lay behind the politics of Marx's revolutionary socialism. The postmodernist rejection of this vision of the future, unmasking it as a 'grand narrative', placed it in the same category as the liberal dreams of complete enlightenment and universal peace between fully rational and autonomous individuals. Marxism was increasingly seen as part of the same Enlightenment project of an impossible liberation of humanity from all its imperfections. At the same time, however, Marx developed a theoretical perspective on the question of the rights of the individual in society that has had an immeasurable positive influence on the critical theories well beyond the confines of socialist politics, including those of postmodernist critics.

Marx's critique of liberal rights

Marx's own hostility to rights is well known, but not always clearly understood. In the political tradition that he inspired, the scepticism and even contempt for the individual rights valued by liberalism are notorious. The

Soviet Marxist justification for downplaying human rights was based on the claim that collective socioeconomic rights – such as the rights to basic shelter, health care and education – were more important to the welfare of individuals as a collective than respect for the more typically liberal negative rights of each and every individual was to those who suffered persecution.

Marx himself was certainly no liberal, but this played no part in his argument against rights. In his criticisms of the natural rights of the French Revolution he was, as is often pointed out, attempting to expose them as mere abstractions masking the true nature of these rights, which were in practice to be extended only to the free activity of the rising bourgeois class, the members of which would have the means to take advantage of them, at the expense of the propertyless majority. More importantly, though, this critique of rights can be linked with his doctrine of commodity fetishism. The fetishism of commodities is for Marx the crucial transformation that occurs in the capitalist economic system when things of different quality are produced for exchange rather than use. In this process, the stamp of equal value on heterogeneous products creates the illusion of homogeneity, such that unequal objects appear as equal.

This 'veil of equality' idea was applied critically to the language of universal rights, such that the main thrust of Marx's criticism of liberal (bourgeois) natural rights was that they were hopelessly irrelevant, because they treated individual people who were in fact different and unequal in their particular characteristics and powers as 'universally equal', thus imposing a veil of generality upon a social world that has to be understood in all its vast array of particularities. In short, what he was criticising was the liberal conception of the individual as a theoretical abstraction in sharp contrast to the reality of concrete individuals. For Marx, the thinking of the supposedly radical liberals was dominated by a conception of the individual that he described as 'monadic', as a self-enclosed entity walled in and separated from its social environment, but most importantly with the social side of its own nature carefully eliminated. This monad is pure egoistic man, which became the model for all the human sciences, from economics to psychology. What Marx was proposing as an alternative model was a concrete conception of humanity, a 'subject' more in tune with the real constitution of human individuals in both their individuated and socialised dimensions. The liberal-bourgeois subject with its natural rights tried to step outside of history to adopt a universal standpoint from which it could confront the injustice and inequality of the premodern world, but the new subject that would carry the revolution forward was rooted in the real historical process of class struggle. There was no talk of rights in this conflict – only a struggle for power and social justice. The important concept that was to exercise so much influence on later social theory was that of egoistic man, the falsely individuated subject of liberal theory. This is the conception presupposed by liberalism from Hobbes's egotistical man to the subject of Rawls's rational contract.

Feminist jurisprudence and the rights of women

Given that women make up roughly one half of the human race, the impact of the wider social phenomenon of feminism upon mainstream jurisprudence is potentially greater than that of any of the other critical perspectives. Over the past forty years feminism has diversified into a richly complex field of theories and research programmes, reflecting many different political positions. Within the confines of legal theory, there has been much overlap and interaction with Critical Legal Studies (CLS), critical race studies and socialist and Marxist theories. The pattern of development has been, in very broad terms, the transition first from the traditional campaigns for equality to more radical forms of feminism in the decades following the upheaval of the 1960s, then somewhat belatedly in the late 1980s to the more confusing world of postmodernist criticism. The original setting in which feminism as a struggle for the rights of women took shape, however, was the liberal tradition of the Enlightenment. The problems confronted and the variety of positions adopted by contemporary feminists writing about law should be seen in the light of their reactions to this liberal tradition.

The subordination of women and the liberal campaigns for equality

Behind the diversity, the one premise upon which all feminists in jurisprudence as elsewhere are agreed is that the fundamental experience of women in society is one of subordination to males. It is in their interpretation of the nature and explanation of this subordination and how to develop a constructive response that there is disagreement. The traditional response, from Mary Wollstonecraft's (1759–97) *Vindication of the Rights of Women* (1792) to the present day, was to confront the male-dominated liberal establishment with its own ideals, demanding that they be extended to all, male and female alike. If the ideals of the Enlightenment are genuinely universal, it was argued, then the recognition of individual autonomy and equal status, or of the right to be treated with reciprocal respect as an end in oneself, could not be restricted to one sex. The much-proclaimed 'rights of man' had, by virtue of their own supreme value of reason and rational consistency, to be applied to women as well. Individual women who argued in this way were at the time almost universally regarded as eccentric and atypical of their sex, which was generally seen as lacking in the quality of rationality essential to the possession of liberal rights. From the standpoint of the overwhelming majority of the male revolutionaries, the explanation of women's subordination lay in nature rather than in the oppression of women by men. For a typical male liberal of the time, there was no inconsistency in denying equal rights to irrational women.

The solid point of reference and platform for women's equality is the long history of campaigning for the public recognition of the inferior position of women in society and under the law, and the legislative and case-law milestones that were a mark of progress in terms of this recognition. The achievement in Britain of universal suffrage in stages by 1928, the gradual breakdown of exclusion from holding public office, from entry into the universities and professions (Sex (Removal of Disqualification) Act, 1919), were fundamental to the cause of basic equal rights. The Equal Pay Act (1970) and the Sex Discrimination Act (1975) are the best known, but among equally far-reaching specific reforms have been those on the rights of married women to own property (The Married Women's Property Act, 1882), the equalisation of custody rights over children (Guardianship of Minors Act, 1971), the right of any woman to take out a mortgage without a male guarantor (1975), the gradual legal recognition of domestic violence and the outlawing of marital rape (1994). These are only the most notable examples of what has been achieved in recent times by relentless campaigning and it is undeniable that they have all been established against deeply ingrained hostility and resistance. These reforms have nevertheless been achieved and have gradually changed the relative status in society of males and females beyond recognition over the past century, a point frequently emphasised by liberal feminists against those who disparage these legal changes as 'merely formal'.

The feminist critical engagement with liberalism

Contemporary feminist reactions to this long slow history of reform has been mixed. Many legal scholars continue to regard it as the main focus for feminist jurisprudence, concentrating their research on specific issues of injustice and inequality. Others, however, have been more sceptical of the value of establishing legal rights, arguing for a more fundamental and thoroughgoing critical analysis of legal theory and practice. In particular, some have argued that the formalities of legal rights are insufficient in the face of the realities of male domination and violence that lie beyond the reach of the law, leaving deeply embedded discrimination and injustice untouched. The universalism of natural rights is said to make no contact with the real lives of individual women, because they are decontextualised and devoid of real content. Beyond this, it has been argued that the achievement of such rights can be not only inadequate but also counterproductive in as far as they create the illusion of a substantive equality that has only been formally recognized. From this point of view, legal rights are seen as a positive obstruction to advancing the cause of equality and justice.

The main objection to feminist liberalism, with its focus on the struggle for recognition of the subordinate position of women, for equal opportunities and full citizen's rights, is the argument that this strategy falls into the trap of demanding parity on terms that have been defined by males, demanding all the same rights, which are typically 'male' rights. The rights as formulated were, it is said, constructed specifically for males. On the face of it, this is a puzzling objection to rights successfully secured, such as those relating to political participation, the right to hold public office and so on. The implication would seem to be that they allow the male domination in these areas to continue unchallenged. The objection, however, runs deeper than this. The claim on which it rests is that gender-bias is built into all the political and legal institutions, and that it permeates the language of politics and especially law so thoroughly that all its fundamental concepts, standards and methods of reasoning are deeply biased against women. The masculine presuppositions embedded in all the legal concepts are said to be so deep-rooted that they are like the air we breathe. So the general idea here is that gender-bias is concealed or subliminal, and it is at this deeper level that it has to be confronted.

Compare this with the kind of masculine bias in law that is overt and visible to everyone on a moment's reflection. The explicit exclusion in the past of women from legal training or higher appointments on the grounds of inherent unsuitability was at the time relatively uncontroversial. Justifications included claims that women had the wrong kind of brains and cognitive abilities, or the wrong pitch of voice to speak in the appropriate tone. Explicit prejudices like these have been dying out, but the language of the law is still regularly criticised for its overt gender bias. One of the common law principles of natural justice states that no 'man' is to be judge in 'his' own cause. The most common example is the standard of 'the reasonable man' as the measure of the kind of behaviour that can be expected by the law. Such expressions, of course, have run right the way through the English language, not just the law. These are relatively superficial grammatical biases, creating an atmosphere of masculinity in the law, which has prompted their recent correction to gender-neutral terminology, such as 'the reasonable person'.

The point of the radical argument is to emphasise bias that is more subliminal than this. The concealment is effected, it is said, by the male judicial 'pretence' of neutrality and objectivity in legal reasoning, in resolving matters of law. The question of whether this pretence is conscious or unconscious is secondary. The claim is that every appearance of neutrality can be maintained while applying rules and standards that have built in masculine assumptions, standards that favour male over female plaintiffs or defendants. To take the most general example, the real concealment is found in the concepts of reason or rationality within the concept of the reasonable man. It is not the overt masculinity of the reasonable 'man', but the covert masculinity of the 'reasonable' man that remains when the term is changed to 'reasonable person'. The deep gender-bias lies in the Enlightenment ideal of reason and the rational individual (supposedly of either sex). The radicals argue that the liberal feminists who aim for parity of legal rights have been setting themselves the aspiration of achieving equality by conforming with male standards of rationality and individualism, accepting the male definition of reason and individuality as the standard point of reference. Adapting Marx's critique of liberalism, radical feminists argue that the fictitious 'individual' of liberalism is an idealised male who exhibits all the characteristics culturally associated with masculinity and suppresses all those associated with femininity. The individual who constitutes the legal subject or person displays the qualities that a patriarchal society values and rewards more highly than the constructed feminine qualities. The characteristics of manliness, virility, strength and independence (exhibiting the male entrepreneurial spirit) are typical of the liberal 'autonomous individual', whereas the virtues of womanliness, patience, gentle submissiveness, care and nurture are marginalised. The ideal is framed in such a way that it is easier for males to conform with or aspire to. Females can only realise their rights by imitating male patterns of behaviour.

The most significant implication of this argument is that the great ideal of liberal feminists, the pursuit of equal opportunities, is only meaningful and realisable for women who can demonstrate masculine abilities, in particular the male conception of rationality, which embodies a particular set of cognitive abilities. Thus, the liberal reformers are on the wrong road, as they submit to the ongoing male-dominated structure of society by accepting the male rules of the game. Against this, the radical feminists are arguing that it is this underlying structure that has to be questioned and challenged.

Difference and sameness

Over the past few centuries, the principal justification of the privileged position of males has been expressed in terms of women's supposed general inferiority and their specific differences from men. The subordination is seen not as oppressive and unjust, but as an inevitable imbalance of rights arising naturally from these biological differences. Resistance to specific legal reforms in areas such as education and employment are linked to the questioning of specific abilities and capacities, such as natural mathematical ability or physical strength. The history of this argument is well known. Directly confronting the arguments for the justifiability of discrimination, feminists generally have argued for male–female identity in the areas relevant to the legislation, and have concentrated on exposing assumptions about female disabilities as male prejudice.

From the more radical point of view that emerged in the 1970s, these liberals were making the mistake of saying 'we are just the same as you'. The result of the shift in emphasis from the overt to the subliminal gender-bias in radical feminist thinking was the reshaping of the debate about difference and sameness. If mere conformity with male standards of reasonableness led only to oppression in another guise, it was perhaps necessary to reconceptualise the basis of the demands for change. It was argued that it should not only be accepted but also emphasised that women are different from men, that they have special characteristics that men do not have, and that this should be the basis for a relationship of mutual respect and concrete rights that related to the individuality of women. 'Cultural feminism', in particular, tried to break the grip of the assumption that made women the 'equals' of men in a sense that threatened their own identity and sidelined their own inherent character and qualities. This line of thought provoked a strong reaction from those who saw it as playing into the hands of male domination. Males have to be contested on their own ground. The abandonment of the insistence on sameness invites misinterpretation and a reinforcement of traditional attitudes of paternalistic protection of 'the weaker sex'.

This debate about difference and sameness has continued, especially in the light of child developmental research, some of which has indicated different patterns of cognitive ability and distinctive approaches to moral reasoning in girls and boys (Gilligan 1982). It has also been partly instrumental in the emergence of the distinctive radicalism of 'dominance feminism', which rejects the debate on difference and sameness as an irrelevant distraction from the main issue of male dominance. According to Catherine MacKinnon, the difference between men and women is that 'men have power and women do not' (1987: 51). In the radical feminist writings of MacKinnon and Andrea Dworkin there is a strong emphasis on physical male violence against women, both in public and in the 'privacy' of the home, as the fundamental fact of women's experience and as the root of the problem.

Feminism and postmodernism

The influence of postmodernist thinking on feminism has been mixed. Its obvious potential for deconstructing and destabilising all the assumptions and norms of what radical feminists see as the central locus of male power in modernity is counterbalanced by the threat it represents to the coherence and stability of their own theories. It is in the nature of postmodernist analysis to be disrespectful of all established 'truths'. Nevertheless, the typical motifs of postmodernist thought appeared in feminist theory as elsewhere some time before it was consciously applied. The influence of Foucault's 'discourses' and analysis of localised power, his histories of the marginalised and oppressed, had obvious resonance for the feminist projects of exposing the hidden ways in which male dominance was perpetuated. Similarly, Derrida's methods of deconstruction, identifying binary oppositions and the privileging of one term over the other, had obvious application to the male–female, reason–emotion, mental–physical distinctions. In more general terms, 1970s feminists tended to fall in with a widespread and rather uncritical absorption of the new 'anti-metaphysics' dogmas, in particular the assumption that foundationalism in epistemology was dead, with all the sceptical and perspectivist conclusions that in postmodernist hands this led to.

When postmodernism was adopted by some as an explicit feminist strategy, it was not only addressed to the problems of articulating women's experiences of oppression, but was also directed at the earlier feminist schools of thought, all of which were seen as trapped within the theoretical framework of modernity, with all its 'grand concepts' and 'grand narratives'. Not only traditional liberals, but also the culture-difference feminists and radical-dominance theories came under the critical spotlight for remaining under the spell of essentialism, the crucial modernist assumption that there is a common core to the experience of being a woman, regardless of her position in society, her relative power or powerlessness, her colour or ethnic background, or her sexual orientation. Postmodernists have sought to place the excluded and marginalised at the centre of theory, emphasising the diversity of the experiences of real individual women in real situations, so they have used the deconstructive techniques to express the reality of particularised and detailed experiences of oppression, which are thought to be as effectively smothered by the generality of the feminist concepts as they are by conventional jurisprudence. The concepts of 'woman' and 'gender' are as much the objects of deconstruction as any other.

Feminist jurisprudence as a whole, however, has been poised uncertainly between the values of Enlightenment modernity and a full embrace of the contemporary postmodernist culture. In the first place, the destabilisation that it brings threatens to disintegrate their own conceptual schemes. 'Feminists should be wary of the siren call to abandon gender as an organising concept' (Barnett 1998: 199). In more general terms, the postmodernist perspectivism, which makes of every truth-claim an ideological construct, undermines the critical feminist positions as effectively as it does the dominant male doctrines. Most importantly, perhaps, there has been a growing recognition that the traditional struggle for equality under the law within a liberal framework established at the very least a solid platform or springboard from which to work for substantive equality as well as formal. The scepticism towards the 'masculine' rights promoted by the Enlightenment, on the grounds that these were designed for the enhancement of male power, has its limits.

Rights in relation to class, sex and race

The main force of the criticisms of liberal thinking on rights, from feminists, Marxists and CLS, lies in their universality and supposed emptiness. These criticisms, while they contain many insights and expose weaknesses in liberal assumptions, are at their most damaging when they go beyond the claim of irrelevance to real problems and criticise the enactment of rights as constituting a positive obstruction to the promotion or defence of the real interests of those whose rights are ostensibly being protected. This is a long-standing theme in the Marxist criticisms of the liberal rule of law and, as we have just seen, it appears in radical feminist theories. It is also a prominent theme in the writings of the critical legal scholars, who have adapted Marx's critique of liberal rights and his concept of the 'monadic' bourgeois individual to a critique of individualist human rights in contemporary law. A strong motif in CLS criticism in the 1980s was the argument that rights as they are understood by liberals in the modern world actually have the effect of deepening the individualistic structure of society, because the preoccupation with legal rights and protections sets up barriers around artificially isolated individuals, denying their essentially social nature and breaking down local relations of community.

This argument has been developed separately by some feminists, but vigorously resisted by others who see the danger in undervaluing what has proved to be the main instrument for the advancement of the cause of gender equality. It may be that the much maligned 'rights culture' does create, among its other effects, divisions and greater distance between individuals, but this is surely not one of its most unwelcome effects. Many people's interests and desires are not served by closer integration with others. The balance between the individual and his or her community is a delicate one. This is a point emphasised by critical race theorists against the radical tendency to disparage individual rights. Patricia Williams, for example, criticises those feminist and critical scholars who are sceptical of rights on the grounds that they seem oblivious to the importance of legal formalities within the world (male and female alike) of black resistance to discrimination and oppression (Williams 1991). She and others have persuasively argued that the attainment of formal equality in law has been the necessary condition for achieving substantive equality. She also sets women's oppression within the different historical context of slave-ownership and the more recent struggles for civil rights, emphasising the different position in which black people find themselves under the formal protection of the law today. This argument can be generalised beyond the contexts of sex and race. Among their many other functions, legal rights serve primarily the purpose of the legitimate protection of vulnerable individuals.

Conclusion

The Enlightenment ideal of the autonomous individual, equal in standing with others and capable of making responsible judgements, is essentially the image of the legally responsible individual with which we are still familiar today. This essentially Kantian conception of the subject has at most been the dominant force within modern ways of thinking; it does not constitute it, as so many undiscriminating critics of 'modernity' seem to believe. It has survived as the dominant way of thinking, despite the relentless assault upon it over the past two centuries by Marxist economic determinism, reducing subjects to the status of bearers of ideology, with their consciousness determined solely by their material existence; by theories of the unconscious – Freudian and post-Freudian – which threaten to undermine conscious agency completely; by radical mechanistic and behaviourist theories that 'abolish' the conscious subject; and by de-centring theories of language that displace the rational subject and represent us as prisoners of the structures of language. The survival of the modern liberal conception of the subject in the popular mind can be seen either as impressive evidence in its favour, or as an indication of the pervasiveness of its ideological power.

Study Questions for Part II

General question: To what extent are the radical critiques of the modern concept of the individual justified?

Further study questions: Assess the impact of these critiques on mainstream theories of rights. How do they differ from mainstream rights-scepticism? Does the emphasis on context-sensitivity effectively undermine the idea of universal rights? Compare the rights-scepticism of the critics of modernity with the rule-scepticism of the legal realists. Explain and evaluate Marx's critique of liberal rights and the monadic concept of the individual. Compare the liberal feminist approach to legal rights with the radical feminist critiques of rights. Are the feminist critiques of the individual and the concept of reason in law justified? Do the postmodernist arguments help or hinder the feminist goal of equality under the law?

Suggestions for further reading

For general reading on the values of liberalism and the Enlightenment, and their postmodernist critics, see the references at the end of Chapter 5.

Sarat and Kearns (1996) and the Oxford Amnesty Lectures in Shute and Hurley (1993) are collections that include a range of critical theories of rights. On Burke's rights-scepticism, see Waldron (1987: ch. 4). On Marx and Marxist theories of law and rights, see Cain and Hunt (1979), Patterson (1996a: ch. 23) and Morrison (1997: ch. 10). 'On the Jewish Question', one of the rare occasions on which Marx spoke explicitly about rights, is reprinted with a commentary in Waldron (1987). McLellan (1973) is a classic introduction to the life and thought of Marx. On Marx's critique of possessive individualism and rights, see MacPherson (1962).

On the CLS criticisms of rights, see Morrison (1997: ch. 16), Douzinas (2000), Patterson (1996a: ch. 7). On critical race theory and rights, see Williams (1991), Morrison (1997: ch. 16) and Davies (1994: ch. 6.4)

On the range of feminist theories and their impact on law and jurisprudence, Barnett (1998) and Davies (1994: ch. 6) are recommended. Also useful are Morrison (1997: ch. 17), Patterson (1996a: ch. 19), Richardson and Sandland (2000), Graycar (1990), Graycar and Morgan (2002), Frug (1992) and Kramer (1995).

Part III

Criminal responsibility and punishment

10 Responsibility and guilt

As a distinct and limited area of the whole of what we call 'the law', criminal law is concerned to control and prevent certain kinds of conduct deemed to be harmful or in other ways undesirable. It has always proved difficult to find a precise definition of a crime that is not circular, which distinguishes it clearly from morally wrongful actions, and in particular from other areas in law that it overlaps, such as the law of torts, or civil wrongs. There are numerous differences, but the main practical one lies in the consequences of the actions, in the civil remedy available or in the punitive sanction. Criminal conduct is probably best described as the kind of conduct – acts or omissions – that the law seeks to discourage or prevent through the threat or implementation of punitive sanctions, whether or not it actually is morally wrong or harmful. It is the unlawfulness of the conduct that is central to the definition.

Criminal law is concerned, however, not only with acts, but also with the states of mind accompanying them. Liability to the sanctions of law can be either 'subjective' or 'objective' in the sense that it is related to the subjective state of the agent's mind, or solely to the act. When it is the latter, liability is said to be 'objective' or 'strict'. The performance of the unlawful act is sufficient to confirm guilt. The established norm in English criminal law is that liability is not strict, but requires proof of a guilty state of mind (*mens rea*) in addition to the unlawful act (*actus reus*). In other words, some degree of fault on the part of the offender is required. This norm is the outcome of a complex doctrine that has evolved in the history of common law. The basic idea is that, in order to be held criminally liable, the agent must have committed an offence freely, knowingly and deliberately. To many legal writers today, full commitment to the doctrine of *mens rea* is – at least in its basic implications – an essential condition for a just legal system.

This interpretation, however, is not self-evident. There are numerous exceptions to the norm of fault-requirement, which are by no means universally condemned as injustices. Strict liability controversially imposed by Parliament in 1994 on owners of dangerous dogs, for example, is thought by many to be wholly justified. This kind of unconditional shouldering of responsibility without fault also exists in civil law, as illustrated by *Rylands* v.

Fletcher (1868), in which a mill-owner was held liable for inadvertently causing the flooding of neighbouring property. This landmark case established a comprehensive rule laying down 'strict liability in the case of the escape of dangerous things from a man's land' (Baker 1991: 277). Furthermore, quite apart from instances in which unconditional liability is stipulated by law, there are numerous grey areas, especially in the context of unlawful injury or killing, in which it is not always readily agreed that lack of *mens rea* should absolve the agent from responsibility. The uncertainty in such cases will be one of the central themes in this chapter.

Free agency and responsibility

One of the fundamental conditions for attributing moral responsibility to anyone for a harmful act they have committed is the assumption that we are talking about a free agent. The general question to be dealt with here concerns situations and circumstances in which we might be inclined to say that, although an act that is normally understood to be criminal has been committed, there is insufficient blame to warrant criminal prosecution because the agents were genuinely not in control of their own actions. In such cases, it is commonly argued, we cannot make the assumption that we are dealing with a free agent. If circumstances place the will of the agent under such pressure that there was no alternative to the course of action taken, it seems that we cannot meaningfully say that a free choice was made. If we cannot say this, then we cannot in all fairness hold the agent liable to punishment. It is this question about the meaningfulness of choices that has to be examined closely.

Excuse or justification

In the context of wrongful or harmful acts, there are many ways in which it can be argued that the agent is blameless. In the case of the volitional argument – that there was no unconstrained will, hence an absence of real choice – the distinction between excuse and justification is vitally important. The distinction is familiar to everyday moral arguments for exonerating harmful behaviour. If the agent is justified, the contention is that despite the harm, no wrong has been committed. A violent act in self-defence, for example, is presented as a justification rather than an excuse. If, by contrast, excusing conditions are cited, the argument is that the act was wrongful but understandable in the circumstances. The claim, for example, that one was in an impossible situation because provoked beyond endurance, is more plausibly interpreted as an excuse than as a justification. With a justification, it is presumed that if faced with the same situation again, one would take the same course of action; with an excuse, which is inherently an admission of human weakness, the tacit argument is that in similar circumstances one would not do it again.

Both arguments of excuse and justification have been employed regularly in legal defences based on necessity or duress. The distinction is important, despite the fact that in many senses the legal consequences are identical. This is because the moral plausibility of any particular defence rests upon a clarification of the different implications of excuse and justification. A justified act is not regarded as wrongful or unlawful, hence the agent is free of blame and criminal liability. An excused act is a wrongful and unlawful act, but the agent is again not liable. The difference is commonly said to lie in the attitude of empathy with the predicament of the offender whose acts are excusable rather than justified. When harmful acts are lawful, the defence does not need to rely on understanding or empathy. This distinction should be borne in mind in the following account of the defences of necessity and duress.

Necessity and duress

These two defences share some common features, but are crucially different in several ways. With the plea of either necessity or duress, it is said that the agent is acting with a constrained will. What we will need to consider for each of these defences is, first, the sense in which it can be convincingly argued that there is no free will, and, second, whether this constraint of the will is more plausibly interpreted as an excuse for admitted wrongdoing, or as a justification that clears the defendant of moral and legal guilt. Acting through necessity is acting under pressure from dangerous natural circumstance. Fear of death in a storm at sea or a mountain blizzard might motivate criminal acts that in any other situation would never be contemplated. The defence is one of necessity when the source of the danger is an impersonal natural force. Acting under duress is acting under pressure from threats by other persons. Fear of serious injury or death at the hands of others might similarly motivate acts that would never otherwise be contemplated. The defence is one of duress when the source of the danger is human. With either defence, the argument is that they were left with no alternative, that they were in some sense compelled to act in the way they did.

Life and death necessity

Situations of extreme danger bring the problems with these defences into sharp focus. When the threat of death is imminent, so the argument goes, the pressure is such that the will as an instrument of free choice is effectively neutralised, and responsibility for one's actions is nullified. Two famous cases will illustrate the problems here.

In the case of *R. v. Dudley and Stephens* (1884), two sailors who had survived a shipwreck had been charged with murder. After drifting in an open boat for twenty days with very little food or water, they had agreed that the only way to survive was to kill the sick cabin boy and eat his flesh. Four days after this, the survivors – including another sailor who had refused to participate in the killing – were rescued. At the subsequent trial, the defence was that the killing was justified by necessity. Against public protest in their favour, Dudley and Stephens were convicted of murder and sentenced to death. Shortly thereafter, they were reprieved and released.

The substance of the argument for the defence of necessity was that, under pressure from a prolonged period of hunger and thirst, the men could no longer be considered free agents. In these extreme circumstances, the course of action they took was the only possible one. In such situations, the will to resist temptation is weakened and the instinct for survival takes over. The only alternative would have been a sacrifice that no one could reasonably be expected to make.

One difficulty with this argument is that it is not clear how it could be construed as a justification. This would require that the killing of the cabin boy was in these circumstances reasonable and lawful. Reference to the instinct for survival seems to constitute an implicit admission that the act could not be justified. It would be more plausible to argue the case for excusing conditions, thereby conceding the wrongful nature of the act, but pleading necessity by virtue of the weakening of the will.

There was little chance, however, that either argument would prevail. The defence that the act was justified by necessity was rejected on the grounds that the law did not recognise the absolute duty to preserve one's own life. According to Lord Coleridge, 'to preserve one's life is generally speaking a duty, but it may be the plainest and highest duty to sacrifice it. War is full of instances in which it is a man's duty not to live, but to die' (Allen 2001: 321). This comment set the tone for later generations of judges presiding over similar cases.

The earlier case of *U.S.* v. *Holmes* (1842) was on the face of it a more plausible candidate for justification by necessity. Holmes was a member of the crew in an impossibly overcrowded lifeboat carrying forty-one survivors from the wreck of an immigrant ship bound for New York. On his initiative, the crew had thrown sixteen passengers overboard in the course of one night, so that the rest would have a chance of survival. Against expectations, the boat did reach safety and Holmes was charged with wilful manslaughter.

In cases like this, there is a natural tendency to obscure the main issue with matters peripheral to the central moral dilemma. Questions about who should have been held responsible, about whether or not lots should have been drawn, about whether it is possible to be certain that a boat is about to sink, all tend to divert attention from the dilemma and how it affects the will. Given the reality of the dilemma – that if a number of people are not sacrificed, everyone will die – then the important question for the issue of responsibility concerns the freedom of action of Holmes and the crew. In what sense can it be said that they had no alternative to this course of action? In what sense were they being 'compelled' to commit these acts? Most prominent among the arguments in defence of their course of action was the 'state of nature' argument. Beyond the reach of civilisation, so the argument goes, normal moral and legal codes do not apply. In a state of emergency, the Hobbesian natural rights to self-defence and self-preservation take over. It is quite unrealistic and unreasonable – it is argued – to apply the moral or legal norms of any particular society in these circumstances.

The main difficulty with this line of argument lies in the inconsistent attitude towards the efficacy of the will. The purpose of the defence of necessity is to establish the virtual disappearance of free will, under pressure of natural circumstances. On the state of nature argument, though, what virtually disappears is not the will but a sense of moral restraint; the will is, if anything, stronger than normal. The choice is for continued life, rather than death. What might be said to disappear is the ability to *direct* the will. If the argument is for justification rather than excuse, then the course of action that will save the greatest number of lives is the rational one. It is the argument for excuse that depends upon the contention that the will is weakened in such situations, because if decisive action such as that taken by Holmes or Dudley is morally wrong and in violation of law, then they must argue that they were not in command of their will to do what was right. The source of the confusion in the arguments in defence of these acts lies in the equivocation between justification and excuse.

In the recent ruling on the case of the conjoined twins (*Re A (Children)*, 2000) (see Chapter 7), the nature of the case was such that justification rather than excuse was called for. The implications of this case for the defence of necessity have to be approached with caution. Although it has been said of this case that 'it is now clear that necessity may be a defence to murder' (Smith and Hogan 2003: 267), it is also true that the judges explicitly warned that general principles should not be extrapolated from the ruling on this highly individualised case. In the judgement of Lord Justice Brooke, the absolute stipulation by Lord Coleridge in *Dudley and Stephens* that the taking of the life of an innocent is ruled out, because it is impossible to judge between the comparative value of lives, is reasoned to be inapplicable in the case of the twins due to the fact that they are making no such judgement, but rather allowing that the unfortunate victim is 'self-designated for a very early death' (Allen 2001: 338). The crucial point is that there is no 'selection' problem here. This is the key difference from a case in which one is selected from a number of possible victims. Coleridge's second reason, that the necessity defence would cut the law loose from morality, is acknowledged in the reasons given by Brooke to represent a moral position still widely subscribed to, but he argues only that the court finds this position less than obvious, adding that it was beyond the court's competence to adjudicate between these philosophies. He nevertheless endorses the principle of using minimal and proportionate evil to avoid inevitable and irreparable evil, thus complementing Ward's conclusion that the law must allow in these circumstances the choice of the lesser evil. The overall effect of these reasons does seem to point in the direction of a general necessity defence, but as we shall see now, the issues with the defence of duress are significantly different.

Acts carried out under duress

Despite the similarity between the defences of necessity and duress, there is a sense in which the connection between duress and free will is less prone to ambiguity. It is plain, for example, how a false confession extracted under duress – under threats of beatings and torture – is invalid because it is not a confession given of one's own free will. Without the intimidation, the false confession would not have been made. It also seems clear that when duress is raised as a defence to a serious criminal charge, what is meant is analogous to the signing of a false confession. Without the threats, the crime would not have been committed.

A key point in the distinction between necessity and duress is that there is an asymmetry in respect of justification and excuse. While it is plausible to argue that necessity can serve either as an excuse for unlawful behaviour or as justified, and hence lawful, it is unimaginable that duress could be anything but an excuse. To argue necessity is to insist that one had to do it, in a sense that at least leaves open the possibility that it was entirely justified. To argue duress is to argue that one was forced to do it, in a sense that immediately suggests that it was contrary to what was willed or desired. The nature of this defence is easier to examine than necessity, because it does not equivocate between excuse and justification. The focus is squarely upon the hopeless predicament of people who find themselves facing impossible choices; the only possible defence is the impossibility of the choice. This is an excuse for the wrongdoing one is forced into; it is not a justification. By its very nature, a crime committed under duress cannot be represented as the right thing to do.

What we need to consider now is the scope of duress. What kinds of act does it apply to? If one were literally compelled to commit a criminal act by, for example, being physically forced to pull a trigger, we have a morally clear reference point. In such a case, it is dubious to speak of an 'act' at all; an act requires more than a muscular contraction. Here one simply becomes the unwilling instrument of another's purpose. If these were the circumstances, there would be no responsibility or blame. What is the situation, though, if the compulsion is less than literal? Can duress still absolve the agent from blame?

The case of *D.P.P.* v. *Lynch* (1975) is the most important one relating to duress in recent years because it unsettled the law and challenged the legal and moral doctrines on duress, before itself being reversed in 1987. The facts of the case were that Lynch was the driver of a car used by a paramilitary group for the killing of a police officer. He claimed that he had nothing to do with the group: that he was acting under duress and that he was convinced he would have been shot if he had not obeyed. These factual claims were not disputed.

The question at the heart of the controversy surrounding this case concerned the apparent injustice of holding fully responsible someone who was acting under such extreme duress. Lynch was initially convicted of aiding and abetting murder, because it was held that the defence of duress was not available for cases involving murder or closely related offences. On appeal to the Lords, a retrial was ordered on the grounds that the jury should have been allowed to consider the defence of duress.

Why was the defence not available at this time? The situation in English law prior to 1975 was that duress was available as a defence to a range of offences less serious than murder, for example, shoplifting or robbery, perjury or other offences not resulting in death. The specific exclusion of duress for murder was a long-established principle in common law, resting on the seventeenth-century authority of Matthew Hale, who had declared that:

> if a man be desperately assaulted, and in peril of death, and cannot otherwise escape, unless to satisfy his assailant's fury he will kill an innocent person then present, the fear and actual force will not acquit him of the crime and punishment of murder, if he commit the fact; for he ought rather to die himself, than kill an innocent.
>
> (Hale 1972)

These words were echoed by the equally authoritative Blackstone (Blackstone 1829), establishing a firm principle in common law. Given the choice between killing and dying oneself, the latter course must be taken.

In overturning these authorities, Lords Morris and Wilberforce insisted that they were not creating new law, but drawing out the principles of the law as a whole. It was argued (by Morris) that the words of Hale were inappropriately extended to cases in which the defendant played a role but was not the actual killer. Wilberforce argued that there was no convincing principle justifying the withdrawal of the defence from the most serious crimes connected with murder. They also pointed to logical anomalies and inconsistencies in the law, whereby, for example, duress might be available on a charge of assault, then suddenly be withdrawn when the victim dies and the charge becomes one of murder. The overall purpose of these arguments was to establish the principle that each case be treated on its own merits and the defence of duress put to the jury, regardless of the seriousness of the charge.

English law on these matters then entered a period of confusion and uncertainty, during which it was unclear whether duress was available as a defence to murder and closely related offences, such as attempted murder, accessory before the fact, or aiding and abetting. The situation was resolved in 1987, when the Law Lords took the unusual step of overruling their own earlier decision, declaring *Lynch* to be unsound law and restoring the *status quo ante*.

What were the uppermost factors in the minds of those deliberating? On the question of authority and precedent, Lord Hailsham and the others in the majority in 1987 disputed the contention by Wilberforce that they were not departing from existing law in the *Lynch* ruling. The authorities of Hale and Blackstone were now firmly reasserted, as was the ruling against Dudley and Stephens. On the question of principle, Hailsham argued that it was the purpose of law to protect innocent lives and set clear standards of behaviour for the avoidance of criminal responsibility. In cases of necessity and duress alike, it never had been accepted that one could take the life of another to save one's own, and it never should be. In all such cases, there was a clear duty to follow the words of Hale and sacrifice one's own life. Morally speaking, this might seem highly demanding, but in recent history – as Hailsham pointed out – there are countless examples of people making this sacrifice. A particularly telling analogy had been drawn earlier by Lord Simon, who argued that it was inconsistent to allow the defence of duress in criminal courts when it had not been allowed to the defendants at Nuremberg when they argued that they had been obeying superior orders.

In terms of policy, admitting the defence of duress to murder was already producing undesirable consequences. Actual killers – as opposed to those like Lynch who were reluctantly assisting – were increasingly pleading duress, claiming to have been terrorised by stronger personalities. The most prominent consideration in terms of policy, though, had already been voiced in earlier dissenting judgements; the general admission of duress for murder would positively encourage gangsters, terrorists and kidnappers to commit murder by proxy.

The reaction to these arguments by those in favour of widening the scope of duress was that the 'terrorist charter' argument was unduly alarmist and unrealistic; that duress in murder cases was only comparable with war crimes if the defendant was the actual killer; and, most importantly, that allowing the defence did not mean automatic acquittal, but rather that it would be left to the jury to decide, on very high standards of proof, whether the circumstances of the case in hand genuinely merited a complete excuse. What was unjust was refusing to put it to the jury at all. These arguments, however, did not prevail.

What is perhaps most noticeable in these arguments is that there are persuasive reasons of policy in conflict with the apparent requirements of justice. Although the Hailsham line of argument was presented in such a way as to admit to no conflict of this nature, it is nevertheless clear that considerations of policy, or recognition of the dangers inherent in admitting the defence, have overridden the principle of guaranteeing individual justice. Given that it is generally agreed that the will has to be free in order to hold an agent responsible for any act, it must be the case that there is no justification apart from considerations of prevention and deterrence for arbitrarily stipulating that duress is to be absolutely excluded at a certain level of seriousness. Whether it stops short of actual murder or of aiding and abetting is beside the point.

Is it true or false, then, that somebody in Lynch's position is morally responsible for the killing carried out with their assistance? It is indisputable that he was causally responsible, hence that his actions were partly instrumental in bringing about the death. This in itself, though, is never enough to establish guilt. Did he also have 'a guilty mind'? This depends on whether his ability to choose was really eliminated. His choice was between assisting in the crime or facing what he believed to be his own certain death. The pressure on the will in such a situation does not amount to literal compulsion, but it can hardly be denied that the ability to choose is severely constrained.

If the doctrine of *mens rea* is sound, and if we accept that the will is virtually neutralised by threats of imminent death in such circumstances, then it must be concluded that the volitional condition was not satisfied and he was not guilty of aiding and abetting murder. The outcome of the decision to restore the situation prior to *Lynch* is that victims of duress in murder cases are taken to be fully culpable and punishable. In terms of the basic principles relating to the justification of punishment, what these prevailing voices are in effect saying is that, although it may be unfair, we cannot afford not to punish people who find themselves in these situations. They need to be punished even if they do not deserve to be. Prevention and deterrence are more important than avoiding a limited amount of injustice.

Intention and responsibility

Intending to cause or inflict harm in one way or another is, generally speaking, a prerequisite of establishing blame or responsibility, whether legal or moral. In a legal context, it is the intention to commit an act prohibited by law that is relevant. The general question concerning intention to be examined here can be phrased as follows. When there is no doubt that a criminal act has been committed, are there any circumstances under which the agent might be exonerated or excused responsibility, on the grounds that the act was unintentional? Conversely, when is the agent guilty in mind as well as in deed, in terms of what he or she means to happen?

Making sense of malice and recklessness

The paradigm case of unintended harm is that of a pure accident. With genuine accidents, it is commonly believed, there are no rational grounds for blame or recrimination. In such cases, it is tempting to assume that the explanation for there being no blame is the absence of malice in the act. In common usage, malice indicates ill will or vindictiveness. This is precisely what is missing in an accidental act that causes harm. As with many other legal concepts, however, the meaning of malice in law is very loosely related to this common usage.

According to a well-established legal definition of malice, it has a very specific meaning that does not require any kind of ill will. What was required, according to Kenny (1902), was *either* 'an actual intention to do the particular kind of harm that in fact was done', *or* 'recklessness as to whether such harm should occur or not', in the sense that the risk of harm was foreseen, but the agent continued regardless. This definition is only contingently related to the more conventional, non-legal meaning of malice. It means either 'specific intent' or recklessness.

None of these terms, however (intention, malice, recklessness), have had a stable meaning in the evolution of English law. Their legal meanings are to some extent interdependent, as we shall see. Two nineteenth-century cases will illustrate the difficulties involved in attributing malice to those whose defences rest on the claim that there was no intention to commit the offence.

In *R. v. Faulkner* (1877), a sailor charged with arson admitted to attempting to steal rum from the spirit room of a ship. In striking a light, he accidentally ignited the rum, which resulted in the complete destruction of the ship by fire. His initial conviction for arson was overturned by the Appeal Court on the grounds that he had neither the actual intent to destroy the ship, nor reckless disregard for such an outcome, because there was no evidence that he believed the stealing of the rum could have such unexpected and dangerous results. Given that arson meant 'unlawful and malicious setting fire to something', the trial judge was considered to have interpreted the word 'malicious' too broadly and intuitively.

One point to reflect on here is that if the subjective interpretation of malice, in terms of what he actually believed, is more in line with common usage than the objective interpretation, in terms of what it would have been reasonable to believe, then it was the Court of Appeal rather than the trial judge that was interpreting the word more intuitively. On the general point, however, they were following a more precise legal definition and ignoring the loose connotations of the word 'malicious'.

The case of *R. v. Martin* (1881) had different implications for the interpretation of malice and specific intent. The Court of Appeal upheld the conviction of a man for the unlawful wounding of a number of people at a theatre. His defence had been that there was no malice in his turning out of the lights and barring of the exit, just 'mischief', and that he had intended to create panic, not to cause injuries. It was explicitly ruled not only that malice required no ill will, and hence that it could include 'mere mischief', but also that it could include acts without the specific intent to commit the kind of harm that actually occurred. It was also held that it was an unlawful act calculated to injure *in the sense that it was likely to injure*.

On the face of it, the rulings in *Faulkner* and *Martin* are inconsistent. What they have in common is the depersonalisation of the concept of malice; the legal concept has nothing to do with personal feelings. Where they seem to be at odds, though, is on the issue of foreseeability of harm. The *Faulkner* ruling rests on the question of what the sailor actually believed about the risk he was taking. The *Martin* ruling, by contrast, was indicating an objective test, in terms of the actual likelihood of injury to the theatre-goers. This tension between the subjective and objective test of malice in terms of foresight and foreseeability has become increasingly significant in more recent rulings on intention.

Kenny's 1902 definition was clearly indicating a subjective test. If there had to be either actual intent or recklessness in the sense that the accused had foreseen the risk and proceeded regardless, the implication was that it was not sufficient to argue that the risk *should* have been foreseen or that 'a reasonable man' *would* have foreseen it. Kenny's definition was endorsed in a dispute over the meaning of malice in the case of *R. v. Cunningham* (1957). The defendant had inadvertently caused an injury to a woman who was sleeping in a room adjacent to a gas meter that he had ripped from the wall in the course of stealing from the meter. As a result of the fracturing of the gas pipe, she had inhaled the escaping gas, and he was charged with larceny and 'unlawfully and maliciously administering a noxious thing', contrary to S.23 of the 1861 Offences Against the Person Act.

Did Cunningham administer the gas 'maliciously'? In common usage, it seems clear that he did not. It played no part in his calculations, and there was no ill will to someone, the presence of whom he did not even suspect. He might still be thought guilty of the injury, despite the absence of this kind of malice, because the act was so obviously dangerous. In legal terms, though, it is not so clear. At the appeal against conviction, the defence cited *Faulkner* as relevant precedent, while the prosecution cited *Martin*.

Cunningham's appeal was allowed, the Lords ruling that the judge had misdirected the jury on the meaning of malice. The judge's direction had been that 'maliciously' (in the wording of the statute) meant 'wickedly': 'doing something which he has no business to do and perfectly well knows it'. The upshot of this direction was that the jury had no alternative but to convict on the second charge if they found him guilty on the first charge of larceny. What he had 'no business doing' was the act of larceny, which was the same act as that which brought about the unintended poisoning. The Lords reiterated the rejection by Kenny and other authorities of the equation of malice with wickedness, and pointed out that, with the proper definition before them, one could not say how a jury would have decided the case on the second charge of maliciously administering the gas. The crucial question would have been whether he had understood the risk and proceeded regardless. This reaffirmation of the 'subjective' test of malice, in terms of what the defendant actually believed, settled the law on this matter for some years. It established what came to be known as the 'Cunningham' test for recklessness.

With the subsequent development of case law, however, there has been more detailed scrutiny of the concept of recklessness. The decisive ruling by the Lords on *R. v Caldwell* (1982), a case involving damage to a hotel and endangering lives with fire, established the wider 'Caldwell' test for recklessness. This was in effect the reinstatement of the objective test for malice (discussed above) in terms of actual likelihood of injury or damage to property. On this test, recklessness was now defined in such a way that encompassed both possibilities – the defendant either saw the risk and proceeded to take it, or gave what was an objectively obvious risk no thought at all, and proceeded to take it. The general idea here is that if you 'close your eyes to the obvious', you are just as guilty as one who sees the risk and ignores it. With the Caldwell test, the prosecution does not have to prove that the risk was actually appreciated by the defendant.

These two subjective and objective 'limbs' of the Caldwell test were supposed to cover every case of recklessness. However, a loophole (known as 'the Caldwell lacuna') soon appeared. The problem arises when a defendant had indeed seen the risk but then discounted it as unlikely and proceeded to take it. This might apply, for example, in cases of dangerous driving, when the driver sees but wrongly dismisses the risk of overtaking on a dangerous stretch of road (*Reid,* 1992), in cases of playing with a partly loaded revolver without realising that the chambers rotate on firing (*Lamb,* 1967), or taking a calculated risk with an exposed electric cable (*Merrick,* 1996). Neither the first nor the second limb of the Caldwell test seems to cover such cases, in which they have not closed their eyes to the obvious; on the contrary, they have seen the risk and miscalculated, but the fact that they calculated and rejected the risk exempts them from the first limb as well. There have been numerous rulings on the lacuna, but the problem has not been resolved. One important ruling to note was the confinement of the lacuna to cases of *bona fide* mistake, with the Lords declaring that grossly negligent mistakes would fall under the second limb of the Caldwell test (*Reid,* 1992).

One point to be clear about is that, although there were some judicial attempts to extend the objective Caldwell test to all offences, it never in fact replaced Cunningham, but merely restricted its application. In the years following the Caldwell ruling there was considerable uncertainty as to how the law stood on this matter. Originally applied to reckless manslaughter (*Seymour,* 1983), this was later explicitly ruled out in *Adomako* (1995). *Caldwell* came to apply mostly to criminal damage and regulatory offences. The subjective Cunningham test was reaffirmed for most offences against the person, including any offence, the statutory terms of which includes the word 'maliciously' and to all offences of assault. In all such cases, the burden of proof continued to rest with the prosecution to establish either intent or subjective recklessness.

The criticisms of the Caldwell definition by lawyers and legal philosophers for this increasing complexity, and the potential for injustice to particular defendants who did not conform with the reasonableness standard, came to a head with the Lords' ruling in *R. v. G. and another* (2003) that the Caldwell test was no longer to apply. The agreed facts of the case were that two boys aged 11 and 12 had set fire to some newspapers on a concrete forecourt while camping unaccompanied by their parents, and had expected them to burn out. The fire spread and caused £1 million worth of damage. The new ruling explicitly restored the Kenny definition and the Cunningham test for recklessness in cases of criminal damage, so that actual awareness of the risk must be proved in all cases. As we will see in Chapter 13, however, this development has not closed the question of the appropriate test for recklessness. At around the same time that the Lords were making this ruling, for example, Parliament was passing the Sexual Offences Act (2003), according to which the sexual offences of rape and indecent assault when carried out reckless as to the victim's consent required an assessment of the reasonableness of the belief that there was in fact consent, in order to constitute a defence. This is a version of the objective test, which runs contrary to the spirit of *G. and another*.

Intention and motive

Motive, in common language, is relatively straightforward. It means a reason behind an action in the sense that it is what moves you to action. The motives for seeking food and drink are hunger and thirst. Intention is a more complex concept involving aims or goal-directedness, conscious deliberation and purposefulness, but its essential meaning can be conveyed by its indication of a design or plan. The intention to seek food and drink is the possession of some kind of design or plan on how to obtain it.

The deliberations of a jury will nearly always involve assessment of intention and scrutiny of motive. Was there evidence of conscious design? Did the defendant mean to do it? Why did he do it? Despite the fact that intention and motive are not near-synonyms, they are often confusingly conflated. The question *why* an arsonist, for example, set fire to a building has no intrinsic connection with the question of whether or not he or she *meant* to do it. A strongly motivated arsonist might as easily start a fire by accident as someone without any motive or desire to start one. Although the two concepts are clearly distinct, we need to understand why they can appear merely as two ways of referring to the same thing.

Motive is usually at most an indicator or symptom of guilt, while intention is a condition of guilt. Motive is in a sense incidental; it is presented only as part of the evidence for the prosecution that the defendant is guilty as charged. Given that a criminal act has been committed, the presence of a motive is neither a necessary nor a sufficient condition of guilt, while intention is normally necessary and sometimes sufficient to establish guilt. A crime without any apparent motive is no less a crime, but a crime that is not intended is in normal circumstances not a crime at all.

With such a clear distinction, it might well be wondered how intention and motive can ever become confused. The manner in which this reversal occurs is not easy to pin down. Consider again the motive behind an act of arson. The motive might be hatred, revenge or jealousy; it may be the wish to frighten, terrorise or kill the occupants; it might be the desire to defraud an insurance company; it might be a protest against the architecture. Any of these reasons might be the correct answer to the question, 'Why did you do it?' Some, but not all, of them would be appropriate answers to the question, 'What did you intend to happen?'

Answers to the 'why' question are also relevant, then, to the intention question. It is directly relevant and indeed central to *mens rea* to establish the extent of what was intended: for example, 'What consequences did you intend?' or 'How far did you mean to go?' The answer might be 'I only meant it as a warning; I didn't mean to kill anyone.' This question and answer relate to intention and responsibility, but also sound like an explanation of motive, of why the act was done. It is the possibility of so much overlap or coincidence between intention and motive that lies at the root of the confusion. The two concepts are logically distinct, but on some occasions the distinction is less apparent than on others. Whatever the motive, certain additional outcomes might be intended. What is immediately relevant here, though, is what the perpetrator intended to happen as a consequence of igniting the building. As far as the guiltiness of mind is concerned, the normal procedure in law is to exclude motive and focus on the intention or purpose of the defendant. The following case illustrates this inclination to exclude motive from account. It also illustrates the ease with which legal reasoning can fall into conceptual confusion.

In a 1947 case (*R. v. Steane*), an Englishman living in Germany at the outbreak of war had succumbed to threats to send his family to a concentration camp, and reluctantly agreed to make broadcasts for German radio. After the war he was charged with treason, the wording of which included the phrase 'doing an act likely to assist the enemy with intent to assist the enemy'. It was argued in Steane's defence that there was no such intent because his true purpose was to protect his family. His defence rested on the assumption that the understandable motive behind the act would exonerate him. Steane did not deny 'doing the act'. Further, the court accepted his explanation as a true account of his reasons for committing the offence.

The general question at issue was whether or not he had a 'guilty mind'. An intuitive non-legal response to this general question might be that there was no subjective guilt and therefore no criminal intention, that he did not intend to assist the enemy even though he was pressurised into doing so.

In his direction of the jury, the trial judge reasoned that while Steane's motive was a worthy and innocent one, his intention was nevertheless to assist the enemy. On this interpretation, the ascription of such intention is nothing more than a morally neutral statement of fact. Objectively speaking, it was reasoned, there was no question that he did intend to assist the enemy, albeit reluctantly. Steane was accordingly convicted of treason, but the conviction was overturned on appeal. The appeal judges took the view that, although it was right to distinguish intention from motive, there was no actual proof of criminal intent, and that the jury was not entitled to assume intent unless they could show that the defendant's actions were not free and unconstrained. On this interpretation, the criminal intent and thereby the *mens rea* were undermined not by motive but by volition. He was deemed not to have performed the act voluntarily. The implication of this decision was that blameless motives were still held to be irrelevant to the question of guilt.

Intention and foresight

With the question of how an agent's foresight relates to responsibility and *mens rea*, we arrive at the heart of the conceptual difficulties raised by intention. Single acts or particular courses of action nearly always have multiple effects, some of which are less obviously connected with the acts than others. These less obvious effects may be perfectly harmless, or they may not. When somebody chooses to follow a certain course of action with one definite outcome in mind, while clearly understanding in advance that this action will also cause other consequences that it is no part of their purpose to bring about, there is evidently a sense in which they are responsible for those secondary side-effects. They have foreseen the consequences and chosen to proceed. When this advance understanding is, for whatever reason, less than clear, there is a problem in determining the extent of responsibility. This is a general statement of the moral problem of unintended consequences, which applies in many different fields, and the complexity of which varies according to the clarity of foresight attributed to the agent.

When the main purpose is lawful, as in the case of a doctor performing a dangerous operation with consent, or administering morphine for the relief of suffering, the doctor is not taken to be responsible for the secondary consequence of the death of the patient, so long as it remains the unintended secondary consequence. When the main purpose is unlawful, involving criminal damage or harm, the question is whether or not there is further blame, and if so to what extent, when the outcome of the unlawful act goes beyond what was fully and explicitly intended. If, for example, an arsonist intends only the destruction of a building, but the fire results in the death of the occupants, the question is whether he or she can be convicted of murder or manslaughter in addition to the arson that was fully and explicitly intended. There are two distinct questions here: (1) does the arsonist in some sense intend the second outcome? And (2) to what extent is the arsonist responsible for the second outcome?

The crucial consideration in any attempt to provide coherent and consistent answers to these two questions is that of the *foreseeability* of the second consequence. There are two extreme points of reference here: (a) it was neither foreseen nor foreseeable; the deaths were entirely unpredictable and accidental, hence – it might be suggested – there is no blame at all; and (b) it was so likely to occur as to be recognised as an inevitable accompaniment of the first consequence, and hence – it might be thought – there is as much blame as if it had been fully and explicitly intended.

These are the two extremes that, in the practical reality of concrete cases, do not often apply. The third possibility (c) lies on a spectrum between these two points; the second consequence was foreseeable with varying degrees of possibility or probability. This would point to the conclusion that there was some degree of blame for the second consequence of the action, the exact extent to be determined by the level of probability.

What we have to ask now is whether there is really a clear-cut distinction between what is 'fully and explicitly intended' and what is anticipated as a possible or probable side-effect. Is the latter in any sense intended or not? In cases of type (a) – cases of genuine accident – it is difficult to see how it could be. With the other extreme (b) – given the certainty with which the outcome is contemplated – it is tempting to say that there is no difference, that the intention is really full and explicit. With the most common type (c), though, we have the difficult problem. What is deeply ambiguous here is whether or not the secondary consequence is clearly envisaged. On the one hand, it is human nature to put unwanted possibilities and dangers out of mind; on the other hand, one is reluctant to accept that in high-risk activities involving the use of fire, dynamite, guns or fast vehicles, the substantial risk of causing fatal injuries can be ignored to the extent that we can say that there was no intention at all to kill.

The traditional solution to this problem was provided by Bentham's distinction between direct and oblique intention. For Bentham, what is directly intended is a consequence, the prospect of production of which plays a causal part in bringing about the action. The consequence is obliquely intended when it is contemplated as likely to follow from the action, but played no causal part in bringing about the action (Hart 1968: 237; Bentham 1970: ch. 8, no. 6). Bentham's purpose here was to extend intention and liability beyond the confines of the directly intended results of acts to include those that are 'contemplated as likely'. Whether this is justified or not, it gives us a clear-cut distinction in as far as it excludes from direct intention anything that is not an inherent part of the plan or design behind the action; however, it does not get us much further with the question of whether the secondary consequence is clearly envisaged. What exactly does 'contemplating' as likely mean?

Glanville Williams's more recent explication of Bentham's distinction solves this by simply stipulating that, in contrast to direct intention, oblique intention is 'something you see clearly, but out of the corner of your eye'. 'Oblique' means that 'it is not in the straight line of your purpose'. He adds that oblique intent is 'a kind of knowledge or realisation' (Williams 1987: 417–21), by which he means that it is known as a moral certainty. The obliquely intended consequence, on this interpretation, is seen clearly as a virtually certain accompaniment of the directly intended consequence. This was not what Bentham had in mind, and it seems closer to our type (b), that of inseparable consequences, which actually applies to very few concrete cases, and which suggests that the 'oblique' intention is, for all practical purposes, full and explicit, which is to say that it is actually intended. The problems with cases of type (c) – the complex cases in which there are varying degrees of perceived risk attached to the act or course of action – remain unresolved.

Another popular interpretation of the direct–oblique distinction is known as 'the failure test'. This is initially more convincing. The question is whether the agent would regard the enterprise as a success or failure in the event of the non-occurrence of the intended consequences. When directly intended consequences do not occur, the enterprise is seen as a failure. With obliquely intended consequences, by contrast, their non-occurrence has no implications either way for success or failure. In the arson case, for example, the plan to destroy the building is not affected by the injury or deaths of the occupants. In the real case of *R. v. Desmond, Barrett and Others* (1868), in which several people were inadvertently killed in an attempt by the defendants to blow up the wall of Clerkenwell Jail, these deaths were not integral to the plan, which was to release the prisoners; the non-occurrence of these deaths would have been compatible with the success of the enterprise.

This failure test is certainly in line with Bentham's meaning, but all it does is provide a practical test for objectively distinguishing between acts in terms of what their agents intend to achieve. It gives no guidance on the question of the extent of their responsibility for the secondary effects that are thus non-essential to the plan, according to their state of mind with respect to these effects. If it does suggest reduced responsibility for this reason, it is misleading, because if the only way to destroy a building is by risking the death of the occupants, the oblique intention is for all practical purposes indispensable to the plan. To say then that the deaths were not required or desired to count the enterprise as a success would – given that they were calculated to be wholly unavoidable – be quite unconvincing.

It follows that the key question for determining the degree of responsibility for secondary effects relates, not to a clarification of the difference between direct and oblique, but to the kind of test that is applied by the courts to establish the *mens rea* requirement for murder. The main issue here is whether the test is a subjective one, in the sense that it is a matter of determining what the defendant actually foresaw and believed about the circumstances in which death was caused; or an objective one, in the sense that it is a matter of determining what was reasonably foreseeable and believable about those circumstances.

If the test for the *mens rea* for murder is subjective, it means that the court has to reach a conclusion from the evidence about the defendant's actual state of mind at the time of the offence. What consequences did he foresee? How likely did he believe them to be? What did he intend when he proceeded with the act? These are the questions to be asked. If, by contrast, the test is objective, it means that it is sufficient for the court to establish what it would have been reasonable to believe in the position of the defendant. What consequences should a reasonable person have foreseen? How likely in fact were they? What can the defendant be taken to have intended, bearing in mind the foreseeability and likelihood of the consequences? These are very different questions. What they indicate is what is known as the test of 'the reasonable man'.

It is important to understand how the law stands on this issue and also to ask which of these tests is more reasonable and fair, in terms of the *mens rea* for murder. Consider first the implications for the case of *Desmond, Barrett and Others*. Did Barrett in fact intend to kill the victims of the explosion? On the subjective test, his own reckoning of the situation and assessment of the risks of using dynamite, his actual foresight of what he expected to happen, would have to be assessed. This is what the prosecution would have to prove. On the objective test, they would only have to prove that any reasonable person would have foreseen the risk of causing injury or death. It would then be assumed that Barrett as a reasonable man must have foreseen it, and hence that he intended it.

This issue became controversial with a Law Lords' ruling on a very different case of 'foreseeable death' in 1961. The facts of *Smith* v. *D.P.P.* were essentially that a man trying to drive away in a car containing stolen goods caused the death of a police officer who was clinging to the door of the car. Gathering speed, the driver zigzagged until the policeman was thrown off, into the path of an oncoming car. Smith returned immediately and claimed that he had not meant any harm, that he had panicked in his attempt to escape.

Smith was convicted of murder and sentenced to death. At the Court of Criminal Appeal, the defence argued that the judge had misdirected the jury by applying the test of the reasonable man, when the test should have been whether he actually intended to cause serious harm or death. The Court agreed and substituted a conviction for manslaughter and a ten-year prison sentence. When the appeal by the Crown went to the Lords, the argument between defence and prosecution revolved around the issue of the appropriate test for *mens rea*.

Did Smith intend to kill PC Meehan? The prosecution argued that the law made a presumption that a man intends the natural and probable consequences of his acts. From that, an intent to cause serious harm or death can be inferred. Any reasonable person would have seen such harm or death as the natural consequence of driving in this manner. Smith was a reasonable man in the sense that he was neither insane nor incapable of forming an intention. Therefore, Smith must have intended serious injury or death. It was no defence to say that he did not actually foresee these consequences.

The case for the defence was that a murder conviction could only be upheld if the intention to cause serious harm or death was actually in the mind of the accused. A central point was their insistence that the presumption of intent (of natural and probable consequences) should be regarded as disprovable by the specific circumstances of the case, in this instance the claim that the defendant was driven by fear and panic. They added that if the reasonable man test is to be used, it must be that of the reasonable man in the position of the defendant.

Faced with these alternatives, the Lords came to the unanimous decision that Smith had been properly convicted of murder, and that it was indeed sufficient to apply the reasonable man test and make the presumption of intent. In rejecting what they called 'the purely subjective approach', they declared that it was self-evidently wrong because it would oblige the jury to take the word of the defendant and acquit him, and that this subjective test would constitute a serious departure from all previous law. This judgement was mainly backed up, oddly enough, by reference to the authority of O.W. Holmes. Holmes had written in 1881 that the law would not inquire whether an offender did actually foresee the consequences or not. For him, the test of foresight was not what this very criminal foresaw, but what a man of reasonable prudence would have foreseen (Holmes 1968). This was an odd authority to cite as representative of 'all previous law', because Holmes was known to be out of step with prevailing legal opinions on objective liability.

What makes it unclear whether this judgement does or does not conform with the principles of the *mens rea* doctrine is the studied ambiguity in the presumption that he intended the natural and probable consequences of his act, as to whether this presumption means that – as a sane and sober man – he must actually have done so, or that if – as a reasonable man acting unreasonably – he did not intend them, then so much the worse for him. This ambiguity pervades the judgement. Even on the former interpretation that Smith must in fact have intended the death, it means that the determination of actual intent is taken out of the hands of the jury. They are simply instructed to make the connection without reference to the defendant's own account of his actions.

Whatever the perceived rights and wrongs of this decision, it was not long before Parliament intervened to overrule it and restore the subjective test by statute, in the 1967 Criminal Justice Act, Section 8. This section implicitly rejected the reasonable man test by laying down that courts or juries were to determine whether a person had committed an offence, not by inferring intent or foresight of results of his actions solely from their natural and probable consequences, but by deciding whether he did intend or foresee them by reference to all the evidence as appears proper in the circumstances. It was this contrast between the presumption of intent and reference to 'all the evidence' that was vital. The totality of evidence included what the presumption was designed to exclude; the defendant's own account of his actions, however apparently unreasonable, are indispensable to the jury's consideration of whether or not there was actual intent to do serious harm or kill. This meant, not that the natural and probable consequences of an act were to be disregarded, but that there was to be no *presumption* that they were intended.

This clarification of the law seemed to have settled the matter in favour of the subjective test, but the following twenty years saw several decisions that appeared to throw doubt upon it. The most important was that of *Hyam* v. *D.P.P.* (1975), a case in which a woman was convicted of murder for having started a fire in which two children died. The act involved pouring petrol and newspaper through the letterbox of the front door and igniting it. On her own account, her intention was only to frighten the occupant – her lover's fiancée – into leaving the neighbourhood. Her defence was that she did not intend to start a full-scale fire, and that there was no intention to harm or kill anyone.

When Hyam's appeal against conviction for murder reached the House of Lords, having been rejected by the Court of Appeal, the conviction was again upheld, but by a narrow 3–2 majority. Included in the ruling was a declaration that the intention to cause death or really serious injury was not required, if it could be shown that the defendant intended to expose a potential victim to the *risk* of such harm. This would be sufficient, regardless of whether the defendant desired such consequences. Hyam, then, was properly convicted of murder, because, although she might not have actually intended harm or the death of her victims, she deliberately placed them at serious risk.

What this amounted to was a substantial extension of the *content* of direct intention, which was now to be understood to include the knowing and deliberate exposure of people to potentially deadly risk. At the same time, as A.S. Kenny has argued (1978), it was implicitly attempting to do away with the direct–oblique distinction, by restricting responsibility to those acts that are directly intended. What this meant was that defendants in Hyam's position had to take full responsibility for such actions, and could – if found to have deliberately created this risk, rather than intending no more than to frighten – be convicted of murder. This further specification about risk was intended by Hailsham as an explanation of why this conviction was legally sound.

Was this a covert attempt to reintroduce the objective test, the presumption that the defendant intends the natural and probable consequences of his or her actions? Did it mean that intent was being imputed to Hyam? It might appear so, if it is interpreted as meaning that, because fire and petrol are so dangerous, she could not possibly have intended less than serious injury. For the same reason, one could have drawn similar conclusions about the danger of the accelerating car in the case of *Smith*. This, however, is a common misinterpretation of the *Hyam* ruling. It was not suggested that Hyam *should*, as a reasonable person, have known the risk. The jury had to satisfy themselves that she actually did know the seriousness of the risk she was exposing the occupants to. The test remained explicitly subjective.

The crucial point is that actual intent always has to be proved. The conditions for establishing the *mens rea* for murder do not point one way or the other for the guilt or innocence of any of these defendants. The crux of the matter is that real actual intention is a necessary *mens rea* condition for murder. In the words of Lord Lane, ruling on a later case (*R. v. Nedrick*, 1986):

> a jury simply has to decide whether the defendant intended to kill or do serious bodily harm. In order to reach that decision, the jury must pay regard to all the relevant circumstances, including what the defendant himself said and did.
>
> (Allen 2001: 90)

Probability and foresight

The law on the question of the *mens rea* required for murder was clarified further and ostensibly settled in the mid-1980s, but not without further complication. There are two connected problems here. First, in the phrase 'natural and probable consequences of an act', does 'natural' mean the same as 'probable'? Second, is the intending of these consequences the same thing as foreseeing them?

For any natural course of events, which can take one turn or another, there are estimates of probability and virtual certainty of possible outcomes of acts. For any dangerous act, such as the firing of a gun, there is usually more than one possible sequence of natural consequences. If the one sequence realised in the actual world involves the death of someone in the line of fire, this outcome will be seen in retrospect as the natural – perhaps inevitable – outcome of the act. If, however, another quite different sequence were to be realised, such as the unexpected harmless deflection of the bullet, it would be seen in retrospect as an equally natural – if unlikely – outcome of the act. The point is that a process is natural regardless of whether it is seen in advance as virtually certain, as fairly probable, or as a remote possibility. Whatever the prediction, a complete chain of cause and effect will still be traceable after the event.

In any of the cases discussed in the last few sections, it seems reasonable to suppose that the degree of probability or certainty of the outcome that did in fact occur should play a vital role in arguments about the evidence for the actual intent. Consider some slight variations on the actual cases. If the constable had died as a result of being thrown back immediately from the car, rather than dragged fifty yards up the road, the much lower likelihood of death would have counted heavily in favour of the defendant. If Hyam's fire had caused deaths only by spreading to neighbouring houses because of a freak change of wind, the evidence of intent to kill would have been very much weaker. The assessment of likelihood, then, in the mind of the defendant and in the judgement of the jury, is an indispensable part of the evidence for intent.

Just as the probability of the consequences of an act is relevant as evidence for intent to kill, so also is the foresight of these consequences. If it is found that the defendant saw that X would probably happen, or was virtually certain to occur, the strength of evidence here would increase in proportion to the level of probability foreseen. The point here is that foresight is evidence of actual intent; it does not actually constitute intent. The existence of intent is inferred from the fact of foresight. It is not in itself sufficient to prove that the defendant foresaw an outcome, whatever the degree of probability or certainty. This proof is a preliminary to drawing the inference from foresight to intent, which is left to the jury.

Conclusion

These are some of the key themes in the question of what determines criminal responsibility, the details of which are regularly disputed in the appeal courts. If the doctrine of *mens rea* is broadly speaking a just one, not only in its basic principles but also in the ways in which it is converted into just decisions, the source of the idea of justice it represents remains an open question. Being subject to evolution in the common law, pronouncements and adjustments to the application of the doctrine by Parliament and the Law Lords have been guided by a concern for precedent and continuity with earlier interpretations, but such adjustment always involves clarification and thereby a new interpretation of what is supposedly already implicit in the law. What should be clear from the sample of cases is that there is a permanent tension within the concept of criminal justice, between the principles of justice as recognised by the *mens rea* doctrine and the perceived requirements of public policy.

Study questions

General question: Is *mens rea* vital to a just legal system?

Further study questions: Can there be criminal guilt if *mens rea* is not satisfied? In what sense should lack of control over one's actions excuse an offender from criminal responsibility? Compare the defences of necessity and duress. In what circumstances should constraint of the will by necessity or duress be a defence against a serious criminal charge? To what extent should we be held legally responsible for the unforeseen or unintended consequences of our actions? Should the courts apply the objective or subjective test in cases of recklessness? Is the Caldwell lacuna an inevitable loophole? Should the causing of death without direct intention be regarded as murder or as manslaughter? What is the purpose of the distinction between direct and oblique intention? Is it defensible or should it be scrapped in favour of the common meaning of intention?

Suggestions for further reading

Major contributions to the analysis of criminal responsibility and the philosophy of action include Hart (1968), Kenny (1978), Duff (1990), Norrie (1993), Katz (1987) and Moore (1993).

On free will, necessity and duress, see Mackie, 'The Grounds of Responsibility', in Hacker and Raz (1977), Norrie (1993: ch. 8), Fuller's (1949) imaginary case of 'the Speluncean Explorers' and Suber's (1998) extension of the same case. See also the selections on 'free will' in Morris (1961: IX).

On intention and foresight, see Bentham (1970: ch. 8), Hart (1968: ch. 5), Duff (1982, 1990), Gavison (1987: ch. 6), Kenny's 'Intention and Mens Rea in Murder', in Hacker and Raz (1977), Glover (1977: ch. 6) and Norrie (1993: ch. 3). See also the selections on 'intention and motive' in Morris (1961: IV).

On strict liability and crimes of negligence, see Hart (1968: ch. 6), Jacobs (1971: chaps 4, 5), Kenny (1978: chaps 1, 3) and Ten (1987: ch. 5), and also Hart's 'Legal Responsibility and Excuses', and Wasserstrom's 'Strict Liability in the Criminal Law', in Kipnis (1977). See also the selections on 'negligence, recklessness and strict liability', in Morris (1961: IV).

Elliott & Wood's Casebook on Criminal Law (Allen, 2001) contains the relevant cases and critical discussions of the problems dealt with in this chapter. Further discussions of the same cases can be found in Smith and Hogan (2002) and Elliott and Quinn (1996).

11 Insanity and diminished responsibility

When the criminal law is dealing with mentally disturbed or insane offenders, is it justified to any extent to hold them accountable and punish them for their criminal offences? This is the basic question to be broached here. What makes it particularly difficult is the enormously variable and problematic nature of the phenomenon of mental disturbance, the popular perception and scientific understanding of which have varied from one society and epoch to another. The practical difficulty in law has always been the articulation of a reliable and stable test for the kind of abnormality or insanity that would, if established, either absolve the defendant from responsibility, or at least reduce the degree of blame.

It is disagreement about the ways in which mental disturbance affects personal responsibility that makes the insanity defence or the plea of diminished responsibility controversial. On the one hand, liberal thinkers in this area regard it as pointless and unenlightened to punish people who, through no fault of their own, are afflicted with the kind of mental condition that leads them to commit harmful acts. Punishing them as if they were responsible agents is no more rational, it is argued, than the medieval practice of putting animals on trial for assault or murder. On the other hand, those with a more sceptical outlook argue that these defences are loopholes through which the guilty escape justice. This kind of scepticism is directed both at the defendants' pleas of insanity, and at the opinions of medical experts. In particular, it tends to involve the belief that moral choices can still be made by many classified as insane or mentally ill. From the liberal point of view, by contrast, it is assumed that it is in the very nature of mental illness that no such choices can be made. This is essentially the controversy, but there are many variations in the arguments, depending on the degree and type of mental disorder.

In this rather stark dispute, the most basic ideas about responsibility and its nullification are not usually contested. Even the most sceptical of critics are inclined to accept that it is not rational to blame anyone for what can be demonstrated to be an entirely unknowing, unintended or involuntary action. What is doubted in practice is that such demonstration is possible, or that perpetrators of evil deeds are genuinely in a mental condition that would justify such a description of their acts. This scepticism is compatible with the further assumption that serious mental disturbance – which under some classifications would count as insanity – does not necessarily involve the kind of cognitive impairment that would affect the ability to make moral judgements and decisions. What tends to be agreed, however, is that where impairment of these faculties is genuine, it should indeed absolve the victims of such illness from responsibility. If the mental disturbance is such that they genuinely do not know what they are doing, or believe themselves to be doing something good, or are wholly incapable of controlling their actions, it would seem impossible in all conscience to brand them as criminals.

Traditional problems with insanity

The problem of when to absolve the mentally disturbed from criminal liability has recurred and evolved throughout the history of Western legal systems. Attitudes to insanity have ranged from the relative tolerance and understanding displayed at times in European societies under the natural-istic influence of Aristotelian science and Galenic medicine, to the mystification of madness and association of it with witchcraft and demon possession in late medieval and early modern Europe. The witch-craze period between 1400 and 1700 was an age of darkness as far as the under-standing of insanity was concerned. In witch trials, which were very frequently prompted by behaviour that would otherwise have been recog-nised as symptomatic of mental illness, the insanity defence was simply unavailable. The symptoms were regarded, not as possible grounds for excul-pation, but as offering further evidence of guilt (Robinson 1996: 55).

It was the philosophical and religious problems of free will that hampered the early modern development of an understanding of insanity. The Christian doctrines of sin and redemption, requiring freedom of action as a condition for reward or damnation, evolved in such a way that the onset of mental illness was seen either as a punishment for past sins or as evidence of possession by evil spirits. Either way, the misfortune was regarded as the responsibility of the victim, who was assumed to have voluntarily consorted with the devil.

The general process of intellectual enlightenment, initiated by Descartes and his contemporaries, and culminating in the eighteenth-century Age of Enlightenment, steadily eroded this entire world-view. With the advance of natural, mechanistic explanations of human physiology, the belief in universal causation in an immanent material world led to a deterministic view of human actions in general. It was within this framework that it became possible to understand, with some semblance of scientific rigour, the various manifestations of mental illness.

One danger here is the temptation to respond to the sceptical attitude to the insanity defence by exaggerating the typical case to be regarded as deserving exculpation. In practice, there is probably no such thing as 'total insanity', or *complete* removal from reality. If the impairment were this severe, it would be difficult to imagine its victim even having the capacity to commit a crime. In ancient society and through much of the history of the common law, there was a tendency to paint insanity in black and white terms, with a caricatured lunatic understood to be completely devoid of reason. The standard test for insanity set by Bracton (1210–68) was the ability to count twenty shillings and name one's own parents. All this established was absolute basic rationality, and what was known as 'the wild-beast test' stipulated that, to qualify as insane, one had to have no more reason than that of such a beast. 'A madman is not able to bargain nor to do anything in the way of business for he does not understand what he has done ... such [mad]men are not greatly removed from beasts for they lack reasoning' (Biggs 1955: 82). In 1581, it was declared by Lambard that 'if a mad man or a naturall foole, or a lunatike in the time of his lunacie ... do kil a man, this is no felonious act, nor anything forfeited by it' (Biggs 1955: 84). Only complete 'lunacy' and total absence of knowledge of good and evil were regarded as grounds for exculpation. It was nevertheless significant that this bare minimum was established, because it meant the recognition in principle of insanity as a defence to murder, even if it applied to very few offenders.

Despite this tendency towards an all-or-nothing approach to insanity, the great common law authorities moved inexorably towards naturalistic explanation. The seventeenth-century classifications of mental disorders by Sir Edward Coke (1552–1634) and Sir Matthew Hale (1609–76) pointed towards complete secularisation of the law. What was increasingly recognised, with the growing influence of medical science, was the different kinds of 'idiocy' and 'dementia' within the category of *non compos mentis*, including the recognition of temporary insanity. Despite Hale's traditional reliance on Holy Scripture and his personal belief in witchcraft, his approach to mental illness and the legal problem of responsibility was guided by the science and medicine of his day (Hale 1972). Throughout this period, however, the test for insanity remained that of a complete deprivation of reason at the time of the offence.

The radical break with the past came in 1800 with the case of *Hadfield*, who had made an ineffective attempt on the King's life at Drury Lane Theatre. A veteran soldier who had sustained severe head wounds, Hadfield was in the grip of a delusion that he was the new messiah, commanded by God to assassinate George III. With the benefit of being defended by the famous advocate Thomas Erskine (1750–1823), and with medical testimony from one of the founders of modern psychiatry, Sir Alexander Crichton, Hadfield was acquitted on the grounds of insanity. Using Crichton's testimony to maximum effect, Erskine succeeded in persuading the court that, in the light of the new science, the traditional law on insanity – requiring total deprivation of reason – was hopelessly outdated. Despite his brain injuries, which had also led him to attempt to kill his own child, Hadfield was in many respects sane and rational. The legal turning point here was that this partial rationality was readily conceded by the defence, who argued that it should not count against the case for insanity. This was because, or so they argued, legal insanity was no longer to be determined by the wild-beast test, but the test of *delusion*. If it could be proved that the defendant was suffering from a specific delusionary belief that caused him to commit the offence, then – notwithstanding his being in other respects sane and reasonable – he was not responsible for the act. What this meant was that partial insanity, in the sense of being judged insane without being completely devoid of reason, was to be recognised by the law for the first time.

The case of Daniel M'Naghten

The case that led to the settling of English law on insanity for more than a century was that of *M'Naghten* (1843). Daniel M'Naghten, charged with the murder of Edward Drummond, secretary to the Prime Minister, Sir Robert Peel, pleaded insanity. It was undisputed that his real target was Peel himself. The defence for M'Naghten was that he was in the grip of an insane delusion that the local Tory Party in his native Edinburgh was conspiring to kill him. Even when he attempted to escape to France, he believed that he was pursued by Tory agents disguised as Jesuit priests. Convinced that Peel, as leader of the party, was personally responsible, he decided that he could only stop the persecution by killing him. The unanimous opinion of the doctors who examined M'Naghten was that this delusion was and remained quite genuine.

The prosecution argued that Erskine (in *Hadfield*) had been wrong to maintain that delusion was sufficient for the insanity defence, when the accused knew the difference between good and evil, as M'Naghten in this case surely did. This argument, however, was overwhelmed by another dazzling display of advocacy in conjunction with the new medical science. For the defence, Alexander Cockburn – the future Lord Chief Justice – quoted extensively from Dr Isaac Ray to discredit all the tests and assumptions of the prescientific age. Crucially, he persuaded the court that the new scientific psychiatry proved beyond all doubt that a man could be 'the victim of the most fearful delusions, the slave of uncontrollable impulses' (Robinson 1996: 168), while still able to function normally in other respects. With regard to M'Naghten, he persuaded them that he had acted under the influence of such a delusion, believing it to be a reasonable act of self-defence. Faced with one-sided medical evidence for the defendant, the judge stopped the trial and gave the jury what amounted to a direction to acquit on the grounds of insanity.

The furore that followed this acquittal was largely due to the belief that M'Naghten – like others before him – was simply a political assassin trying to escape justice by taking the insanity defence. Given that the 1840s was a time of growing unrest and revolutionary agitation, this was not entirely implausible. In response to this controversy, Queen Victoria – herself a victim of three assassination attempts – intervened by demanding from the House of Lords a clarification of the law on insanity. Five questions on the test for criminal responsibility in cases of insanity were then put by the Lords to the sixteen most senior judges. The answers delivered on behalf of the majority by Lord Chief Justice Tindal became the text known subsequently as 'the M'Naghten Rules'.

The formulation of the M'Naghten Rules

Over the years since the Hadfield decision, the law had dealt with insanity cases in an *ad hoc* manner, with various cases decided on apparently contradictory principles. What the authors of the M'Naghten Rules now sought to lay down was a clear guideline on how the law stood and on how juries were to be instructed. The meaning of the text that emerged from their deliberations on the history of common law on the subject was not entirely clear. The main difficulties arose from the abandonment of the clear-cut rationality tests of Bracton and Hale, the intrusion into law of medical science and the problem of understanding partial insanity and delusion. In other words, the conceptual difficulties started when the law began to take mental disorders seriously and to formulate general principles to guide the legal response to these disorders. Bearing this in mind, it is hardly surprising that the Rules that were laid down in these circumstances were not a model of clarity.

The main preoccupation of the questions and answers was to clarify the law on cases of partial delusion, in which offenders 'are not in other respects insane' (Allen 2001: 216). Three main issues arose from the judges' answers to questions about the criminal responsibility of such offenders:

- the offender's knowledge of the nature and quality of the act;
- the offender's knowledge of right and wrong, moral and legal;
- the excusability of the act that the offender believed himself to be committing.

The central point in the Rules is the judges' opinion that the insanity defence can only succeed if it is proved that:

> at the time of committing the act, the accused was labouring under such a defect of reason, from disease of the mind, as not to know the nature and quality of the act he was doing, *or*, if he did know it, that he did not know he was doing what was wrong.
>
> (Allen 2001: 216)

What they appear to mean here is that he must either not know what he is doing, in the sense that he does not understand that he is killing, or he does not know that this act of killing is wrong.

On the matter of knowing right from wrong, the answers are ambiguous. On the one hand, the judges reply that a partly deluded offender is punishable 'if he knew at the time of committing such crime that he was acting contrary to law'. On the other hand, switching to the language of moral value, they concede that the offender is punishable if 'conscious that the act was one that he ought not to do', if this coincides with violation of the law.

The most important point here concerns the distinction between the offender having general awareness of the difference between right and wrong – which indicates no more than the antiquated rationality test – and, more specifically, his 'knowledge of right and wrong, in respect to the very act with which he is charged'. In other words, he might have complete moral integrity without understanding that his own act is wrong, because of the nature of his delusion. M'Naghten and Hadfield, like many others, knew perfectly well that murder was wrong, but did not regard their own acts as murder. If the offender has the more specific understanding, the judges decided, then he is punishable. The question of knowing the law of the land, which virtually all offenders will be aware prohibits murder, obscures this issue of specific understanding.

The third point is the most difficult. The fourth question had asked whether a person committing an offence as a consequence of an insane delusion as to existing facts is thereby excused. The judges replied by dividing possible cases of delusion into two categories, those in which the imagined facts would have excused the act, and those in which they would not. 'We think he must be considered in the same situation as to responsibility as if the facts with respect to which the delusion exists were real' (Allen 2001: 217). Had the situation actually been as he in his deluded state imagined it, the criminal liability that would then have obtained is applied to the situation in which he now finds himself. The example given in the Rules is that if he believes himself to be responding legitimately to a deadly threat, he will not be held liable. If, on the other hand, he believes himself to be avenging an injury to his character or fortune, he will be held liable. This is how it would be if there were no delusion. In place of the plea of self-defence, those in the position of M'Naghten, for example, can plead insanity. Those who imagine themselves to be avenging an insult cannot.

Criticisms of the M'Naghten Rules

Despite the resilience and longevity of these Rules as the legal test for the insanity defence, they have been subjected to relentless criticism since their adoption in the 1840s. There are several types of criticism, coming from different directions.

The most general criticism is that, due to the ambiguity and vagueness of the language, especially on the legal–moral distinction, they are open to multiple interpretation that undermines their credentials as a clear and reliable guideline. Coupled with this is the criticism that they fail to provide general principles adequate to the task of dealing with the variety of particular cases that the courts have to face. The vagueness especially applies to the concept of *knowing*. 'Knowing' the nature and quality of the act can be taken to indicate a literal understanding that, for example, guns are potentially lethal; or it can be taken in the more complex sense of appreciating the implications of the act of firing a gun. If the usage of the word is such that it can be taken either way, interpretation can be either factual or normative. This applies also to the phrase 'nature and quality'. This is interpreted by some to mean simply that the agent understands what he is doing, the two words being taken as near-synonyms. By others, it is interpreted as meaning an understanding of the nature of an act as what it factually *is*, and seeing the *moral* quality of the act. This confusion of factual and normative, it is commonly suggested, will inevitably lead to inconsistent interpretations of what the Rules require.

A more specific criticism relates to the coherence of the delusion test. The division of delusion into two categories – those in which the act would be justified if the imagined facts were real, and those that would not – is initially plausible, but on closer analysis is not entirely clear. One aspect of this criticism is that this rule is based on an artificial compartmentalisation of beliefs, implying the kind of distinctions that only an unimpaired rational mind can draw. With the partially insane, the ability to distinguish between life-threatening situations and relatively harmless ones is precisely what is said to have been lost or at least impaired. If someone commits murder in the belief that it is an appropriate response to an imagined insult, would this really be any less insane a delusion than that of one who believes himself to be defending his life? With all such delusions, the ability to make rational discriminations is at least seriously impaired. There is, furthermore, a deeper problem here. Is it really intelligible to instruct sane members of a jury to assess the excusability of an act carried out in the deluded belief that, for example, the defendant is the new messiah commanded by God to sacrifice himself, or that his victim is an agent of Satan, as if these 'facts' were *real*?

Historically, the most significant criticism of the Rules is that, in their tests for liability, they are narrowly and exclusively cognitive. They are said to be narrowly cognitive in the sense that they treat the state of knowing in a very restricted way, ruling out any emotional component of knowledge. It is therefore sufficient that defendants have formal knowledge of the nature and quality of the act, without needing full realisation and understanding. The Rules are said to be exclusively cognitive in that they focus solely on the cognitive, to the exclusion of other aspects of the defendant's state of mind, in particular, the volitional.

As we saw in the last chapter, one of the basic conditions for *mens rea* is that, at the time of the offence, there is an unconstrained will. If this freedom of will is absent or severely constrained, it is assumed to be an injustice to hold the agent responsible for the act. We also saw, however, that this was deeply problematic in the context of the defences of necessity and duress. It is no less so with the insanity defence. Most critics of the M'Naghten Rules have focused their fire on the absence of the volitional condition, which is simply ignored in the Rules, thereby – the critics argue – opening up a wide gap for unjust convictions.

It is undeniable that the sole concern of the Rules is with what the agents believe and understand about what they are doing and about the rights and wrongs of it. There is no provision for offenders whose mental disturbance consists in their inability to prevent themselves from committing offences that they fully understand to be criminal and morally wrong. The criticism has been based on the claim that a large proportion of those who should be excused on grounds of insanity can be shown to be suffering from this kind of inability, rather than a demonstrable cognitive impairment. They might know perfectly well how bad the act is, but be unable to control themselves. For such offenders, treatment is said to be more appropriate than punishment. The most prominent demand of the campaign for the amendment of the Rules has accordingly been the inclusion of an 'irresistible impulse' clause, whereby those who are demonstrably incapable of resisting criminal impulses are also treated as insane.

Before we consider the problems with the irresistible impulse argument, it should be noted that this was not a post-M'Naghten innovation or an expression of an ultra-liberal interpretation of mental illness based on modern psychiatry. It was a response that arose immediately in Britain and the USA to the M'Naghten tightening up of the legal definition of insanity. In fact, it does no more than hark back to the original challenge to the anachronistic rationality test in Erskine's speech in 1800 and Cockburn's advocacy for M'Naghten in 1843. Each of these – rightly or wrongly – understood the new medical science to have demonstrated a close link between 'fearful delusions' and 'slaves of uncontrollable impulses' (Robinson 1996: 168). A volitional insanity defence, then, should have arisen naturally from the admissibility of partial insanity as a defence. Instead, the M'Naghten Rules closed the door on it.

Defences of the M'Naghten Rules

Defences of the Rules have been aimed in two directions: at those who regard them as too broad and liberal, allowing the insanity defence to offenders who do not merit it; and at those who see them as too restricted and illiberal, unjustly condemning as criminal and often executing too many mentally ill offenders.

The charge of ambiguity and vagueness can come from either direction. It can be argued by critics that this looseness of language allows too much discretion for the judicial direction of juries, allowing judges to exercise their own bias for or against those taking the insanity defence. Or it can be argued that this indeterminacy results in unreliable general principles, inevitably leading to inconsistency and injustice. Against either of these criticisms, defenders of the Rules have seen this indeterminacy as the virtue of flexibility, rather than as the vice of ambiguity. It enables the court to deal with the unique facts of each individual concrete case appropriately.

As far as the charge of incoherence is concerned, there is no real answer other than to deny it and reassert the validity of the delusion test. If it is true that the Rules do not make good sense, it would seem that there is no convincing answer to the case for replacing them. A very general reply to this is that the Rules have provided a legal definition of insanity, rather than a medical one. As such, they are concerned not with a definitive distinction between the sane and the insane, but rather with a delicate balancing act between the requirements of justice and the need to protect the public from the criminally insane. What this involves is a practical decision within the legal profession on who is to be held criminally responsible and who is not. Bearing this in mind, it is said to be impossible to formulate general principles that are perfectly coherent.

Within the English legal system, resistance to the century-long campaign for an irresistible impulse amendment to the M'Naghten Rules has been implacable. A parliamentary bill in 1923, proposing the addition of a clause that it be proved that the defendant was capable of conforming his action with the law, was defeated in the House of Lords. Several recommendations in later years were also emphatically rejected. The reasoning behind this peculiarly English scepticism towards the idea of impulses that cannot be controlled is very complex, but there are three main types of argument.

The first and most obvious objection, frequently voiced in Parliament, is that the admission of irresistible impulse would have the effect of increasing the number of insanity defences beyond an acceptable level. In one sense, this implies that too many sane and cunning people would be capable of exploiting this defence; in another sense, it implies that the defence itself would be suspect, because even people genuinely subject to irresistible impulse should not be excused; everyone should be responsible for their own impulses – especially when the impulses are murderous – irresistible or otherwise.

A second type of argument questions the intelligibility of the concept of irresistible impulse. Kenny, for example, has argued that an impulse is by definition something that can be resisted (Kenny 1978). He argued further that, if there really is such a thing as the kind of compulsive behaviour that would remove criminal responsibility, it would have to be a literally unstoppable causal force. The test he suggests for such a force is that the agent would be compelled to perform these irresistible acts even if a policeman was standing next to him. People who display enough cunning to avoid the attention of the law cannot be deemed to be out of control of their own actions.

This scepticism was also voiced by Barbara Wootton (Wootton 1981), arguing from a quite different point of view that all criminals should be treated rather than punished. Her influential argument in this context was that one should not be too ready to infer from the fact that an impulse *has* not been resisted, to the conclusion that it *could* not have been resisted. The assumptions she challenged were that impulses are always overwhelming, rather than mere temptation; that the more evil the impulse, the more difficult it must be to resist.

In Britain, sceptical arguments such as these against the introduction of irresistible impulse as a defence have prevailed. The significance of this issue, however, was radically altered by two pieces of legislation, the 1957 Homicide Act and the abolition of capital punishment in 1965.

Diminished responsibility and the 1957 Homicide Act

Instead of any amendment to or clarification of the M'Naghten Rules, a new special defence of diminished responsibility, adapted from Scottish law, was introduced into English law in 1957. This was partly a response to the long-standing dissatisfaction with the Rules, designed as it was to cover cases that do not involve the kind of cognitive impairment required for the full insanity defence. Insanity was and remains a complete defence – under the same Rules – which if successful leads to acquittal and confinement for life in a psychiatric hospital. In such cases, there is no responsibility. With the plea of diminished responsibility, the defendant is pleading not guilty to murder, but guilty to manslaughter on the grounds that he is less than fully responsible for his action. It is this reduction, this partial responsibility, that constitutes the important innovation. The defendant is held to be less than fully culpable, by virtue of what is now called 'abnormality of mind', in place of the much more specific 'defect of reason' in the M'Naghten Rules.

This plea has largely replaced that of insanity, because it leads to a definite prison sentence, rather than an indefinite confinement under the 1959 Mental Health Act. Until the abolition of capital punishment in 1965, defendants successful in either defence avoided the death sentence.

According to Section 2 of the 1957 Homicide Act, any person accused of killing or being a party to killing:

> shall not be convicted of murder if he was suffering from such abnormality of mind – whether arising from a condition of arrested or retarded development of mind or any inherent causes or induced by disease or injury – as substantially impaired his mental responsibility for his acts and omissions in doing or being a party to the killing.
>
> (Allen 2001: 528)

The key points here are abnormality of mind and substantial impairment of responsibility. What a jury is called upon to decide is, first, whether there is such abnormality, and, second, whether this has led to sufficient impairment of the defendant's responsibility to merit a reduction of the verdict from murder to manslaughter. At the same time, it must be found that there is sufficient responsibility – it is diminished, not negated – to merit a sentence appropriate for manslaughter. In reaching these decisions, the jury is expected to take into account the evidence of medical experts only as one component of the evidence as a whole, including all witness statements and the demeanour of the defendant.

The 1957 Act, then, has replaced the 'insanity or nothing' situation with an alternative flexible enough to counter many of the criticisms of the M'Naghten Rules. The criterion of mental abnormality, replacing the strictly cognitive test, is deliberately phrased in such a way that juries are free to interpret it as emotional instability or constrained will, if they believe that this is enough to prove substantial impairment of responsibility. When a judge in 1961 attempted to exclude these non-cognitive factors, he was overruled on appeal (Bavidge 1989: 26). It was also through the 1957 Act that irresistible impulse was tacitly admitted, as acknowledged in the ruling on *Byrne* (1960), in which it was accepted that the 'inability to exercise will power to control physical acts', providing this inability results from the kind of mental abnormality specified in the Act, is allowable as a defence to murder (Allen 2001: 533).

Conclusion

What this reform of the law has amounted to in practice is a recognition that both mental disturbance and responsibility are a matter of degree, and a belief that the borders of insanity are grey areas in which the good sense of the jury, with the benefit of all evidence available, is the most reliable method for determining the presence of abnormality and the degree of responsibility. Historically speaking, this is a long way from the wild-beast test. Neither the 1957 Act nor the M'Naghten Rules require the defendant to be entirely devoid of rationality. The tension between liberal and sceptical responses to mentally disturbed offenders persists, but the test for criminal liability remains distinctively legal.

Study questions

General question: Is there a coherent and fair rationale behind the current excusing conditions for insane and mentally disturbed offenders?

Further study questions: Are the M'Naghten Rules consistent with the doctrine of *mens rea*? Is the delusion test a reasonable one? Is the criticism that the Rules are narrowly and exclusively cognitive justifiable? Was the exclusion of the volitional clause of *mens rea* from the insanity defence justifiable? Should an 'irresistible impulse' defence excuse an offender from criminal responsibility? Has the introduction of the concept of diminished responsibility solved all the problems raised by the M'Naghten Rules?

Suggestions for further reading

Recommended general works on insanity and the law are Robinson (1996), Reznek (1997), Fingarette (1972), Fingarette and Hasse (1979), Bavidge (1989) and Schopp (1991). There are also important analyses in Hart (1968: chaps 8, 9), Jacobs (1971: ch. 2), Ten (1987: ch. 6), Norrie (1993: ch. 9), Murphy (1979: chaps 9–11) and Kenny (1978: ch. 4). Porter (1987) and (2002) are excellent short histories of insanity.

For further information and analysis of the M'Naghten Trial and Rules, see Robinson (1996: ch. 5), Keeton (1961), West and Walk (1977), and Biggs (1955: ch. 4). See also the selections on 'legal insanity' in Morris (1961: VIII). The M'Naghten Rules are reprinted in numerous anthologies, including Morris (1961: 395), as well as in *Elliott & Wood's Casebook on Criminal Law* (Allen 2001: 4.1), which also contains other relevant cases and critical discussion of the problems dealt with in this chapter.

12 Theories of punishment

The institution of state punishment is so widespread in the contemporary world that the question of justifying its very existence does not often arise. This is partly because the answer seems so obvious. Without any structure of positive sanctions in place, it is assumed, normal social transactions could not be governed by law. Without any mechanism for coercion or enforcement of legal norms, we could hardly speak of a legal system at all. Close analysis of the justification of punishment, however, reveals serious tensions, not only between competing theoretical perspectives but also between conflicting practical attitudes on questions about what kinds of punishment are morally acceptable. Various defences of the existing systems offer inconsistent accounts of the principles underlying punishment. They also collide with proposals for penal reform and even with frankly abolitionist arguments. What philosophical analysis over the last few centuries has aimed at is a clear examination of the principles in conflict here.

The problem of justification

We need first to remember why state punishment requires justification. Like many other common practices, punishment is at least *prima facie* problematic because it involves the kind of treatment that in any other context would be morally indefensible. As is well known, the history of the practice of punishment has spanned the full range, from the mildest of penalties to the most cruel and inhumane treatment imaginable. Even in an age when we like to think that most state punishment is relatively humane, policies such as the death penalty or imprisonment, involving the deprivation of life or liberty, clearly stand in need of justification.

It has often been found instructive to compare this question about justifying punishment with other, non-punitive instances of state coercion, which are also in their very nature morally problematic. Any state action or policy that involves the apparent violation of individual rights requires a special justification. Emergency measures in times of national crisis, the introduction of military conscription or national service, the Prevention of Terrorism Act and other suspensions of specific civil liberties are generally agreed to be subject to special justification. Non-punitive coercion also includes practices such as the rationing of scarce resources, the requisitioning of property or internment of enemy citizens in wartime, compulsory purchase and the enforced quarantine of blameless victims of contagious diseases. None of these examples normally involve punishment or penalisation; nevertheless all of them are, to say the least, morally questionable and need to be justified.

Apart from the obvious consideration that the question of whether such measures can be justified will depend on the specific circumstances in each case, it at first seems that there is only one type of justification available, that of reference to ends and the invocation of 'necessary evil'. The greater the danger to be averted or the greater good to come out of the action — in terms of public safety, public health or national security – implies that the ends are desirable enough to outweigh the distress or inconvenience involved in the means. The assumption, then, is that the only justification available for such 'harsh measures' is based on an instrumental, means–ends type of reasoning.

Does it follow that the practice of state punishment is of the same order as these other questionable practices and that justification must follow the same instrumental route? Some philosophers have certainly thought so. Surely, it might be argued, the victims of such policies are blameless and, if such treatment can be justified, then the punishment of the guilty can *a fortiori* be justified along the same lines.

To show that this argument is too peremptory, we need to look more closely at the claim that all morally questionable acts can only be justified by instrumental reason. Is it possible to justify such an act without any refer-ence at all to the good that will come out of it? One way to argue this would be to deny that the act was in fact morally questionable, or 'an evil' in itself. To argue that an activity is 'perfectly justified' is often to claim that there is nothing wrong with it, that those who disapprove are entirely mistaken. In a wider context, this is frequently said in defence of 'victimless' crimes, where no harm has been done. Another way, however, is to accept that in normal circumstances the act would be indefensible, but that in these unusual circumstances it is justified in itself as a response to another act. Thus, one might argue that 'a justified outburst' or 'justified anger' at an unwarranted attack on oneself or another is a morally appropriate response to provoca-tion and contemplated without any view to the future. This could, of course, be represented as covertly instrumental, in that the justification is derived from the intention to defend one's interests, character or reputation. The ends again justify the means. This tendency, however, to reduce all justifica-tions to forward-looking ones, with reference only to goals or objectives, obscures an important normative distinction.

To take the most serious example as an illustration of how this occurs, consider the procedures for justifying a military war against a clearly identi-fiable evil. For genuine justification here – as opposed to rationalisation before or after the fact – one has to present compelling reasons for taking one course of action rather than another. To justify the resort to war, it is clear that the means employed must be a considerably lesser evil than the evil the war is intended to put a stop to. In addition, it needs to be shown that the response is appropriate and proportionate to the threat, that there are no effective alternatives to achieve the same objective, that non-combatant casualties are kept to a minimum, and that overall there is a realistic chance of success. Above all, though, the crucial condition for a just war is the antecedent one that the cause is just, that the war is genuinely against 'a clearly identifiable evil'.

While the instrumentalist strain of reasoning behind such justifications is predominant, this should not obscure the rival normative claim that the basic reason for morally endorsing a war precedes any instrumental thinking. Before any calculations of the prospect of success, or acceptance of the constraints aimed at minimising the negative consequences, the fundamental point is that it is already justified by the cause. For intrinsicalist thinking, the justification already exists; the course of action is justified by what has happened, such as an act of unprovoked aggression, not by predicted outcomes. As a chosen course of action, the war is claimed to be right in itself, not by virtue of events beyond itself. Having *the moral right* to fight a war is quite distinct from whether or not it is a good idea. Clear statements of war aims, though highly desirable, are quite distinct from an evaluation of the initial moral and legal legitimacy of the war. Entitlement precedes practicability.

Instrumental and intrinsic angles on justification do not necessarily conflict in practice, but there is a strong tendency in philosophical analysis for the partisans of each side to attempt to eliminate or marginalise the other, arguing about where the 'real' justification is to be found. The difficulty here lies in the fact that, while these two perspectives can frequently complement one another, they can and do easily come into direct conflict. This is sometimes represented as the clash between principle and pragmatism, or between idealised and realistic justification. This is not entirely appropriate, because it is easy to see how advocates of the two positions can swap roles in this respect, with the intrinsicalist prepared to justify anything for the sake of the just cause, and the instrumentalist with an eye to the future insisting on proper restraints in the conduct of the war.

Punishment justified by its effects

Something very similar to this kind of moral conflict and confusion lies behind the disputes over the justification of punishment. Given that state punishment can involve extremely harsh treatment, which in normal circumstances (which is to say, without good cause) would be regarded with horror, philosophers who adopt the instrumentalist outlook insist that the only justification for such drastic measures must lie in the compensating benefits that will come out of it. The standard practice of imposing long periods of imprisonment for serious crime, for example, can only be justified if this practice as a whole is at least partly instrumental in the reduction or control of crime. If it cannot be justified with reference to these or some other social goals, then punishment inflicted for its own sake would be seen as nothing more than pointless cruelty, and hence manifestly unjustified. The basic requirement of justification is that the punishment has some definite purpose.

What this purpose might be varies enormously. To define it as the reduction of crime is the most general statement of the purpose of punishment, thus understood. For this reason, this perspective is often referred to as 'reductivism' (Walker 1991). This objective is in turn justified in terms of more general moral aims, such as the need for personal security and the opportunity to fulfil human potential. This in turn is justified until we reach a goal – such as the utilitarian standard of the general happiness – that does not need to be justified in any other terms. That is to say, we reach a goal that has non-instrumental value.

The reductivist aim is itself broken down into many specific penal strategies, with widely varying moral implications. The most obvious preventive strategy is the use of temporary or permanent confinement – either in prison or psychiatric hospital – to neutralise or incapacitate dangerous offenders. Consequently, the most basic justification of punishment is the need to remove offenders from society. Taken in isolation, this justification is morally equivalent to the enforced quarantine of carriers of deadly diseases. Second, one of the central reductivist strategies is the threat or the implementation of punitive sanctions in order to discourage or pre-empt the need for punishment. What this involves is the use of punishment as a deterrent, in a specific form to deter its recipient from reoffending, and in a general form to discourage others from committing the same kind of offence.

In addition to the goals of prevention and deterrence, reductivist strategies have included various attempts to adjust the behaviour of persistent offenders. The ideal aim here is to achieve the rehabilitation or reintegration of the offender into society. This rehabilitative ideal takes us beyond the scope of the standard consequentialist theories of punishment, primarily based on prevention and deterrence, because it ranges from the kind of moral education and reform strategies that see punishment itself as the agent of such effects, to approaches that regard the adjustment of the offender's behaviour as a preferable alternative to punishment. The latter includes the belief that offenders can be 'cured' of their criminal tendencies by various kinds of aversion therapy. Overall, though, this general goal of rehabilitation still exemplifies a broadly instrumental approach to the problem of justification, in that it rests on the assumption that this is the only way to justify either openly punitive practices or compulsory reformative alternatives.

The instrumental justification of punishment requires that at least one of these strategies lies behind its practice. The condition of its justification is that the evil of punishing is outweighed by one or more of these compensating benefits.

Justifying punishment retrospectively

For those who look exclusively to the present and the past for justification, the good that may come out of the practice of state punishment is contingent or incidental to the justification. Whether or not there exists a right to punish depends on what has already happened. The various social and individual benefits of the practice – the prevention and reduction of crime, the creation of greater peace and security, the effects on the offenders and their victims – are recognised as important considerations in themselves, but also as outcomes to be encouraged quite independently of the legitimacy of punishing. The right, in other words, precedes the good. The right to punish is derived from the offender's breaking of the law, or from his or her violation of the rights of others. How exactly the right to punish is derived from these past events rather than from projections into the future is, for the retrospectivist, the crux of the justification problem.

The main issue for retrospectivists, then, is how far they succeed in fixing a strictly non-consequential horizon. In its purest versions, the committing of a crime is both necessary and sufficient for the justification of punishment. The crime in some sense calls for or demands a punitive response. The classic statement of this claim was made by Hegel (1770–1831), who represented both crime and punishment in terms of the negation or annulment of its opposite. Punishment is justified because it nullifies or makes nothing of the crime; it negates it both legally and morally. This is why, morally speaking, it can be done, and why it has to be done; the state has both the right and the duty to punish.

This was one version of what is known as retributivism. Although the literal meaning of 'retribution' concerns the idea of the duty of repayment or reparation for wrongs committed, the connotations attaching to this ancient term are much wider. The core concept of the traditional theories of retribution is that of desert, indicating the principle that punishment should be given to people according to what they justly deserve, rather than to what we may feel is necessary for purposes of deterrence or rehabilitation.

Most of the other key retributive concepts revolve around this one. The right to retaliate with equivalent force against intentional violations of the moral code as enforced by the law is intrinsically linked with the idea that wrongdoing deserves punishment of the same level of seriousness as the offence. The general idea that retributive justice is the proper goal of punishment, rather than consequentialist calculations of outcomes, is also based on the idea of just deserts. Desert lies behind the retributive belief that the suffering inflicted by the punishment on the guilty is not an intrinsic evil to be regretted, but on the contrary a desirable state of affairs. This can only be so if those who have inflicted suffering on others can be said to deserve to suffer themselves. Each of these elements of the retributive justification is essentially backward-looking; the repayment, the retaliation, the deserved sufferings for past wrongs, all seem to be purely retrospective in their frame of reference.

Several other elements combine to produce the standard retributive justification. One of the more prominent is the Kantian insistence that the precondition of just punishment is that it treats offenders with respect for their dignity and capacity for free choice. Treating offenders as ends in themselves is the positive requirement here, but what is perhaps more important is what this prescription rules out, the use of others 'merely as a means' for greater social objectives.

Criticisms of the traditional theories

The most general and fundamental criticism of the forward-looking, instrumental approach is the claim that it is unjustifiably lenient in its implications for penal policy, that it releases the state from its obligation to punish crime in accordance with desert. Retributivists argue that, if desert is removed from the justification, nothing is left to prevent inappropriately light sentencing for serious crime. The role played by desert in this respect cannot be taken over by deterrence, because it is precisely the restriction of the goal of punishment to this unpredictable factor that destabilises the entire institution of state punishment.

It may at first seem paradoxical that the other main type of criticism focuses on the personal dignity and rights of those who are liable to be punished by consequentialists. The first aspect of this line of criticism is the belief that we – or the state – owe it to the offenders themselves to punish them as if they were free reasoning agents. If offenders are punished in accordance with factors extraneous to the fact and nature of their crime, or their degree of culpability, the implication is that they are being treated – contrary to the Kantian dictum – merely as a means to an end, rather than as responsible human agents. This idea that it is morally repugnant to regard people merely as objects for manipulation is applied generally to the practice of punishment, but it is thought especially relevant to the forcible re-educative and 'curative' rehabilitation programmes favoured by some consequentialists. A typically retributive view is that even the most severe punishment is less dehumanising than this kind of 'treatment'.

The second aspect of this line of criticism is that there is an irresistible logic whereby the unrestricted pursuit of utility leads to outright injustice. This is a criticism applied much more broadly to utilitarianism as a moral theory, but it becomes particularly focused in the philosophy of punishment. The danger in this respect is quite clear. If the administration of punishment, especially in sentencing, were to be guided solely by considerations of social policy and expediency, calculating the best probable consequences for society as a whole, there would be no limit to the potential injustice suffered by individuals or minority groups for the sake of the general good. There would be no restraint on favouritism or victimisation, or on the nature of the punishment. Even the complete absence of guilt would provide no good reason for not punishing, if the occasional scapegoating of the innocent could be shown to be in the public interest. This, it is often said, is the logical conclusion of making the justification of punishment purely forward-looking. The overall criticism is that, when the core requirements of guilt and desert are removed, there remains no steadiness of purpose or stability in the philosophy of punishment. Every policy is subject to variation and experimentation.

It is in their attack on this inherent lack of control or limitation on the instrumentalist approach that retributivists score most heavily. Their insistence that prospective benefits – even the prospect of the complete elimination of a particularly threatening crime – do not give the state the right to punish, that this can only be derived from the prior fact and nature of the crime and what the criminal thereby deserves, puts them in a position to make the retributivist case persuasive by virtue of its focus on the injustice of punishing the innocent, which makes an almost universal appeal to moral intuition.

Weaknesses of retributivism

The weaknesses found in traditional retributivism fall under three headings: (1) doubts about its status as a moral justification; (2) problems with intelligibility; and (3) problems of rationality. Overall, it has been argued by critics that retributivism is morally dubious, that its key concepts are incorrigibly vague or ambiguous, and that it is based on feeling rather than reason. It will become clear that these sets of problems are interconnected, but it is important first to isolate them as distinct weaknesses.

The moral status problem

This is seen by many consequentialist critics as the basic and decisive one. Retributivism, it is said, does not really qualify as a moral theory of justification at all, because it is based on the premoral instincts to retaliate and take revenge. What this sanctions is the taking of sadistic pleasure in the self-righteous infliction of suffering. The point of constructing a modern moral theory is to civilise our instincts, not to give them free rein by institutionalising them.

Traditional retributivists hold that the state draws not only the right but also the duty to punish exclusively from the fact and nature of the crime, rather than from any benefits the punishment might produce. The duty as well as the right to punish is strictly backward-looking. This is the source of the most damaging criticisms of the retributive case. If the duty arises solely from what cannot be undone, it is argued, the state has no moral alternative but to exact retribution, regardless of the good or evil that may come out of it, even if a non-punitive response would be manifestly preferable. In this respect, it is argued, they are saddled with an outdated superstition, that every crime must be paid for, regardless of exonerating circumstances. On this line of reasoning, the logical conclusion of retributivism is a completely irrational and vindictive insistence on punishment for its own sake.

The retaliatory character of the retributivist justification is central to Kant's philosophy of punishment and is rooted in the ancient biblical doctrine of *lex talionis*. A standard line of defence against the criticism that retributivism is rooted in an Old Testament morality of vengeance, from which we should long since have distanced ourselves, is that even in the original sources these maxims were intended to civilise rather than to urge vengeance. The idea is that the 'eye for an eye' maxim was a judicial rule aimed at limiting revenge to inflicting equivalent harm – that is, to take no more than an eye – rather than insisting that justice demands the taking of revenge. It has to be said that there is little support for this interpretation in the relevant passages, which do seem to insist upon responding punitively, rather than urging restraint in the response. It is quite possible, of course, that both meanings can be intended simultaneously. Even on the softer interpretation, however, the question of whether the returning of 'like for like' is really a moral response remains unresolved.

Although appeals to intuition are frequent in this debate, they do not seem to take us much further, because there is a deep intuitive conflict on this matter. While some find it self-evident that a serious offence intrinsically merits an equally serious punishment, others find it intuitively obvious that punishment for the sole purpose of retribution is pointless, that it serves no useful or civilised purpose. The retributive reply that the point of punishment is that it serves the purpose of criminal justice is met by the response that this is a particular, outdated and severe conception of justice that is inappropriate to a modern humane society.

Problems with intelligibility

In addition to the claim that the retributive attitude is morally reactionary, the second major weakness identified by critics is that all attempts to develop a systematic elucidation of its key concepts have led only to deeper mystification. What does it really mean, for example, to say that a criminal 'deserves' to suffer or be penalised for the crime? Does it mean any more than that we believe they ought to suffer for it? If so, how does this 'ought' mysteriously arise from the fact or nature of the crime? Why should it not be derived from, for example, the need to prevent and deter other such crimes?

The retributivist reply to this is complex. On the face of it, one might imagine, it is easy to argue that desert, like acknowledgement or gratitude, is an essentially retrospective concept and is intuitively intelligible as such. The difficulty that remains, however, is that of showing that it makes sense to say that either a moral right or an obligation to punish can be generated by the simple reflection that we commonly use this retrospective concept.

More specifically, what is the reasoning behind the retributive claim that the punishment should 'fit' or 'match' the crime? In the context of the death sentence for murder – 'a life for a life' – it is conceded by critics that this is at least intelligible; however, what would the matching sentence be for fraud, for treason, for rape? The idea of even a rough correspondence in this sense between a crime and its punishment is said to be of little practical value. Ultimately, it is argued, the retributive language of desert is mere rhetoric to mask the absence of an intelligible justification.

The standard retributivist reply to this criticism as a whole is that the intelligibility of desert as a justification is exhibited in the principle of proportionality, the violation of which – handing out disproportionate punishment – is a clear injustice. To punish a minor theft, for example, more severely than an armed robbery is manifestly unjust. Starting from such examples, it is easy to construct parallel scales of seriousness in criminal offences, on the one hand, and penalties or sentences, on the other. That one should match the other is a requirement of desert, not of any consequentialist calculation.

There are basically two problems with this. The first is that any ranking of criminal offences according to desert is controversial. Which is the more serious, meriting more serious punishment: robbery with violence, or a non-violent crime such as fraud, the illicit proceeds of which are much greater? Second, even if a scale of desert is settled, this only solves the problem of the relative severity of the punishment. It does not fix the level of the mean, which in practice is relative to the standards of a particular society. Nor does it fix the range (minimum and maximum) or the spread (ratio of one offence to another) of the scale. A retributivist might well reply that the very recognition of these problems amounts to a tacit admission that desert is the appropriate basis for justification. The consequentialist can in turn reply that the principle of proportionality gives us at most a justification for treating some offences as more serious than others; the scale might as easily be applied to the appropriate degree of disapproval or reprimand, as to the institution of punishment. What this demonstrates, however, is that the justification is difficult, not that the idea of desert as justification is unintelligible.

The most notoriously vague aspect of the retributivist account originates in Hegel's theory that the punishment constitutes an annulment of the crime. The idea at the heart of this theory is that the act of punishment constitutes a denial of the legitimacy of the criminal act, in Hegel's dialectical terms, a rightful negation of the criminal negation, leading to a moral reaffirmation of the legitimacy of the rightful order. Although this perhaps comes the closest to a purely retributive justification, problems of intelligibility have frequently been voiced. How can punitive action nullify or 'make nothing of' an offence in which death or permanent injury has been caused? How can the situation prior to the crime be restored? These objections, however, rest upon a misinterpretation of the sense of negation intended by Hegel. It is not the offence itself that is annulled or 'cancelled out', it is the implicit claim to a morally and legally invalid legitimacy that is 'made nothing of'. For Hegel, the dialectical process of crime and punishment is a struggle for the recognition of the validity of the moral order that has been challenged. The justification of punishment is purely retrospective because it is drawn solely from the challenge to the moral and legal authority of the state.

Problems of rationality

In addition to doubts about moral soundness and intelligibility, the third type of weakness commonly attributed to the retributive approaches is the absence of a rational basis for the justification of punishment. The problem here is that, even if we can make it clear what is required for a retributive justification and give an intelligible account of the state's right and duty to punish without reference to consequences, we cannot give any good reasons for preferring this justification, without such reference. The best that can be done is to clarify by example the intuition that the guilty deserve 'to be brought to justice'. The problem here is that most phrases that seem to capture the elusive meaning of the retributive justification are highly emotive ones. The general charge in terms of rationality is that retributivism is entirely dependent on intuition and the negative emotions of anger, resentment and hatred. An important accompanying criticism is that attempts at elucidation depend too much on symbol and metaphor, not enough on reasoned argument.

There are essentially two ways in which retributivists can reply to this. They can either accept that retributivism is not rational, but argue that it is nevertheless morally defensible, or they can reject the instrumentalist model of rationality and argue that a rational account of retributivism can be given. With the first approach, it can be argued that the retributive emotions, properly controlled and channelled by law, express a wholly legitimate response to crime and that this in itself constitutes a justification. The reason for preferring the retributive justification is that it is held to be psychologically and morally realistic, in that it conforms with the sentiments of disapproval or abhorrence that most people feel in response to serious crime. This approach questions the assumption that justification as such has to be rational (Mackie 1985: ch. 15).

The second way is more difficult. It is insufficient – though quite correct – to point out that retributivists do not lack reasoned arguments; the question is about the basis of these arguments. What has to be shown here is that a strictly non-consequential justification can sensibly be called a rational one. If 'rationality' simply means 'thinking in terms of consequences', any non-consequential thinking becomes irrational by definition. If, on the other hand, its meaning is wider than this, including retrospectivist thinking in terms of pre-existent rights and the duty to respect them for their own sake, then the constraints on the application of the narrower rationality will themselves be seen as an integral part of rationality, rather than as emotive constraints.

Modifications and compromises

It should be clear from the discussion to this point why, unless one side gives way on an important point of principle, the two positions cannot be simply combined into a unified theory of punishment. There have nevertheless been numerous attempts, especially in the second half of the twentieth century, to modify the theories in such a way that they might complement one another. The idea behind the 'mixed theory' is to search for a common ground on which some of the opposing elements can be synthesised into a coherent theory that will either reflect the reality of existing legal practices or provide the basis for realistic proposals to reform the current system. From this standpoint, neither the instrumental justification nor the retributive one in their pure and intransigent versions are seen as realistic in either sense.

There are three important possible structures for the mixed theory to adopt. It can be (1) retributive in its basic justification, making concessions to the demands of social policy; (2) instrumentalist in its basic justification, making concessions to one or more of the retributive principles; or (3) more radically innovative in that the basis of justification is extended across both areas, so that both retributive justice and social value are necessary conditions, but neither alone are sufficient.

Strong and weak retributivism

The first option has been a very popular one. What the moderation of retributivism involves is the distinction between a maximum version, insisting on both the right and the duty of the state to punish, and a minimum version that relinquishes the duty, insisting only on the prior right to punish and the forfeiture by the criminal of the right not to be punished. The main advantage of this is that it avoids the range of criticisms relating to its moral status. On the minimum interpretation, the state only exercises its right when there actually is a non-retributive point, which is to say that it takes a flexible approach to prosecution and sentencing, allowing that consequential considerations can override the *prima facie* duty to punish.

The maximum interpretation is clearly indicated by the traditional versions of retributivism. Kant's insistence on the solemn duty to execute every last murderer (1887: 194–201) is the paradigm case of strong retributivism. Hegel's theory of annulment also implies the inseparability of the duty and the right to punish; the theory is an explanation of why the state is morally obliged as well as entitled to invalidate the crime. It cannot let the offence stand. The case for minimalism, however, has been defended by modern retributivists such as Ross (1930), Armstrong (1961) and Mundle (1954).

There is certainly some plausibility in arguing that the minimal thesis is more in line with actual practices; the commuting of sentences and reprieves, the royal prerogative of mercy, the powers of the Home Secretary, judicial discretion and mitigation of severity of sentence have played a prominent role in the history of the English legal system, and also many prosecutions are not held to be in the public interest. In short, the right to punish is not always exercised. Against this, however, some sentences have been mandatory and many offences are not regarded as subject to discretion.

The relevant question here, however, is about the kind of principles in operation. Flexibility and mitigation of sentence tend to be desert-based – focusing on degrees of responsibility – rather than consequentialist. To the extent that this is true, the mixed theory is not a concession to consequentialism at all. If, on the other hand, the theory were to accept the principle that consequentialist considerations should govern sentencing as a proposal for systematic reform, it would be making so many radical concessions that it would be difficult to see it as retaining any more than a formal commitment to retributivism. Either way, the minimal version, abandoning the duty to punish, does not seem to provide a basis for a real compromise. The dilemma we are left with is that, while the Kantian strong version is too strong, the weak version either makes no real concessions or virtually dissolves as a retributive theory.

Lex talionis *and unfair advantage*

A different kind of attempt to modify the retaliatory character of retributivism is represented by theories that shift the justification from the doctrine of *lex talionis* to the idea that desert is based, not on the right of the state to retaliate against offenders, but on the right and duty to remove the advantage unfairly gained by the offender's refusal to play by the rules. The duty is towards those who have not taken similar advantage, those on behalf of whom the state acts, and the focus is on the injustice towards the law-abiding. Offenders deserve to suffer in a measure equivalent to their offence, not by virtue of an ancient moral law commanding such equivalence, but because the failure to cancel the advantage is an injustice.

This line of thought is aimed at defusing the criticism that retributivism is based solely on the vengeful emotions. The idea that the suppression of unfair advantage is morally mandatory is aimed, not at changing the substance of the theory, but at providing it with rational rather than emotional backing and thereby making it more intelligible.

Consequentialist compromises

There are a number of important theories that are explicitly instrumentalist in their basic assumptions, but that are designed specifically for the purpose of reconciling this kind of justification with retributivism. The two most influential were developed by Rawls (1955) and H.L.A. Hart in 1959 (Hart 1968).

The essential feature common to each of these theories was the claim that the problem of justification in punishment theory cannot be expressed by one question – such as 'How is punishment justified?' – but must address a more discriminating set of questions, the answers to which are different in kind. It is the difference between these answers that is supposed to create the ground for a compromise, or for a combined theory of punishment.

Rawls's opening distinction is between (1) any practice or system of rules, such as a game, a governing assembly or the institution of punishment, and (2) a particular action falling under these rules, such as a move in a game, a parliamentary enactment or a judicial decision, any one of which is governed by the relevant system of rules. Justifying a practice, Rawls argued, is quite different from justifying any of its instances. With the practice of punishment, what we are determining is the initial purpose of setting up the institution and punishing anybody at all. This, he claimed, can only be justified in utilitarian terms, as furthering in some way the interests of society. Nobody, he believed, would want to argue that the very *purpose* of punishment was to match wrongdoing with suffering. With a particular instance of punishment, by contrast, the conviction and sentencing of an individual lawbreaker can only be justified in terms of that individual's guilt, or the fact that he has broken the rules of the practice.

What Rawls was arguing was that it would be inappropriate to try to justify any such punitive action in forward-looking, consequentialist terms. While the legislator laying down the law looks to the future, the judge applying the law looks to the past. In this way, Rawls argued that utilitarians and retributivists both have a legitimate point, and that the two perspectives can be combined by recognising this distinction.

Hart's starting point is similar to that of Rawls, in that he distinguishes between a 'general justifying aim' behind punishment as a whole, and the specific principles of justice guiding and restricting the application of punishment. He then rejects retribution as the general aim and argues that it is legitimately to be found in the principles constraining the operation of utility. This he describes as 'retribution in distribution', which he finds morally defensible. The main feature of this distributive justice is the requirement that guilt is a necessary condition of punishment. Punishment as a whole is justified in the first place – as it had been in Rawls's version – by the general justifying aim of its beneficial consequences, primarily crime reduction. What Hart was seeking, in his own words, was 'the middle way between a purely forward-looking scheme of social hygiene and theories which treat retribution as a general justifying aim' (1968: 233). One of Hart's central themes was the need to untangle the conceptual confusion caused by utilitarians and retributivists alike in failing to see the distinction between the general justifying aim and the principled constraints upon it.

Both Rawls and Hart worked on the assumption that, if the implications of these distinctions could be made clear, only the most intransigent of old-fashioned retributivists could fail to see that the justifying aim must be consequentialist, especially given the recognition of the real place of the retributivist principles in the practice of punishment. The implication that they both attached great importance to, that the problem of punishing the innocent could be avoided by combining the utilitarian general aim with 'retribution in distribution', was thought to be decisive. That these assumptions were unduly optimistic was to be clearly demonstrated by the retributivist revival in the 1970s. The main practical concern in this revival was to reinstate the priority of desert over deterrence as the fundamental justification.

Punishment as communication

The theme of expression and communication implicitly runs through all the literature on punishment. Even where it is not explicit, the idea of a negative value judgement embodied in or accompanying the punishment is present in any attempt to justify it. In recent times, the close attention given to the communicative aspect of punishment as its inner meaning has been developed in order to find the source of the conflict between the different perspectives on justification.

Communicative theories have been predominantly but not exclusively retributivist. The idea that the inherent meaning of punishment is to convey a message of emphatic denunciation, whether to the offender, the victim of the crime, or the society in whose name the state punishes, can as easily be interpreted as having an instrumental function (as serving the ends of crime prevention or moral education) as being an end in itself. This kind of theory has nevertheless been associated mainly with the retributivist revival since the early 1970s, with attempts to clarify, reinforce or amend the traditional versions of retributivism. The commitment of many of the new retributivists to theories of communication should be seen partly as an attempt to move the debate forward, partly as a continuation of the old project of defending the moral respectability and rational intelligibility of punishment as retribution.

Robert Nozick: connecting with correct values

Robert Nozick's retributive theory is an attempt to do both, to illuminate the old tradition within the framework of a distinctive communicative theory. For Nozick, 'retributive punishment is an act of communicative behaviour' that communicates the unwelcome message to the offender, 'this is how wrong what you did was' (Nozick 1981: 370).

Taking as a guiding structure the simple formula $r \times H$ (degree of responsibility, multiplied by actual harm done), Nozick argues that retributive punishment is justified to the extent that a wrongdoer intentionally causes harm. The retributivist claim that the intentional committing of the crime is sufficient justification is expressed by Nozick in his central argument that the unwelcome message of wrongness forcefully delivered by punishment constitutes a reconnection with correct values of those who have flouted them through criminally harmful acts, thereby disconnecting themselves from these values.

Recognising the retributivist need to detach the justification from any hint of instrumental objectives, Nozick contrasts his own version with what he calls teleological retributivism, which looks primarily for a positive effect on and a response from the offender. Despite the forward-looking aspect and the reformative implications, this is still retributive because it is a message of condemnation merited by the wrongdoing. On his own version of reconnection, however, the retribution is justified even if the message is entirely unsuccessful. All that is required is that the message is sent and received. In cases where the message has no effect, the connection is still imposed via punishment. 'The act of retributive punishment itself effects this connection' (Nozick 1981: 374). To be punished is to be connected. Like most previous retributivists, Nozick regards a positive response by the offender to the message as a valuable bonus, but unlike them he describes this as an *intensification* of what is already achieved without it.

The difficulty many have found with this lies in the highly teleological flavour of the phrase 'reconnection with correct values', which sounds as though it must depend on a project of moral improvement. Despite his denials that any reformative goals, successful or otherwise, are necessary for this justification, Nozick's purely non-teleological retributivism remains difficult to interpret.

What he seems to mean by this is that, right from the outset, the imposition of punishment is an involuntary connection with correct values of those who have broken and resisted this connection, thus 'flouting' correct values. This enforced connection is already justified solely in terms of connecting even if the offender subsequently comes nowhere near to understanding or responding to the message and is determined to reoffend as soon as released. If the offender does show signs of internalising the correct values, exhibiting understanding and remorse, what is happening is not something qualitatively different, it is the connection – already in place – beginning to work.

One thing Nozick is trying to defuse is the standard criticism that punishment without beneficial results is pointless. What he is implicitly denying in his insistence on the continuity of the communicative behaviour of the punisher is the radical breach between intrinsic and instrumental value and justification. As he sees it, the latter might or might not emerge from the former.

Jean Hampton: defeating the wrongdoer

The retributive emphasis on rights is of particular importance to the attempts to interpret the tradition in the light of the idea of punishment as communication. The pressure from instrumentalist criticism is resisted by viewing retributive punishment as the legitimate sending of a message that responds to criminal violations or infringements of the rights of others. The justification originates in the criminally coercive invasion of rights, rather than in the instrumental value of the denunciatory message.

Jean Hampton places the issue of rights violation at the centre of her communicative theory. Following up Nozick's theory of connection or 'linkage' to correct values, she is less concerned with detaching the justification from moral reform or other penal policies than with explaining punishment as an inherently justified response to the rights-violating message sent out by the offender, and to explain why the state is at fault if it fails to respond with the appropriate message. Her essays rest on Kantian ideas about respect and human value; they offer a modern interpretation of the *lex talionis* and of the Hegelian theory of annulment (Murphy and Hampton 1988).

Hampton's central idea is that of 'inflicting a defeat' on the wrongdoer, whose violation of the rights of others is seen as sending out an objectively demeaning message of domination or mastery over the victim. The reason tough punishment, inflicting suffering in equal measure to the seriousness of the violation, is essential to the communication of the message is that the defeat must be a real one, rather than a merely symbolic denunciation. When society fails to deliver the appropriate punitive action, we allow ourselves as a whole, and the victim in particular, to be demeaned and defeated.

The message conveyed by the wrongdoer who invades the rights of another is that the other is of less personal worth than he or she actually is. At the same time as it expresses a diminishment of the worth of the other, the wrongdoer's message lays false claim to his or her own superior worth. It is the rightful correction of this false representation of their relative worth that justifies the punishment. The purpose of retributive punishment is to bring down the exaggerated claims about the offender's worth, while at the same time, through the same act, reasserting and restoring the worth of the victim. If the state fails to administer punishment sufficiently serious to bring about this defeat, it implicitly endorses the false representation of the relative worth of the rights of invader and victim.

Hampton calls this representation of relative worth 'false evidence of mastery'. It is this evidence, she argues, that is the proper object of Hegelian annulment. The negation of the evidence for a distorted representation of the relative worth of offender and victim restores the true picture in the same way that a scientific disproof of misleading evidence uncovers the true picture of a natural reality. It does not make the evidence disappear; it simply discredits it and shows that it does not prove what it appears to prove. This 'refutation' can only be achieved through punishment, because this is the only practical demonstration of the invalidity of the evidence and vindication of the victim's true worth. To punish is to force the would-be master to suffer defeat at the hands of the victim or the victim's agent. No amount of verbal or symbolic denunciation can inflict this defeat.

The point of Kant's insistence that the failure to punish every murderer implicates the entire community in the crimes left unpunished is explained by Hampton as a general insight into the significance of the message conveyed by punishment. In terms of her theory of false evidence, she argues that, when we abandon the retributive goal of punishment, we condone the false evidence for the inferior worth of the victim, because it stands undefeated. In allowing it to stand, we 'acquiesce in the message it sent about the victim's inferiority'.

Her reinterpretation of *lex talionis* is that this is a formula demanding that the wrongdoer suffer a defeat on a similar scale to the one he or she has inflicted. Hampton argues that this should be restricted to the principle of proportionality, whereby the greater the offence the greater the defeat needed to reassert the victim's value. What she claims can be removed from the traditional doctrine is the severity of the 'eye for an eye' demand for equivalence, for the punishment to match the crime. The retributive punishment designed to nullify the demeaning message can be constrained by upper limits determined by the Kantian demand for the respect for the humanity of the wrongdoer, even when the wrongdoer has not shown similar respect for the humanity of others. She argues that this demand for respect imposes a ceiling on the severity of punishment, the function of which is to defeat without dehumanising and degrading. By rooting her demand for these humane upper limits to punishment within her own theoretical framework, rather than in *ad hoc* consequential reasoning, she seeks to avoid the old criticisms that retributivism is by its own logic necessarily barbaric.

Hampton's account as a whole certainly throws light on how the Kantian and Hegelian theories can be plausibly interpreted in line with contemporary penal policies, and it has radical implications both for minimum and maximum sentences. The idea that only punishment and the actual 'lowering' of the offender can deliver a real defeat of the criminal offence is perhaps more convincing than earlier retributivist accounts; it probably comes closer than most theories to bridging the gap between the rational case for denunciation of wrongdoing and the case for hard penal treatment.

There are, however, several serious problems. It is dubious that the restriction of *lex talionis* to proportional punishment, relinquishing the idea of it 'matching the crime', counts as a retaliatory principle at all. It is not even clear why it is distinctively retributive, as we shall see in the next section. Second, there is a stronger than usual emphasis here on personal worth and the lowering of personal value. This kind of account is at its most convincing in the context of offences against the person. When the emphasis is on crimes with victims who suffer irreversible physical or psychological damage, it is easier to find this justification plausible. It is more difficult to extend it to the full range of crime. Is it really plausible to interpret ordinary offences of theft as attempts by criminals to elevate themselves above their real moral status and to demean their victims? How does it fit impersonal crime, in which the victims are anonymous? The unfair advantage explanation seems more appropriate to such cases.

Instrumentalist censure and reprobation

For instrumentalists, the important question about the message communicated by punishment is how this expression of disapproval or condemnation can be most effectively used. Thus, Walker and Padfield (1996: 116) describe it as one sentencing strategy among others, aimed specifically at increasing disapproval of the offence and increasing respect for the law. Braithwaite and Pettit (1990: 160–4) regard the censure or reprobation of the offender as an integral part of punishment, but only for the purpose of what it can achieve in terms of reducing crime and protecting people's freedom. They reject what they term the 'intrinsic reprobationism' of Nozick, von Hirsch and others, all of whom promote the idea that reprobation is a good in itself. In particular, they argue that the need for effective denunciation or reprobation does not support the retributive insistence on some degree of hard treatment, on the grounds that this can only be justified as a last resort, when prevention and public safety demand it.

Desert and deterrence in sentencing

One of the intractable difficulties that seems to have defeated the retributivist imagination is the problem of devising a method to determine the general level of what is deserved. It is much easier to find consensus on the question of relative desert, on which kinds of offender and offence deserve greater or less punishment than others, than it is to set the average level, reflecting the initial equivalence between the punishment and the crime. How do we determine, for example, whether the respective punishments for burglary and armed robbery should be five years and ten years imprisonment, or five months and ten months? This 'absolute' question is sometimes obscured by the arguments for proportionality in sentencing.

More recent theories of desert have focused on the question of how deterrence-based sentencing stands in relation to the desert requirements in terms of both equivalence and proportionality. Given that deterrence is the central factor in the attempts to control or reduce crime, the crucial question concerns the compatibility between this goal and the pursuit of justice in the sense of adhering to both of these principles. It should be noted that the orthodox judicial opinion in Britain and the USA today is that this requires a delicate balance between rights and social policy, and that this balance is largely achieved.

For some theorists, it is a question of which way the balance should be tilted, towards maximising crime reduction or safeguarding justice. For others, this balance is wholly fictitious, concealing the reality that in many areas of crime hard decisions have to be made, seriously compromising either the reductivist strategy or the demands of justice. Alan Goldman (in Simmons *et al.* 1995) has argued that a paradox or dilemma presents itself as soon as we compare the requirements of deterrence and desert. Given that the rate of apprehension and conviction for any type of crime is always less than perfect and often very low, those who in fact are caught and punished have to pay the price for the low rate of conviction, by serving sentences that are always greater than the crime would otherwise merit in terms of the principle of equivalence. The paradox is that, while the resulting injustice, which is tantamount to punishing the innocent, is quite intolerable, the relaxation of this policy, allowing a massive increase in the criminal violations of the rights of innocent victims, would be equally intolerable. Goldman's conclusion is the unremarkable one that the only appropriate response is to increase levels of detection and attack the socio-economic roots of crime.

He deals with three possible objections to this account of sentencing practices. The 'exceptive clause' argument, that the excessive punishments are justified by the harms greatly outweighing the rights, is rejected on the grounds that there is nothing exceptional about them. The 'fair warning' objection, that if excessively harsh penalties are well-advertised, then the criminal has only himself or herself to blame for ignoring the warning, is rejected on the grounds that this would justify any degree of punishment, however extreme, which it clearly would not. The 'lynch mob' objection, that the criminals are themselves being protected from angry public reaction by excessive punishment, is rejected on the grounds that such reactions would justify punishing the vigilantes rather than the criminals.

Given the premises of the argument, these replies sound persuasive. The assumptions Goldman is making, however, are certainly questionable. We have to ask whether effective deterrence in general really requires more punishment than is deserved. The more usual retributive objection to deterrence is not that it is inherently excessive but that it has a destabilising effect on justice, in that it fluctuates according to current social circumstances and type of crime rather than according to equitable criteria. The retributivist conclusion is that lower sentences than desert demands are as common as sentences in excess of desert. With unusual crimes that are unlikely to be emulated, the need for deterrence is negligible, but the retributivist still insists that there must be an equivalence between harm intentionally caused and the punishment. With exceptionally long sentences, such as the 'life tariff', it is quite plain that desert outlives the need for deterrence. What Goldman's argument assumes is that the general level of desert is actually very low, relative to current sentencing practices, such that it will always be less than what is needed for deterrence. The mistake behind this is the assumption that the imperfect rate of detection and conviction is the only factor governing the operation of deterrence. It is, however, often applied quite independently of such considerations, for example to discourage the spread of a new kind of fraud, which would have nothing to do with making people suffer additionally for those who have not been caught.

Another argument that works against the Goldman paradox is found in the influential 'desert-band' theory put forward by Norval Morris (Duff and Garland 1994). This takes the edge off the equivalence problem by introducing flexibility into the determination of how much punishment any particular crime merits. If the attempt to determine the level of punishment deserved is not burdened with the assumption that there must be a precise equivalent, a range can be established, within which the punishment is morally acceptable in terms of desert. Desert is seen as a limiting principle, setting 'the outer limits of leniency and severity which should not be exceeded'. Thus one might argue that, for example, a particular kind of serious assault merits at least six months, at most two years imprisonment, rather than fixing it at exactly two hundred days. With a rigid equivalence principle such as Hegel's, one day too many or too few would be an injustice. Morris's intention is to promote a sentencing practice whereby there is room for manœuvre or 'fine tuning' within this desert-band, applying lower or higher sentences for purposes of incapacitation and deterrence. This, for Morris, is the model upon which discretionary sentencing should operate.

How does this work against the Goldman paradox? The overall point of Morris's argument is that retributive justice does not have to clash with the pragmatic goals of crime reduction, which can be accommodated within the desert-band. It means that increasing the sentence within the minimum–maximum range solely for purposes of deterrence does not constitute an injustice. It does not mean that the tension is eliminated, because there is still an upper cut-off point beyond which deterrence strategies should not go, and a basic minimum that should not be ignored. Thoroughgoing consequentialists will still reject this as an obstacle to rational social policy. It has the potential, however, to reduce the tension between desert and deterrence.

Morris's desert-band theory has greater appeal, in that it offers both an explanation and a kind of justification of common sentencing practices, but it faces serious objections, the most obvious of which is that it merely shifts the problem of determining equivalence from an exact point to a range. Why, for example, should the range itself be fixed at two to four years, rather than four to eight? Why, indeed, should it be a prison term at all? Why not a ten- to twenty-minute severe reprimand?

Even if one accepts that the substitution of a range for a precise point facilitates the intuitive setting of equivalence, Morris's theory faces other objections from a retributivist position. There is, for example, nothing to prevent the range of deserved punishment from being manipulated and overstretched to accommodate grossly unjust sentences. It also explicitly sanctions inequality in sentencing and violates the principle of proportionality. Morris defends his rejection of the principle that 'like cases should be treated alike' on the grounds that equality in law is at most a guiding principle, to be balanced against other values and suspended whenever outweighed.

This was exactly the point that was rejected by von Hirsch (1993) in his defence of the 'commensurate desert' principle, which links the idea of just deserts with the principle of proportionality and 'commonsense notions of equity', ruling out disparate sentences for identical offences. Norval Morris's desert-band theory is unacceptable, he argues, because it holds the principle of equal treatment to embody merely one value among others, to be dispensed with whenever desirable on utilitarian grounds. Von Hirsch, by contrast, insists that there should be a presumption in favour of the principle of commensurate deserts, that it should have *prima facie* controlling effect on sentencing, only giving way in exceptional circumstances.

Conclusion

The intention throughout this examination of the justifications has been to dispel some of the misconceptions surrounding the debates on punishment, in particular the one that sees two well-defined camps in stark opposition. At the same time, I have tried to show that there are nevertheless two very different modes of moral thinking about punishment, as there is with war and other instances of serious state coercion. Any well-informed reflection on the theory and practice of sentencing reveals a permanent tension between these two ways of thinking.

The search for a coherent link between these two approaches will certainly continue, but what most contemporary philosophers are anxious to avoid is a repetition of past mistakes, the most obvious of which is a simplistic endorsement of the uneasy compromise embodied in the contemporary institutions of punishment, combining the goal of controlling and reducing crime with retributive 'elements' in sentencing. The search continues, not so much for a 'mixed theory' that tries to establish a compromise between incompatibles, but rather for the articulation of a unified theory that combines the two sides, if not into a single position, at least into a framework in which genuine dialogue is possible. What is sought is a realistic theory that tries to root the justification in the kind of punishment which is the least ineffective, holding out some prospect of actually working towards the achievement of its basic goals, which in themselves neither exclude the proper concern with blame and desert, nor set up the kind of institutional framework that will systematically violate any of the principles of justice highlighted by the retributivists.

Study questions

General question: Can punishment be justified? If so, how?

Further study questions: Compare the merits and defects of forward-looking and backward-looking justifications of punishment. Is it possible to synthesise them into a single theory of punishment? What place should the concept of desert have in a theory of punishment? Might it be possible to base a theory of punishment solely on deterrence? Should levels of sentencing be fixed according to desert or deterrence? Does Nozick's communicative theory make better or worse sense of retribution? Is the Hegelian theory that punishment annuls the crime, intelligible? Evaluate Hampton's version of annulment theory.

Suggestions for further reading

Outstanding general books on the philosophy of punishment include Honderich (1976), Hart (1968), Lacey (1988) and Ten (1987). More introductory accounts can be found in Lyons (1984: ch. 5), Harris (1997: ch. 5) and Murphy and Coleman (1990: ch. 3).

Very useful anthologies of influential traditional writings and modern essays include Grupp (1971), Acton (1969) and Duff (1993). Two anthologies are particularly useful for the more recent developments in this area, the Duff and Garland reader (1994) and the *Philosophy and Public Affairs Reader* (Simmons *et al.* 1995).

Any attempt to attain a comprehensive view of twentieth-century and contemporary philosophy of punishment should begin with the hard core of influential arguments contained in these anthologies. The key passages from the classics are in Kant (1887: 194–201), Hegel (1942: 68–73) and Bentham (1970: 158–73).

In the early to mid-twentieth century, the most significant writings were those of the mixed theorists Ewing (1929), Rawls (1955) and Hart (1968); and the defences of retributivism by Mabbott, Mundle and Armstrong (Acton 1969).

As a representative sample of late twentieth-century writings, one should read Murphy (1979, 1987), Andenaes (1974), Kleinig (1973), Cottingham (1979), Mackie (1985: ch. 15), Primoratz (1989), Nozick (1981: ch. 4), Hampton (1984), Murphy and Hampton (1988), Walker (1991), Braithwaite and Pettit (1990) and von Hirsch (1993). On particular problems relating to sentencing, see Walker and Padfield (1996), Gross and von Hirsch (1981) and Duff (1993: part IV).

13 Crime and modernity

Scandals in criminal justice in the Western liberal democracies today tend to be linked not only with high-profile miscarriages of justice, with outspoken comments by eccentric or controversial judges, with false convictions and the imprisonment or execution of the innocent, but also with standing abuses such as the inappropriate judicial treatment of the mentally ill, or the unfair aspects of standard trial procedures, when they are said to be inherently biased or discriminatory against women or ethnic minorities. Such problems are serious, but the agenda of the theories critical of modernity in criminal law is more probing than this. It is not just that the idealised theory of equal justice for all sometimes comes into conflict with the practice in the criminal courts. Radical critics claim that even in theory the system of criminal justice in modern legal systems does not stand up to examination, because it rests on internally inconsistent foundations and flatly contradictory attitudes towards justice. This constitutes a fundamental challenge to the principles of criminal justice as discussed over the last three chapters. In this final chapter, I will critically assess this challenge.

Enlightened liberalism and its critics

What exactly is under attack here? The first point is that the general framework of the principles of criminal law today is provided by the doctrine of *mens rea* that emerged from the liberal individualism deeply associated with the Enlightenment, and from the English common law tradition. In accordance with the Enlightenment ideal of the rational, autonomous individual, the fundamental liberal assumption behind the *mens rea* doctrine is that every individual who is subject to the sanctions of the legal system is a free, rational agent, self-aware and consciously deliberating and acting on choices, hence presumed to be fully responsible unless proven otherwise. The free rationality of this agent is of special significance to criminal law, because the praise and blame that come with it generate specific conceptions and doctrines of fault and punishment, and it is the absence of this rationality that governs the law on insanity. The second point, as was made clear by the cases considered (Chapters 10–11), is that there is always a tension between the recognition of *mens rea* as vital to a just legal system, on the one hand, and the judicial and governmental perceptions of the needs of public policy in terms of public health and safety, on the other. The doctrine of *mens rea*, then, is only one component of the system of criminal justice. Some see it as the idealised component, the feature that gives the system its character as an essentially just one, comprising a set of ideals that can be aspired to but not always wholly achieved.

The range of radical criticism

The range of radical criticism of this picture of criminal law as a precarious balance between individual justice and the protection of the public is very broad. Critics have attacked both its general principles and their application in great detail. The criticism ranges from Marxist and Critical Legal Studies (CLS) historical analysis of criminal law as essentially an instrument of class oppression, designed primarily for the protection of private property, to feminist critiques of the masculine assumptions behind its theory and practice, to postmodernist deconstructions of all the doctrines, theories and concepts that sustain criminal law. As with legal theory in general, a critical approach to the concept of the individual as the 'legal subject' is prominent. Deconstructing this subject involves an analysis of privileging and marginal-isation. Questions of power are again central, revealing in particular the influence of Marx, Nietzsche and Foucault. Understanding the philosophy of crime and punishment purely in terms of power means not only the unmasking of ulterior motives and drives behind the institutions and ideologies associated with them, but also the reduction of the language of rights, justice and justification to expressions of the hierarchical relations of power in contemporary society. It means that all the liberal assumptions about the courts judging whether or not defendants are responsible for their actions, or juries determining whether or not defendants are sane according to law, or the general defensibility of the rationale behind sentencing, while not exactly meaningless, are at best to be regarded as indications of self-deception, and at worst as the cynical manipulation of public opinion. So let us see how this critical perspective on the criminal law is built up.

The individual and society

For most of the critical theories, the autonomous rational individual presup-posed by liberalism is a myth designed to legitimise the state and the legal system. Marx's critique of liberalism and its 'monadic' individual, abstracted from its social relations, is the single most influential idea in modern critical theory. This individual is said to be a relatively recent creation, an artificial construct, projecting the idea of a self-contained, isolated individual person who plays, among other roles, that of the central subject of the criminal law. As a rational, deliberating individual, seeking only his own interest, he can choose to conform his behaviour to the moral law and the law of the land, or face the punitive consequences. This 'person', it cannot be emphasised enough, is a fiction. The real individual, by contrast, is a concrete person, embedded in a social context of family, environment and social class, exhibiting a unique combination of individuated and socialised characteristics. According to its critics, it is the almost universal tendency of modernity (or, for Marxists, bourgeois ideology) to superimpose this fictitious conception of the individual upon the vast diversity of concrete individuals and thus to arrive at a 'subject' suitable for the purposes of criminal law.

Intentionalism and determinism

One of the central lines of criticism the critical legal scholars of recent times is largely derived from this contrast between the real and fictitious conception of the individual or the person. One prominent criticism is that there is a contradiction at the heart of liberal legal ideology on the question of free will and determinism, as it applies to human action in society. The question concerns the contexts in which people have real choices and those in which they do not. In criminal law, this age-old metaphysical problem comes into sharp focus. The reasonable assumption is that blame and criminal liability are completely dependent upon the presence or absence of these choices, but it is often not clear how to draw this distinction. A prominent CLS criticism is that liberal legal reasoning on these matters is completely confused, to such an extent that it makes criminal law, like every other area of law, radically indeterminate.

There are several versions of this criticism, but Mark Kelman's is representative and has been influential (Kelman 1987). His argument is essentially that in liberal society nearly everyone tends to oscillate between the two poles of 'intentionalist discourse' and 'determinist discourse'. His distinctive thesis is that most people, including lawyers, are drawn simultaneously to both descriptive accounts of the same course of events and find themselves compelled to accept one and suppress the other, while always remaining aware of what has been suppressed. Only at the outer extremes do we find philosophers or lawyers fixing exclusively on one pole or the other, either asserting universal responsibility and blame for all acts, regardless of pressure of circumstance, duress, illness, etc., or at the other extreme denying blame entirely by asserting universal determinism and negating personal agency.

Despite the implausibility of these extremes, what the criminal law is said to do is privilege the intentionalist discourse over the determinist, the latter being subordinated and arbitrarily confined to particular acceptable areas, so that the standing presumption is always one of a perfectly free agent. The fictitious 'monadic' self is imposed when it is thought necessary to uphold an intentionalist discourse, in order to show that free choices could have been made. When such choices are assumed, offenders are legitimately punishable. A version of the alternative socialised self is substituted when excuses are thought appropriate – so that the self is seen as helplessly caught up in a causal chain of events beyond its control. In the modern liberal mind, there is an uncomfortable oscillation between these two discourses, as if everyone were aware of the arbitrary nature of the division of human action into these two domains. The result is a deep indeterminacy in criminal law as practised in the liberal democracies. This allows the criminal law to become a political battleground between leftist judges who interpret human actions as literally 'products' of their circumstances, thus excusable, and more conservative judges interpreting the same actions as outcomes of the unconstrained individual will.

Nevertheless, beneath the surface of this political conflict, we find agreement on the basic liberal commitment to the idea of the substantiality of the self as a metaphysical entity, a fixity that is only in specified circumstances 'causally dissolved' by the pressures of social life. The realistic alternative obscured by these abstractions, according to Kelman, is to see the self as a 'crossroads, a locus where things occur, a place in which action is just one result of past actions, known and unknown' (1987: 112), a concrete view of the self that is supposed to be neither determinist nor intentionalist, at least in the usual senses of these terms. What we need to consider now is the extent to which this critique can be upheld in relation to the central problems with the doctrine of *mens rea* (as laid out and discussed in Chapter 10).

Free agency, criminal intention and **mens rea**

According to the critical scholars, then, the main body of criminal law rests upon the assumption of a mythical legal subject, a typical self-sufficient individual who from his position of isolation is able to engage morally with the world beyond his island. He is capable of perfect self-control, is morally equal in standing with all others and in full possession of all his rational faculties. From the standpoint of mainstream jurisprudence, this picture of the legal subject is a caricatured exaggeration of what is a wholly reasonable and necessary normative framework in which to develop general and specific principles of criminal justice. Without such assumptions about individual autonomy and rationality, it would be impossible to justify a system of punishment that respects the rights of the individual. Such assumptions are built into the very idea of criminal justice. For the critical theorist, however, this response misses the point not only about what concrete individuals are really like, but also about the naturalisation of a conception that is really historically specific and relative. The assumptions embodied in the essentially fictitious picture of the individual in society today, far from being natural and inevitable, are said by the critics to be anachronistically rooted in the age in which liberal ideology was born, an age of *laissez-faire* capitalism, colonialism and extreme individualism, in which property-owners constituted a small minority, slavery was still legal and flourishing, starvation wages were paid to legally free labourers and women of all races had virtually no rights. The new conception of the individual was an idealised character drawn from the educated, privileged élite. This was the age in which the principles of liberal justice took shape and it has left a lasting mark upon them (Norrie 2001).

The function of the *mens rea* doctrine stipulating conditions of responsibility is to distinguish those who are to be blamed for their harmful and criminal acts from those who are not. In the case of mental illness, it also distinguishes the fully from the partially responsible, or those who are less than fully culpable. Generally speaking, the defendant is required to have acted freely, knowingly and intentionally. On the specific question of freedom and unconstrained action, it is in the context of the defences of necessity and duress that the central tensions in the attitudes of the law come into sharp focus. In the classic case of *Dudley and Stephens* (1884), the 'freely' chosen actions of the starving sailors who murder the cabin boy are both condemned and mitigated. There was and remains a deep ambivalence about their guilt or blamelessness and about whether a private defence of necessity should be available at all. In such cases, there is usually a conflict between sympathetic public opinion and the harsh rulings of the courts, but there are also divisions within legal opinion. In a more recent incident, a decision not to prosecute survivors of the *Herald of Free Enterprise* (1987), when there was evidence that a man inadvertently obstructing their exit had been deliberately killed in the scramble to escape the sinking ship, seems to have been prompted by the realisation that under existing law they would have no defence to a charge of murder, and that this would be widely regarded as unacceptable (Smith 2002: 273), given the circumstances that many lives had been saved at the expense of one, who was going to die anyway. As noted in Chapter 10, the recent ruling (*Re A*, 2000) on the case of the conjoined twins indicates that the law might be shifting in a direction more in line with public opinion.

For the CLS critics, this legal uncertainty is symptomatic of the deep confusion and incoherence of the criminal law (Norrie 2001: ch. 8). Situations of extreme necessity or duress – as in the case of *Lynch* (1975), in which the defendant was forced at gunpoint to assist in a murder – are said to explode the myth of the rational, autonomous subject, but at the same time the courts are more disposed to find them guilty than not guilty, for reasons of expediency. The idea that people in such extreme situations of need or danger can be viewed in terms of the Enlightenment ideal as autonomous agents in full possession of their rational capacities, making carefully reasoned decisions, is seen as completely unrealistic. Such agents, the critics say, do not exist anywhere outside of the philosophical and legal imagination, let alone in the middle of an emergency. In Kelman's terms, the courts and lawmakers have readily at their disposal the discourses of intentionalism or determinism, so that the actions of the defendants can be set within the framework of either voluntaristic decisions or of a chain of events beyond the agent's control, according to the inclination of the judges or drafters of the law.

Intention and insanity

Intention and motive

With this kind of critical approach, all the elements of the *mens rea* doctrine fall under scrutiny. The concept of intention in particular is deconstructed to show how it has developed to serve particular political objectives. According to Norrie, the artificial distinction between intention and motive was originally drawn in such a way that any aspect of poverty could be eliminated as a defence, no matter how extreme the circumstances of cold or hunger, so that the threat to property would be defused, leaving the common law with a distinction that would be applied indiscriminately (2001: ch. 3), from relatively trivial offences such as criminal trespass, to the most serious such as treason and murder. With the separation of intention and motive, the most relevant aspect of a defence to criminality is said to be removed, resulting in a prominent principle of law that flatly contradicts its own proclaimed concern for individual justice. In excluding motive as a defence, the criminal law divests itself of the only element that could make coherent moral sense of criminal justice.

Intention and recklessness

CLS critiques of the common law tests for recklessness tend to focus on the unsettling of criminal law in recent decades on the question of whether the test should be subjective or objective for all offences. To reiterate, if the test is subjective, the prosecution has to prove that the defendant was actually aware of the risk implicit in the action that caused the harm. The 'subjectivity' is relative to the actual state of mind. If the test is objective, the prosecution only has to prove that the defendant ran an obvious risk that should have been apparent to any reasonable man/person. According to the subjective Cunningham test (1957), the jury had to be satisfied that the defendant had actually seen the risk and proceeded regardless. With the establishment of the Caldwell test (1982), the stringency of this requirement was relaxed for offences against property, so that the jury had to be satisfied that either the defendant saw the risk or the risk was of such a nature that as a rational agent he should have seen it. The implication was that if he closed his eyes to the obvious risk, he was as guilty of acting recklessly as if he had actually seen it. Finally, the so-called 'Caldwell lacuna' or loophole concerns cases that neither the subjective nor the objective test seem to cover. When the defendant does see the risk of, for example, pulling the trigger of an apparently unloaded gun, but then disregards the risk for what he erroneously believes to be good reasons and proceeds to run the risk, it cannot be proved with either test that he is guilty of recklessness.

The controversy that the *Caldwell* ruling caused has had several dimensions. Many have seen it as an application of common sense to an area of law that had been long overdue for reform. Given the difficulty of seeing into the defendant's mind, especially to determine such an intangible and passing state of mind as recklessness, rather than the more enduring intentions that leave marks on the person's behaviour, the serviceability of the reasonableness standard was obviously an attraction. The plain fact that this would make it easier to get convictions, though, counted both in favour of the new test and against it. It was argued by critics that it would open the door to unlimited injustice in obtaining automatic convictions regardless of the subjective qualities of the defendants in each case, given that the reasonableness test was applied to young people and schizophrenics to whom it was completely inappropriate. It also raised some odd anomalies, such as the implication that personal injury would be easier to raise a defence against than criminal damage. If A recklessly takes out B's eye with an air-rifle and damages B's spectacles in the process, the application of the Caldwell test would result in the conviction of A for the damage but not for the injury, thus raising a fundamental doubt about the distinction. Some have responded to this by arguing that Caldwell should be universalised and applied to all offences, a suggestion that has so far been wisely resisted. Its introduction in the first place was also criticised at the time for pre-empting the authority of Parliament, which it was claimed had ruled out such a test. It was also criticised for blurring the distinction between recklessness and what was traditionally seen as the less culpable category of inadvertent negligence.

The wrangle over these two tests, which matches quite closely the similar dispute over the tests for the *mens rea* for murder, has been criticised by CLS scholars on numerous grounds. The main point in Norrie's historical analysis (2001: ch. 4) is his argument that the Cunningham and Caldwell versions of recklessness rest upon concepts of subjectivity and objectivity that are juxtaposed against each other rather than synthesised (thus allowing space for the Caldwell lacuna to appear), and that they are limited and distorted conceptions, the inadequacies of which can be explained by the nineteenth-century attempts to positivise the criminal law by eliminating the moralistic language of the common law, which had made it increasingly difficult for juries to determine guilt. The heritage for modern criminal law is an overrestricted concept of subjectivity and an overbroad concept of objectivity. The concept of subjectivity as embodied in Kenny's 1902 definition of malice and the *Cunningham* ruling is too narrow because it excludes what should properly be seen as subjective (such as the failure to take proper care by an agent who is well capable of it, even if he gave it no thought), rather than being shifted to the realm of objective negligence or recklessness. In Duff's colourful example, the bridegroom who 'genuinely' forgets to attend his own wedding is subjectively guilty; there is no need in such cases to resort to the imaginary 'reasonable man'. This narrowness in turn provokes the overextended concept of objectivity, counting as 'objectively' culpable what really could have been avoided. The result is a depth of conceptual confusion in the law that cannot be untangled by formulating ever more refined tests for recklessness. What is required is a genuine synthesis in a unitary understanding of recklessness in relation to intention, within the context of a social consensus on the kinds of risks that it is justifiable to take. Without such a consensus, there is no possibility of such a synthesis.

The decision in *R. v. G. and another* (2003) (see Chapter 10), overruling *Caldwell* for cases of criminal damage, was at least in part a response to the relentless criticism by 'subjectivists' that it had opened the door to ever-increasing complexity on the law on recklessness, and to serious injustice to young offenders and the mentally unsound. This reinstatement of the subjective test without any revision or readjustment, however, will almost certainly perpetuate the problems in the more typical cases featuring adults of sound mind who claim never to have seen an obvious risk in their behaviour. The switch from the objective to the subjective does nothing to counter the criticisms that either test taken in isolation is inevitably defective.

Intention and foresight

As is well known, the *mens rea* for murder, resting on tests to distinguish it from manslaughter, underwent regular reassessment and adjustment in the second half of the twentieth century. At the heart of the problem in this area lay a collision of views on how the guilty mind in cases of homicide should be established, in terms of what was intended and what the defendant foresaw. The eventual, more or less stable outcome of the disputes and reversals on this question was a test for murder that incorporated both the subjective and the objective test, in as far as it retained the fundamental *mens rea* principle that the actual state of mind in terms of intention and foresight had to be proved, but also allowed the jury to infer actual intention (to cause at least grievous bodily harm) from what was objectively foreseeable by 'the reasonable man', along with the rest of the evidence.

There have been many detailed criticisms of this and subsequent minor adjustments to the law on this issue. CLS criticisms have been mixed, but the general tenor of the criticism is that the uncertainty and wavering are symptomatic of a deeper malaise in the law, that they point to an indeterminacy that opens the law to political manipulation. Norrie's argument (1993: 52–7) is that the perpetual narrowing and broadening of the definitions of intention and foresight have served the purpose of enabling the judiciary to switch almost at will between the requirements of individual justice and the interests of state policy and social control. The elaborate pretence of following legal logic is designed to bridge the gap between legal ideology and the social reality, given that the facts of all the cases of homicide under consideration over these years are so radically different.

Critical perspectives on criminal law and insanity

In mainstream jurisprudence, the orthodox framework for the law relating to insanity is, as its critics point out, predominantly rationalistic. The fundamental idea governing legal thinking in this area is that individuals beyond the age of majority who lack reason (the great Enlightenment virtue) are not legally responsible – they are legally insane. This, it should be remembered, does not necessarily mean that they are medically insane, or that all those found medically insane are legally insane. Insanity is defined as a distinct legal category. It is a question of what the law is to regard as the kind of mental impairment that will be accepted as negating responsibility. It was partly the recognition of the unrealistically strict dichotomy between the presence and absence of the faculty of reason that led to the 1957 introduction of the distinct defence of diminished responsibility through impairment of the mind, thus allowing a gradation of insanity and responsibility. Nevertheless the concepts of the reason and rationality of the individual remain at the centre of legal thinking in this area.

Twentieth-century medical research and psychiatric theorising on sanity and madness underwent transformations more far-reaching than at any earlier times, but it occupies a domain quite distinct from that of the law. In general cultural terms, the impact of modern theories of the unconscious on the understanding of madness has still not been fully absorbed. More radical anti-establishment theories derived from existentialism and existential psychoanalysis (such as the anti-psychiatry movement), or the philosophies of Nietzsche and Foucault, have deeply influenced criticisms of the social and legal treatment of the insane. Scientifically and medically, however, there is no real consensus on even the most basic features and causes of mental disorders. There is no common thread running through the radical critiques of the modern treatment of insanity, but a number of features are prominent. Most are united in the claim that the medical heritage of the Enlightenment is anything but humane and 'enlightened'. On the contrary, it is seen as the increasingly repressive and dehumanising exercise of institutional power for the sake of social control, rather than the well-being of the patient. One of the basic beliefs behind many of these critiques is that the rationalistic language of the law on insanity and responsibility carries all the uninterrogated assumptions of modernity. From this point of view, the labelling of some people by others as 'insane' is the focal point of a power struggle, through which the self-designated 'sane' dominate and exclude others. 'Sanity' itself is as much a construct as 'insanity', identified as its assertion is with the excessively rationalistic mind. Madness is seen as a holistic condition, which cannot be diagnosed or treated as a malfunction in one isolated aspect of the whole person, such as the capacity to reason.

Some of the CLS writers have drawn extensively upon these sources to present a picture of English and US law on insanity that is sharply at odds with the mainstream interpretation. The most cogent of these accounts is developed by Norrie, who focuses on the concepts of rationality and power. Citing Foucault's histories of the early modern transitions in the treatment of madness (Foucault 1967) and the new practice of confinement of the insane, in conjunction with the rise of psychiatric science, Norrie identifies the struggle for power between the psychiatric and legal professions as the key to understanding contemporary law on insanity. The real struggle, he says, is seen in the advance of scientific psychiatry invading the domain of lawyers, whose professional interest lies in retaining control over the definition of insanity. Historically, the conflict developed in the nineteenth century when the focus on moral education and reform of the asylum inmates gave way to the emergence of scientific medical expertise in theories of underlying organic causes behind the various types of mental illness. Although the two professions were united in their interests as agents of social control in their own respective domains, they came into inevitable collision over their fundamentally opposed approaches to insanity. If, for a scientific psychiatrist, insanity is a matter of physiological causation in the brain, the medical evidence takes the matter out of the hands of the court (as was evident as early as the cases of *Hadfield* (1800) and *M'Naghten* (1843)).

Furthermore, the organic causes could attack the will or the emotions as much as the cognitive abilities, thus potentially rendering the legal rationality tests virtually irrelevant. This is why in Britain the legal profession has resisted encroachment by psychiatry upon the law on insanity. The causal physiology is seen as a threat to the liberal conception of the rule of law, with its presumption of the liberty of the individual, which was increasingly regarded as an object of scientific control and manipulation. It is also seen as having implications throughout the criminal law, in as far as 'sickness' models of crime were applied, negating the very idea of individual responsibility and retributive punishment. In the USA, by contrast, psychiatry has made greater inroads into the legal domain, since the Durham ruling in 1954, creating the 'product test' for insanity, according to which the defence has only to prove that the criminal conduct was caused or produced by the mental disorder. Irresistible impulse has also been incorporated as a complete defence, in the USA and elsewhere, rather than as a mitigating defence as in Britain.

The overall point of this account is that, if the current state of the law on insanity is shaped by this professional power struggle, the official version of the function of the law, in terms of individual justice and public safety, is nothing but a legitimating ideology. Norrie illustrates this by linking insanity and mental illness in general with social and economic status. It is not so much that its distribution is directly caused by factors of class, sex and race as that there is a deliberate and explicit legal strategy to decontextualise all forms of madness by focusing exclusively on the question of presence or absence of rationality in the individual, removed from the environment in which the condition developed. As in every other area of law, individuals are regarded by liberalism as self-enclosed 'monads', in abstraction from the social relations within which they have their true meaning.

Feminist criticisms of criminal law

One of the most obvious facts about crime is that most of it is committed by males. There is therefore insufficient evidence for the comparison of treatment of male and female defendants in the criminal courts to substantiate any strong conclusions about the fairness or unfairness of this treatment. Feminist research in this area focuses more on the general experience of the criminal law by women, who are of course no less the victims of crimes than males. The research has revolved around male sexual violence against women, in particular, domestic violence and rape. Apart from this focus on issues of special significance and concern to women, however, feminist jurisprudence also extends to critical analysis of the general concepts and principles upon which the criminal law rests, including the doctrine of *mens rea* and the principles behind the legal defences.

As in other areas of law, the question of judicial impartiality and even-handedness features prominently in the feminist criticisms. Almost the defining characteristic of the liberal ideal of justice is the principle that it is unfair to apply different rules to different classes of people, whether this involves gender, social class, race or any other irrelevant feature. The principle of applying the same rules to males and females is seen as a question of basic equality and justice. It would be unfair, for example, for the *mens rea* for murder or the test for recklessness to be different according to the sex of the offender. The problem for feminist critics is their perception that this apparent balance does not lead to fairness at all. On the contrary, it is argued, this formal equality, if uncritically and rigidly applied, can reinforce the substantive unfairness that is already present in criminal law, embedded in the legal concepts. In real life, a difference between a typical woman's options and those of a typical man can make the operation of legal principles completely unfair. This argument can be illustrated with the two central examples, domestic violence and rape.

As a social problem, violence against women in the home has tradition-ally been treated as a domestic issue, reinforced by the private–public distinction in law. Criticism of this distinction is the basis of the feminist analysis of this problem. Wives and partners of violent males have had very little substantial protection from the criminal law. The main criticism lies in the disparity between the low levels of prosecution of male perpetrators of violence and the treatment of women who react violently against it. In cases of murder in response to long-term domestic violence, one point at issue concerns the possible defences, which include the complete defence of self-defence (leading to acquittal) and the partial defences of provocation or diminished responsibility, which are the two 'mitigating' defences leading to reduction of the charge of murder to a conviction for manslaughter. Self-defence is defined so narrowly, in particular with the stipulation that it must be a response to an immediate threat to one's life that it is almost impossible to run as a defence, especially given the relative physical power of the average male and female. The alternative defences, provocation or dimin-ished responsibility, are regarded as inadequate because they only mitigate the offence, and are inherently biased against women by virtue of the stand-ards of reasonableness that they rest upon.

The main criticism, though, addresses the distinction between intention and motive, which we have already seen criticised by the critical legal scholars. The feminist arguments against the exclusion of motive from the defences in criminal law are that it works against female defendants because it deprives them of any reasonable line of defence to the kind of crime that is almost exclusive to women. In cases of murder in response to long-term abuse and violence, the conceptual separation of intention and motive is said to be unfair, because it abstracts one discrete mental state (whether they meant to kill) from the other, morally crucial one, of why they formed the intention, or what drove them to it. The law is designed to exclude motivation by despair, which is the most common female reaction to such a situation.

The law on rape is one of the most contentious issues, because feminists argue that it is here that all the gender-bias, both overt and covert, comes sharply into focus. As is well known, cultural prejudices about female sexual behaviour and norms of femininity colour the atmosphere of rape trials. Attempts at character assassination are commonplace and there is an imbalance between attitudes towards male and female sexual histories. In short, the much-reported experience of rape victims is that it is they, rather than the accused, who are on trial. In the feminist critical writings on the law on rape, the problem of consent in relation to *mens rea* has been central. This problem has several dimensions, but there are two important points to concentrate on here. Part of the definition of rape is sex with one of the parties withholding consent. It was ruled in *R. v Olugboja* (1982), a case in which two women were terrorised into submission, that consent was no defence to rape. This was a clarification of the law that meant in effect that it was actual consent under duress of threats that was no defence, that submission did not imply consent and that the prosecution did not have to prove that the victim physically resisted. On the question of whether the defendant 'believed' that the woman was consenting when she clearly was not, however, recent law has been much more problematic.

In an earlier case (*D.P.P. v. Morgan*, 1976) Lord Hailsham notoriously ruled that a man who genuinely but mistakenly believed that a woman was consenting to sex was not guilty of an offence. His argument that the principles of *mens rea* had to be applied evenly regardless of gender sounded entirely fair and reasonable. As in other non-sex-related cases involving males or females, the subjective test of recklessness had to establish the actual state of mind of the defendant at the time of the offence, rather than the objective test of what it was reasonable to believe. Thus, it had to be established that a man charged with rape did actually believe or realise that the woman was not consenting, regardless of how unreasonable this belief might be. The objective standard, he said, would undermine the presumption of innocence. Among the numerous feminist criticisms of this ruling, some have focused on the sudden readiness of a male judge to abandon the cherished standard of the reasonable man in a context in which its application would favour female victims (Barnett 1998: 277). Others have argued that existing law did not in fact dictate the selection of the subjective test for this type of offence, and that the underlying principles would equally have allowed the imposition of the objective test. Each of these interpretations is questionable, given the state of the law at that time on recklessness, but the imposition of the objective test was, of course, exactly what was done a few years later (*Caldwell*, 1982) for a specified class of offences against property, with considerations of social policy overriding the subjective test. Apart from the question of the perceived importance for social policy of the problem of rape in comparison to the security of property, this raises all the problems laid out by Norrie (see above) in relation to the excessive narrowness of the subjective test for recklessness. In the context of rape, does it really make sense to allow a defendant who, against however much evidence to the contrary, has chosen to believe that a woman is actually consenting, is 'subjectively' guilty of no offence? The conceptual problems with defining recklessness unambiguously are accentuated here, but the core of the feminist argument, that the bias in favour of males can be concealed by the appearance of judicial impartiality, does seem to be vindicated. It was not until the Sexual Offences Act (2003), which stipulated that a jury must be convinced that a man's belief that a woman was consenting was a reasonable one, that this particular injustice was eliminated.

It is the way in which this concept of reasonableness operates in criminal law, however, that remains one of the principal targets of feminist criticism. It features prominently in all the defences. In judging guilt and innocence, or degrees of responsibility and grounds for mitigation of sentence, the standard of behaviour is what can be expected of a reasonable man or person. With necessity and duress, it is a question of what could be expected of a person of 'reasonable fortitude'. With self-defence, it is a question of what constitutes 'reasonable force', and of what a reasonable person would have done in the circumstances. In cases of provocation, it is a question of the kind of provocative acts that might induce a reasonable person to suddenly and temporarily lose self-control. According to the feminist criticisms, all of these are defined in such a way that they implicitly refer to male standards of reasonableness, making one assumption after another about the substantive equality of power between males and females, when the opposite is manifestly the case.

An assessment of the critical theories

As noted at the outset of this chapter, the real force of the radical criticisms lies in their charge that even at a deep theoretical level the modern systems of criminal justice are defective, and that it is not just a failure of putting sound principles into practice that leads to tangible injustices in the courts. We have to ask now whether this is borne out by the arguments and examples given by the radical critiques, and if so, whether or not it is fatal to the credibility of a liberal theory of criminal justice. A plausible answer is that to an extent it is borne out, that one can concede many of the insights into the problems and inconsistencies in the presuppositions made within mainstream criminal law and jurisprudence, but without allowing the conclusion that, for example, the rule of law is an empty ideology or that the criminal law is nothing but an instrument of oppression rather than of justice.

On each of the specific criticisms of the principles and operation of the *mens rea* doctrine, a common feature is that problems and dilemmas are exposed without a positive solution being proposed. Let us consider again the essential points in each area. On the question of agency in the defences of necessity and duress, it may well be that cases such as these raise intractable dilemmas that have to be dealt with pragmatically by the courts. It is widely agreed that the state of law on these defences is inconsistent and overdue for radical overhaul. Norrie and Kelman, among others, have highlighted some of the conceptual problems effectively, but the basic moral problem is a deep one. The question of the value of human life and of the justifiability of killing the innocent creates a deep moral schism in contemporary society and poses dilemmas that cannot be resolved by utilitarian numerical calculations. These dilemmas are arguably not created by particular societies, by the ascendancy of an economic class or by male domination. They are the inevitable outcome of serious moral reflection in any pluralist liberal society that does not impose uniformity on moral thinking.

The problems relating to *mens rea* and intention also run deep. Both CLS and feminist critics have criticised the separation of intention and motive as morally counterintuitive and as an expedient for the protection of property and/or male domination, by expelling from the main trial process the one factor that could lead to acquittal. The separation of the process of determining guilt or innocence from the secondary process of sentencing in the light of mitigating factors, however, does have a purpose, which cannot be reduced to these charges of expediency and cynicism. The admission of blameless motive as a substantial defence, which if successful would lead to acquittal, would almost certainly create more problems than it solved. Would it really be satisfactory to allow a standard defence to offences against the person, based upon honourable or blameless motive, given that the intention was to harm? Norrie's argument that the present state of the law makes a cold-blooded contract killing morally equivalent to a mercy killing motivated by compassion (2001: 39) only illustrates the problems with the mandatory life-sentence for murder, which could be reformed with lower minimum sentences for euthanasia and possibly other forms of homicide. The case for root-and-branch reform of the intention–motive distinction has simply not been made.

The problems and inconsistencies in the law on intention in relation to recklessness are undeniable. Many contradictory stands have been taken by judges and legal writers in recent years on questions of criminal liability in relation to the thorny problem of how and where to set the boundaries of intentionality in relation to, for example, drunkenness, dangerous driving or the use of firearms. The distinction between criminal negligence and reck-lessness has been particularly problematic. It can be argued against the CLS critiques, however, that this difference of opinion and lack of certainty is an inevitable feature of any society and its legal system, rather than specifically of the modern liberal legal systems. The tension may in part be the conse-quence of attempting an almost impossible balancing act between assumptions about autonomy and responsibility, on the one hand, and the need for consideration of public safety, on the other, and this tension may in certain respects be more acute at some times and in some systems than others, due to specific social conditions, but this does not vindicate the CLS thesis that the law is entirely incoherent or radically indeterminate.

Similar problems appear in any critical assessment of the radical critics of the law on insanity. In mainstream criminal jurisprudence the evolution of the law on insanity has to be understood in terms of the *mens rea* doctrine, but as any examination of this history will reveal, the standard *mens rea* requirements of cognitive and volitional competence are constantly balanced against consideration for public safety, even where this is not explicit. One of the problems with the critical theories is that genuine concern for public safety is systematically interpreted as social control, as if there were no concern for justice within the legal system or for humane and beneficial treatment within the psychiatric profession at all. The argument that because legal reasoning conceals relations of power and struggles between vested interests, then there are only relations of power and no real values at stake is invalid. The whole of human affairs and human interac-tion can be described in terms of power, if one is determined to do so, but this is only one description from one particular angle. There is more to it than this.

Conclusion: Enlightenment values and the rule of law

Resistance to the sweeping criticisms of the systems of criminal justice in the liberal democracies has revolved around a defence of the independent value of the rule of law, regardless of its origins. It is certainly arguable that the development of procedural rights in the eighteenth century was intrinsically linked with the interests of the privileged few in their battle against the old order, but this does not undermine their real value to real individuals. The security of the individual citizen from arbitrary arrest, imprisonment and torture has an impact on the realities of criminal law in a liberal society, quite independently of how fictitiously liberals conceptualise 'the indi-vidual'. An illuminating example of this can be seen in one of the milestones in the struggle for women's rights. In the case of *R. v. Jackson* (1891) a woman estranged from her husband had been abducted and imprisoned by her husband. The remedy at law was for her relatives to apply to the court for *habeas corpus*, legally compelling the husband to release her. This unprecedented action established the common law principle that such imprisonment of married women was not legal, an outcome that was only made possible by the liberal rule of law. It may be objected that such legal remedies were only in practice available to the educated élite, but it can hardly be denied that such developments constituted a real advance in the cause of women's equality.

In assessing the values of the Enlightenment it is also necessary to separate them from the political and social conditions with which they were contemporaneous. While it is true that there were glaring contradictions between the grand universalism in the proclamations of human rights and the practical, and in some senses legal, denial of those rights to the lower classes, to women and to black slaves, there were at the same time liberal reform movements to change these social and economic conditions. The 'empty' ideal of universality was an essential presupposition behind these reforming ideals. The concept of the autonomous reasoning individual, although formulated in abstract terms, was also indispensable as a general formulation, as was the idea that each of these autonomous individuals was equal in standing, even while this flatly contradicted the social reality of differences in social status.

The principle of autonomy has, as we have seen in the critical writings, given rise to numerous problems, but one of the most general problems in criminal law – not just in critical legal scholarship – is that the obvious truth that autonomy as the capacity for self-governance is a matter of degree, that people vary enormously in the type and quality of their rationality, is frequently overridden by the assumption that one either has this capacity or one does not. The generally unexamined assumption is that there is an implicit standard of sufficient degree of autonomy (rationality, specific cognitive skills, ability to choose, etc.) for the ascription of responsibility. As we have seen repeatedly, the traditional standard of the reasonable man is notoriously implausible for assuming a general norm to which everyone and no one conforms. However, when suitably adjusted to 'the reasonable person', it seems hard to avoid the conclusion that, despite the problems highlighted by feminist critics, some such generality is inescapable when formulating a standard that everyone is presumed capable of. The liberal ideal of the autonomous self may be a fiction, but it is also an inescapable one. It is undisputed that a new conception of the self emerged in the early seventeenth century, a new dimension of inwardness and individuality, which had momentous political and philosophical consequences. It was linked with, among other things, the growing awareness throughout the following centuries of individual human rights. What is not generally agreed is that this new idea of 'the individual' was simply the ideological product of the capitalist mode of production, or the latest strategy to perpetuate male domination.

Study questions for Part III

General question: Are the radical critics of modernity justified in their attack on mainstream criminal law theory?

Further study questions: Explain the role of the rational, autonomous individual as the subject of criminal law and assess the critics' arguments that it leads to incoherence and radical indeterminacy. Does the *mens rea* doctrine stand up to the scrutiny of the radical critics? Does the deconstruction of intention and the intention–motive distinction undermine the assumptions behind the *mens rea* doctrine? Do the CLS critiques of the tests for reckless-ness resolve the problems surrounding the subjective–objective wrangle? Are the radical criticisms of the law on insanity convincing? Explain the distinction between overt and covert gender-bias. How justified are the feminist critiques of the legal concepts of reasonableness and rationality in the context of domestic violence and rape?

Suggestions for further reading

For general reading on the values of liberalism and the Enlightenment, and their postmodernist critics, see the references at the end of Chapter 5.

The essential background in criminal law is provided by the cases, critical discussions and proposals for reform in *Elliott & Wood's Casebook on Criminal Law*, Allen (2001) and the Smith and Hogan textbook on criminal law, Smith (2002). Elliott and Quinn (1996), *Criminal Law* is also useful.

The most relevant Marxist and CLS writings on criminal law referred to in this chapter are Norrie (2001) and Kelman (1987: ch. 3).

The most useful examples of feminist perspectives on criminal law are Lacey *et al.* (2003), Graycar and Morgan (2002), and Nicolson and Bibbings (2000). See also Barnett (1998: chaps 11 and 12) on criminal law in relation to domestic violence and rape.

On the radical critiques of the modern treatment of insanity in general, the most influential writings are found in Foucault (1967), Szasz (1960) and Laing (1965). For critical discussions of insanity in relation to criminal law, see Reznek (1997) and Norrie (2001). These should be compared with the more orthodox accounts referred to in Chapter 11.

Appendix: cases and statutes cited

Cases

Brown v. Board of Education (1954) 347 U.S.
Donoghue v. Stevenson (1932) A.C. 562; House of Lords
D.P.P. v. Hyam (1975) A.C. 55; House of Lords
D.P.P. v. Lynch (1975) A.C. 653; House of Lords
D.P.P. v. Morgan (1976) A.C. 182, House of Lords
D.P.P v. Smith (1961) A.C. 290; 3 W.L.R. 546; 3 A11 E.R. 161
Hadfield (1800) 40, George III, Howell's State Trials, Vol. 27, 1281–1356
Henningsen v. Bloomfield Motors Inc. (1960) 32, N.J. 358, 161 A.2d 69
M'Naghten's Case (1843) 10 C. and F. 200; 8 E.R. 718
R. v. Adomako (1995) 1 A.C. 171; 3 W.L.R. 288
R. v. Byrne (1960) 2 Q.B. 396;3 W.L.R. 440
R. v. Caldwell (1982) A.C. 341, House of Lords.
R. v. Cunningham (1957) 2 Q.B. 396, C.C.A.
R. v. Desmond, Barrett and Others (1868) 11 Cox C.C. 146, C.C.C.
R. v. Dudley and Stephens (1884) 14, Q.B.D. 273
R. v. Faulkner (1877) 13 Cox C.C. 550; I.R.C.C.C.
R. v. G and another (2003) U.K.H.L. 50, 3 W.L.R. 1060, 4All E.R. 765
R. v. Jackson (1891) 1 Q.B. 671
R. v. Lamb (1967) 2 Q.B. 981; 3 W.L.R. 888
R. v. Martin (1881) 8 Q.B.D. 54
R. v. Merrick (1996) 1 Cr. App. R.130
R. v. Nedrick (1986) 1 W.L.R. 1025; 3 All E.R. 1, C.A.
R. v. Olugboja (1982) Q.B. 320
R. v. Reid (1992) W.L.R. 793; 3 All E.R. 237
R. v. Seymour (1983) 2 A.C. 493; 3 W.L.R. 349
R. v. Steane (1947) K.B. 997; 61 L.J.R. 969
Re A (Children) (Conjoined Twins: Medical Treatment) (No. 1) [2000] 4 All
    E.R. 961.
Riggs v. Palmer (1889) 115 N.Y. 506, 22 N.E. 188
Rylands v. Fletcher (1868) L.R. 3 H.L. 330
U.S. v. Holmes (1842) 25 Fed. Cas. 360

Statutes

The Married Women's Property Act (1882)
Sex (Removal of Disqualification) Act (1919)
Rent Restriction Act (1920)
Homicide Act (1957)
Mental Health Act (1959)
Criminal Justice Act (1967)
Equal Pay Act (1970)
Guardianship of Minors Act (1971)
Sex Discrimination Act (1975)
Human Rights Act (1998)
Sexual Offences Act (2003)

Bibliography

Acton, H.B. (ed.) (1969) *The Philosophy of Punishment*, London: Macmillan.

Adams, D.M. (ed.) (1992) *Philosophical Problems in the Law*, Belmont, CA: Wadsworth.

Allen, M.J. (2001) *Elliott & Wood's Casebook on Criminal Law*, 8th edn, London: Sweet & Maxwell.

Altman, A. (1986) 'Legal Realism, Critical Legal Studies, and Dworkin', *Philosophy and Public Affairs* 15: 205–35.

Andenaes, J. (1974) *Punishment and Deterrence*, Ann Arbor, MI: University of Michigan Press.

Aquinas, St Thomas (1948) *Selected Political Writings*, ed. A.P. D'Entreves, trans. J.G. Dawson, Oxford: Blackwell.

—— (1988a) *On Law, Morality and Politics*, eds R.J. Regan and W.P. Baumgarth, Cambridge: Avatar Books.

—— (1988b) *On Politics and Ethics*, ed. and trans. P.E. Sigmund, New York and London: W.W. Norton.

Aristotle (1924) *Rhetorica*, trans. W.R. Roberts in W.D. Ross (ed.), *The Works of Aristotle*, Vol. XI, Oxford: Clarendon Press.

—— (1948) *Politics*, trans. E. Barker, Oxford: Clarendon Press.

—— (1985) *Nicomachean Ethics*, trans. T. Irwin, Indianapolis: Hackett.

Armstrong, K.G. (1961) 'The Retributivist Hits Back', in H.B. Acton (1969) *The Philosophy of Punishment*, London: Macmillan.

Atiyah, P.S. (1983), *Law and Modern Society*, Oxford and New York: Oxford University Press.

Atiyah, P.S. and Summers, R.S. (1987) *Form and Substance in Anglo-American Law: A Comparative Study of Legal Reasoning, Legal Theory and Legal Institutions*, Oxford: Clarendon.

Austin, J. (1995 [1832]) *The Province of Jurisprudence Determined*, Cambridge: Cambridge University Press.

Baker, C.D. (1991) *Tort*, 5th edn, London: Sweet & Maxwell.

Baker, J.H. (1990) *An Introduction to English Legal History*, London: Butterworths.

Barnett, H. (1998) *Introduction to Feminist Jurisprudence*, London and Sydney: Cavendish.

Barry, B. (1973) *The Liberal Theory of Justice*, Oxford: Clarendon Press.

Bavidge, M. (1989) *Mad or Bad?*, Bristol: Bristol Classical Press.

Bechtler, T.W. (1978) 'American Legal Realism Revaluated', in T.W. Bechtler, *Law in a Social Context: Liber Americorum Honouring Professor Lon Fuller*, Dordrecht: Kluwer.

Bedau, H. (ed.) (1969) *Civil Disobedience: Theory and Practice*, New York: Pegasus.
—— (ed.) (1991) *Civil Disobedience in Focus*, London and New York: Routledge.
Benditt, T.M. (1978) *Law as Rule and Principle: Problems of Legal Philosophy*, Brighton: Harvester Press.
Bentham, J. (1970 [1789]) *An Introduction to the Principles of Morals and Legislation*, eds J.H. Burns and H.L.A. Hart, London: The Athlone Press.
—— (1987 [1843]) 'Anarchical Fallacies', in J. Waldron, *Nonsense upon Stilts: Bentham, Burke and Marx on the Rights of Man*, London: Methuen.
Beran, H. (1987) *The Consent Theory of Political Obligation*, Beckenham, Kent: Croom Helm.
Bertens, H. and Natoli, J. (eds) (2002) *Postmodernism: The Key Figures*. Malden, MA, and Oxford: Blackwell.
Beyleveld, D. and Brownsword, R. (1986) *Law as a Moral Judgement*, London: Sweet & Maxwell.
Biggs, J., Jr (1955) *The Guilty Mind: Psychiatry and the Law of Homicide*, Baltimore, MD: The Johns Hopkins University Press.
Bix, B. (1993) *Law, Language and Legal Determinacy*, Oxford: Clarendon.
—— (1996) *Jurisprudence: Theory and Context*, London: Sweet & Maxwell.
Blackstone, W. (1829 [1765]) *Commentaries on the Laws of England*, vols I–IV. London: Sweet & Maxwell.
Bobbio, N. (1990) *The Age of Rights*, trans. A. Cameron, Oxford: Polity Press.
Boucher, D. and Kelly, P. (eds) (1994) *The Social Contract from Hobbes to Rawls*, London: Routledge.
Braithwaite, J. and Pettit, P. (1990) *Not Just Deserts: A Republican Theory of Criminal Justice*, Oxford: Clarendon.
Brown, J.M. (1977) *Gandhi and Civil Disobedience*, Cambridge: Cambridge University Press.
Burke, S. (1998) *The Death and Return of the Author: Criticism and Subjectivity in Barthes, Foucault and Derrida*, Edinburgh: Edinburgh University Press.
Cahoone, L.E. (ed.) (1996) *From Modernism to Postmodernism: An Anthology*, Cambridge, MA, and Oxford: Blackwell.
Cain, M. and Hunt, A. (1979) *Marx and Engels on Law*, London: Academic Press.
Campbell, J. (2001) *The Liar's Tale: A History of Falsehood*, New York and London: W.W. Norton & Co.
Campbell, T. (1988) *Justice*, London: Macmillan.
Cicero (1928 [54–52 BC]) *De Republica and De Legibus*, trans. C.W. Keyes, London: Heinemann.
Clark, M. (1990) *Nietzsche on Truth and Philosophy*, Cambridge: Cambridge University Press.
Cohen, M. (1984) *Ronald Dworkin and Contemporary Jurisprudence*, London: Duckworth.
Coleman, J. and Paul, E.F. (1987) *Philosophy and Law*, Oxford: Blackwell.
Connor, S. (ed.) (2004) *The Cambridge Companion to Postmodernism*, Cambridge: Cambridge University Press.
Cornell, D., Rosenfeld, M. and Carlson, D. (1992) *Deconstruction and the Possibility of Justice*, New York and London: Routledge.
Cotterell, R. (1989) *The Politics of Jurisprudence: A Critical Introduction to Legal Philosophy*, London and Edinburgh: Butterworths.

Cottingham, J.G. (1979) 'Varieties of Retribution', *Philosophical Quarterly* 29 (July): 238–46.

—— (1987) 'Just Punishment', *Proceedings of the Aristotelian Society* (Supplement), 1987: 41–55.

—— (1996) (ed)*Western Philosophy: An Anthology*, Oxford: Blackwell.

Critchley, S. (2001) *Continental Philosophy: A Very Short Introduction*, Oxford and New York: Oxford University Press.

Cross, R. and Harris, J.W. (1991) *Precedent in English Law*, Oxford: Clarendon.

Daniels, N. (1975) *Reading Rawls*, Oxford: Blackwell.

Davies, H. and Holdcroft, D. (1991) *Jurisprudence: Texts and Commentary*, London: Butterworths.

Davies, M. (1994) *Asking the Law Question*, Sydney: Sweet & Maxwell.

Deflem, M. (ed.) (1996) *Habermas, Modernity and Law*, London: Sage Publications.

D'Entreves, A.P. (1951) *Natural Law: An Introduction to Legal Philosophy*, London: Hutchinson [2nd edn 1970].

Devlin, P. (1965) *The Enforcement of Morals*, Oxford: Oxford University Press.

Dews, P. (1987) *Logics of Disintegration: Post-Structuralist Thought and the Claims of Critical Theory*, London and New York: Verso.

Dias, R.W.M. (1985) *Jurisprudence*, London: Butterworths.

Dinwiddy, J. (1989) *Bentham*, Oxford: Oxford University Press.

Douzinas, C. (2000) *The End of Human Rights: Critical Legal Thought at the Turn of the Century*, Oxford and Portland, OR: Hart Publishing.

Douzinas, C. and Warrington, R. (1994) *Justice Miscarried: Ethics, Aesthetics and the Law*, New York and London: Harvester Wheatsheaf.

Duff, A. (1982) 'Intentions, Responsibility and Double Effect', *Philosophical Quarterly*, January.

—— (1990) *Intention, Agency and Criminal Liability: Philosophy of Action and the Criminal Law*, Oxford: Blackwell.

—— (1993) *Punishment*, Dartmouth: Aldershot & Brookfield.

Duff, A. and Garland, D. (eds) (1994) *A Reader on Punishment*, Oxford: Oxford University Press.

Dworkin, G. (ed.) (1994) *Morality, Harm and the Law*, San Francisco and Oxford: Westview Press.

Dworkin, R. (ed.) (1977a) *The Philosophy of Law*, Oxford: Oxford University Press.

—— (1977b) *Taking Rights Seriously*, London: Duckworth.

—— (1986) *Law's Empire*, London: Fontana.

—— (1989) 'Liberal Community', *California Law Review* 77(3) (May): 479–87; reprinted in Dworkin, G. (1994).

Dyzenhaus, D. (ed.) (1999) *Recrafting the Rule of Law: The Limits of Legal Order*, Oxford and Portland, OR: Hart Publishing.

Edmundson, W.A. (2004) *An Introduction to Rights*, Cambridge: Cambridge University Press.

Elliott, E. and Quinn, F. (1996) *Criminal Law*, Harlow, Essex and New York: Addison-Wesley Longman Ltd.

Ewing, A.C. (1929) *The Morality of Punishment*, London: Kegan Paul.

Feinberg, J. (1973) *Social Philosophy*, Englewood Cliffs, NJ: Prentice-Hall.

Fingarette, H. (1972) *The Meaning of Criminal Insanity*, Berkeley, CA: University of California Press.

Fingarette, H. and Hasse, A.F. (1979) *Mental Disabilities and Criminal Responsibility*, Berkeley, CA: University of California Press.

Finnis, J. (1980) *Natural Law and Natural Rights*, Oxford: Oxford University Press.

——(ed.) (1991) *Natural Law*, Vol. I and Vol. II, Aldershot: Dartmouth Publishing Company.

Fish, S. (1994) *There's No Such Thing as Free Speech and It's a Good Thing Too*, New York and Oxford: Oxford University Press.

Fitzpatrick, P. (1992) *The Mythology of Modern Law*, London and New York: Routledge.

Fitzpatrick, P. and Hunt, A. (eds) (1987) *Critical Legal Studies*, Oxford: Blackwell.

Flathman, R.E. (1973) *Political Obligation*, London: Croom Helm.

Fleming, J. (1994) *Barbarism to Verdict: A History of the Common Law*, Sydney: HarperCollins.

Fletcher, G.P. (1996) *Basic Concepts of Legal Thought*, New York and Oxford: Oxford University Press.

Foucault, M. (1967) *Madness and Civilisation: A History of Insanity in the Age of Reason*, London and New York: Tavistock [Routledge 1989].

—— (1977) *Discipline and Punish: The Birth of the Prison*, London: Allen Lane

Frank, J. (1949 [1930]) *Law and the Modern Mind*, New York: Coward McCann; London: Stevens & Sons.

Frey, R.G. (ed.) (1985) *Utility and Rights*, Oxford: Blackwell.

Friedmann, W. (1944) *Legal Theory*, London: Stevens & Sons.

Frug, M.J. (1992) *Postmodern Legal Feminism*, New York and London: Routledge.

Fuller, L.L. (1949) 'The Case of the Speluncean Explorers', *Harvard Law Review* 62(4): 616–45.

—— (1964) *The Morality of Law*, New Haven, CT, and London: Yale University Press [revised edn 1969].

Gabardi, W. (2001) *Negotiating Postmodernism*, Minneapolis and London: University of Minnesota Press.

Gavison, R. (ed.) (1987) *Issues in Contemporary Legal Philosophy: The Influence of H.L.A. Hart*, Oxford: Clarendon.

George, R.P. (ed.) (1992) *Natural Law Theory: Contemporary Essays*, Oxford: Clarendon.

—— (ed.) (1996) *The Autonomy of Law: Essays on Legal Positivism*, Oxford: Clarendon.

Gilligan, C. (1982) *In a Different Voice: Psychological Theory and Women's Development*, Cambridge, MA: Harvard University Press.

Glover, J. (1977) *Causing Death and Saving Lives*, London: Penguin.

Golding, M. and Edmundson, W. (2005) *The Blackwell Guide to the Philosophy of Law and Legal Theory*, Oxford: Blackwell.

Golding, M.P. (1975) *The Philosophy of Law*, London and Englewood Cliffs, NJ: Prentice-Hall.

——(1984) *Legal Reasoning*, New York: Borzoi Books.

Goldman, A.H. (1979) 'The Paradox of Punishment', *Philosophy and Public Affairs* 9(1) (fall), reprinted in Simmons *et al.* (1995).

Gould, C.G. (2003) *Constructivism and Practice: Towards a Historical Epistemology*, Lanham, MD: Rowman & Littlefield.

Gray, J. (1996 [1983]) *Mill on Liberty: A Defence*, London: Routledge.

Gray, J. and Smith, G.W. (eds) (1991) *J.S. Mill 'On Liberty' in Focus*, London: Routledge.

Gray, J.C. (1921 [1909]) *The Nature and Sources of the Law*, New York: Columbia University Press.

Graycar, R. (ed.) (1990) *Dissenting Opinions: Feminist Explorations in Law and Society,* Sydney: Allen & Unwin.

Graycar, R. and Morgan, J. (2002) *The Hidden Gender of Law*, 2nd edn, Sydney: The Federation Press.

Greenawalt, K. (1987) *Conflicts of Law and Morality*, Oxford and New York: Oxford University Press.

Gross, H. and von Hirsch, A. (eds) (1981) *Sentencing*, Oxford and New York: Oxford University Press.

Grupp, S.E. (1971) *Theories of Punishment*, Bloomington, IN: Indiana University Press.

Guest, S. (1992) *Ronald Dworkin*, Edinburgh: Edinburgh University Press.

Gutting, G. (ed.) (1994) *The Cambridge Companion to Foucault*, Cambridge and New York: Cambridge University Press.

Haack, S. (1998) *Manifesto of a Passionate Moderate*, Chicago and London: University of Chicago Press.

Hacker, P. and Raz, J. (1977) *Law, Morality and Society*, Oxford: Clarendon.

Hagerstrom, A. (1953 [edited essays from 1916–39]) *Inquiries into the Nature of Law and Morals*, ed. K. Olivecrona, trans. C.D. Broad, Stockholm: Almqvist & Wiksell.

Hale, M. (1972 [1680]) *History of the Pleas of the Crown*, London: Professional Books Ltd.

Hall, J. (1938) *Readings in Jurisprudence*, Indianapolis: Bobbs-Merrill Co. Publishers.

Halpin, A. (1997) *Rights and Law: Analysis and Theory*, Oxford: Hart Publishing.

Hampton, J. (1984) 'The Moral Education Theory of Punishment', *Philosophy and Public Affairs* 13(3) (summer): 208–38.

—— (1986) *Hobbes and the Social Contract Tradition*, Cambridge and New York: Cambridge University Press.

—— (1997) *Political Philosophy*, Boulder, CO, and Oxford: Westview Press.

Harding, A. (1966) *A Social History of English Law*, London: Pelican.

Harris, J.W. (1980) *Legal Philosophies*, London, Edinburgh, Dublin: Butterworths [2nd edn 1997].

Hart, H.L.A. (1961) *The Concept of Law*, Oxford: Clarendon [revised edn 1995].

—— (1963) *Law, Liberty and Morality*, London: Oxford University Press.

—— (1968) *Punishment and Responsibility*, Oxford: Clarendon.

—— (1982) *Essays on Bentham*, Oxford: Oxford University Press.

—— (1983) *Essays in Jurisprudence and Philosophy*, Oxford: Clarendon.

Hawkes, T. (1977) *Structuralism and Semiotics*, London: Methuen.

Hegel, G.W.F. (1942 [1821]) *The Philosophy of Right*, trans. T.M. Knox, Oxford: Clarendon.

Henberg, M. (1990) *Retribution: Evil for Evil in Ethics, Law and Literature*, Philadelphia, PA: Temple University Press.

Hobbes, T. (1962 [1651]) *Leviathan*, London: Collins.

Hohfeld, W.N. (1919) *Fundamental Legal Conceptions: As Applied in Judicial Reasoning*, ed. W.W. Cook, New Haven, CT, and London: Yale University Press.

Holmes, O.W. (1897) 'The Path of the Law', *Harvard Law Review* 10: 457–78; reprinted in Adams (1992).

—— (1968 [1881]) *Common Law*, London and Melbourne: Macmillan.

Honderich, T. (1976) *Punishment: The Supposed Justifications*, London: Penguin.

Hook, S. (ed.) (1964) *Law and Philosophy: A Symposium*, New York: New York University Press.

Horton, J. (1992) *Political Obligation*, London: Macmillan.

Hume, D. (1972 [1739]) *A Treatise of Human Nature*, London: Fontana.

Hunt, A. (ed.) (1992) *Reading Dworkin Critically*, New York and Oxford: Berg.

Hunt, L. (1991) *Nietzsche and the Origin of Virtue*, London and New York: Routledge.

Hutcheson, J. (1929) 'The Judgment Intuitive', *Cornell Law Quarterly* 14: 274–8; reprinted in Adams (1992).

Israel, J.I. (2001) *Radical Enlightenment: Philosophy and the Making of Modernity 1650–1750*, Oxford: Oxford University Press.

Jacobs F.G. (1971) *Criminal Responsibility*, London: Weidenfeld & Nicolson.

Jameson, F. (1972) *The Prison-House of Language*, Princeton, NJ: Princeton University Press.

Jones, P. (1994) *Rights*, London: Macmillan.

Kant, I. (1887 [1796]) *The Philosophy of Law*, trans. W. Hastie, Edinburgh: Clark.

Katz, L. (1987) *Bad Acts and Guilty Minds: Conundrums of the Criminal Law*, Chicago and London: University of Chicago Press.

Keeton, G.W. (1961) *Guilty but Insane: Four Trials for Murder*, London: Macdonald.

Kelly, J.M. (1992) *A Short History of Western Legal Theory*, Oxford: Clarendon.

Kelman, M. (1987) *A Guide to Critical Legal Studies*, Cambridge, MA, and London: Harvard University Press.

Kelsen, H. (1957) *What is Justice?*, London: University of California Press.

—— (1970 [1934]) *Pure Theory of Law*, trans. M. Knight, Berkeley, CA: University of California Press.

—— (1973) *Essays in Legal and Moral Philosophy*, ed. O. Weinberger, trans. P. Heath, Dordrecht and Boston: Reidel.

Kennedy, D. (1976) 'Form and Substance in Private Law Adjudication', *Harvard Law Review* 89: 1685–1778.

Kenny, A. (1978) *Free Will and Responsibility*, London: Routledge.

Kenny, C.S. (1902) *Outlines of Criminal Law*, ed. J.W.C. Turner, 19th edn, Cambridge: Cambridge University Press, 1966.

Kipnis, K. (ed.) (1977) *Philosophical Issues in Law*, Englewood Cliffs, NJ: Prentice-Hall.

Kleinig, J. (1973) *Punishment and Desert*, The Hague: Martinus Nijhoff.

Kolakowski, L. (1968) *Positivist Philosophy: From Hume to the Vienna Circle*, Harmondsworth: Pelican Books.

Kramer, M. (1991) *Legal Theory, Political Theory, and Deconstruction: Against Rhadamanthus*, Bloomington, IN: Indiana University Press.

——(1995) *Critical Legal Theory and the Challenge of Feminism: A Philosophical Reconception*, Lanham, MD: Rowman & Littlefield.

——(1999) *In Defence of Legal Positivism: Law without Trimmings*, Oxford: Oxford University Press.

Lacey, N. (2004) A Life of H.L.A. Hart: The Nightmare and the NOble Dreamer, Oxford: Oxford University Press

—— (1988) *State Punishment: Political Principles and Community Values*, London and New York: Routledge.

Lacey, N., Wells, C. and Quick, O. (2003) *Reconstructing Criminal Law: Text and Materials*, London: LexisNexis UK.

Laing, R. (1965) *The Divided Self*, Harmondsworth: Penguin.

Lee, K. (1989) *The Positivist Science of Law*, Aldershot: Avebury.

Leiser, B.M. (1973) *Liberty, Justice and Morals: Contemporary Value Conflicts*, New York and London: Macmillan.

—— (1981) *Values in Conflict: Life, Liberty and the Rule of Law*, New York: Macmillan.

Lessnoff, M. (1990) *Social Contract Theory*, Oxford: Blackwell.

Levin, D. (1999) *The Philosopher's Gaze: Modernity in the Shadows of Enlightenment*, Berkeley, CA: University of California Press.

Leyden, W. von (1981) *Hobbes and Locke: The Politics of Freedom and Obligation*, London: Macmillan.

Llewellyn, K. (1930) *The Bramble Bush*, New York: Oceana Publications.

Lloyd, D. (1964) *The Idea of Law*, London: Penguin.

Locke, J. (1924 [1690]) *Two Treatises of Civil Government*, London: Everyman.

Lyons, D. (1984) *Ethics and the Rule of Law*, Cambridge: Cambridge University Press.

—— (1993) *Moral Aspects of Legal Theory: Essays on Law, Justice and Political Responsibility*, Cambridge: Cambridge University Press.

Lyotard, Jean-François (1984) *The Postmodern Condition: A Report on Knowledge*, Manchester: Manchester University Press.

MacCormick, N. (1978) *Legal Reasoning and Legal Theory*, Oxford: Clarendon.

—— (1981) *H.L.A. Hart*, London: Edward Arnold.

—— (1982) *Legal Right and Social Democracy*, Oxford: Clarendon.

MacCormick, N. and Weinberger, O. (1986) *An Institutional Theory of Law: New Approaches to Legal Positivism*, Dordrecht: Kluwer.

McCoubrey, H. (1987) *The Development of Naturalist Legal Theory*, New York: Croom Helm.

MacIntyre, A. (1981) *After Virtue: A Study in Moral Theory*, London: Duckworth.

Mackie, J.L. (1977a) *Ethics: Inventing Right and Wrong*, London: Penguin.

—— (1977b) 'The Third Theory of Law', *Philosophy and Public Affairs* 7(1) (Autumn): 3–16, reprinted in Mackie (1985).

—— (1985) *Persons and Values*, Oxford: Clarendon.

MacKinnon, C. (1987) *Feminism Unmodified*, Cambridge, MA: Harvard University Press.

McLeod, I. (1999) *Legal Theory*, Basingstoke and London: Macmillan.

McLellan, D. (1973) *Karl Marx: His Life and Thought*, London and Basingstoke: Macmillan.

MacPherson, C.B. (1962) *The Political Theory of Possessive Individualism*, London and New York: Oxford University Press.

McWilliams, P. (1996) *Ain't Nobody's Business if You Do: The Absurdity of Consensual Crimes in Our Free Country*, Los Angeles: Prelude Press.

Mansell, W., Meteyard, B. and Thomson, A. (2004) *A Critical Introduction to Law*, 3rd edn, London, Sydney and Portland, OR: Cavendish.

Marmor, A. (1997) *Law and Interpretation: Essays in Legal Philosophy*, Oxford and New York: Oxford University Press.

Midgley, M. (2004) *The Myths We Live by*, London and New York: Routledge.

Mill, J.S. (1972a [1859]) *On Liberty*, London: Everyman.

—— (1972b) [1861]) *Utilitarianism*, London: Everyman.

Mitchell, B. (1970) *Law, Morality and Religion in a Secular Society*, London: Oxford University Press.

Montefiore, A. (ed.) (1975) *Neutrality and Impartiality*, New York and London: Cambridge University Press.

Moore, M.S. (1993) *Act and Crime: The Philosophy of Action and Its Implications for Criminal Law*, Oxford: Clarendon.

Moore, R. (1978) *Legal Norms and Legal Science: A Critical Study of Kelsen's Pure Theory of Law*, Honolulu: University Press of Hawaii.

Morris, H. (ed.) (1961) *Freedom and Responsibility: Readings in Philosophy of Law*, Stanford, CA: Stanford University Press.

Morrison, W. (1997) *Jurisprudence: from the Greeks to Postmodernism*, London: Cavendish.

Mulhall, S. and Swift, A. (1996) *Liberals and Communitarians*, 2nd edn, Oxford: Blackwell.

Mundle, C.W.K. (1954) 'Punishment and Desert', in H.B. Acton (1969) *The Philosophy of Punishment*, London: Macmillan.

Murdoch, I. (1992) *Metaphysics as a Guide to Morals*, London: Chatto & Windus.

Murphy, J.G. (ed.) (1971) *Civil Disobedience and Violence*, Belmont, CA: Wadsworth.

—— (1979) *Retribution, Justice and Therapy: Essays in the Philosophy of Law*, Dordrecht and London: Reidel.

—— (1987) 'Mercy and Legal Justice', in J. Coleman and E.F. Paul, *Philosophy and Law*, Oxford: Blackwell.

Murphy, J.G. and Coleman, J.L. (1990) *Philosophy of Law: An Introduction to Jurisprudence*, San Francisco and London: Westview Press.

Murphy, J.G. and Hampton, J. (1988) *Forgiveness and Mercy*, Cambridge: Cambridge University Press.

Nickel, J. (1987) *Making Sense of Human Rights: Philosophical Reflections on the Universal Declaration of Human Rights*, Berkeley, CA: University of California Press.

Nicolson, D. and Bibbings, L. (eds) (2000) *Feminist Perspectives on Criminal Law*, London: Cavendish.

Norrie, A. (1993) *Crime, Reason and History: A Critical Introduction to Criminal Law*, London: Weidenfeld & Nicolson.

—— (2001) *Crime, Reason and History: A Critical Introduction to Criminal Law*, 2nd edition, London: Butterworths.

Novick, S.M. (1989) *Honourable Justice: The Life of Oliver Wendell Holmes*, New York: Dell.

Nozick, R. (1974) *Anarchy, State and Utopia*, Oxford: Blackwell.

—— (1981) *Philosophical Explanations*, Oxford: Clarendon.

Oderberg, D.S. (2000a) *Applied Ethics: A Non Consequentialist Approach*, Oxford: Blackwell.

—— (2000b) *Moral Theory: A Non-Consequentialist Approach*, Oxford: Blackwell.

Olivecrona, K. (1971 [1939]) *Law as Fact*, London: Stevens & Sons.

Owen, D. (1994) *Maturity and Modernity: Nietzsche, Weber, Foucault and the Ambivalence of Reason*, London & New York: Routledge.

Pateman, C. (1979) *The Problem of Political Obligation: A Critical Analysis of Liberal Theory*, Chichester and New York: John Wiley & Sons.

Patterson, D. (ed.) (1996a) *A Companion to Philosophy of Law and Legal Theory*, Oxford, UK: Blackwell.

—— (1996b) *Law and Truth*, New York and Oxford: Oxford University Press.

—— (ed.) (2003) *Philosophy of Law and Legal Theory: An Anthology*, Oxford: Blackwell.

Paul, J. (1981) *Reading Nozick: Essays on Anarchy, State and Utopia*, Oxford: Blackwell.

Perry, M.J. (1998) *The Idea of Human Rights: Four Inquiries*, Oxford: Oxford University Press.

Porter, R. (1987) *A Social History of Madness: Stories of the Insane*, London: Weidenfeld & Nicolson and Phoenix.

—— (2000) *Enlightenment: Britain and the Creation of the Modern World*, London and New York: Allen Lane.

—— (2002) *Madness: A Brief History*, Oxford and New York: Oxford University Press.

—— (2003) *Flesh in the Age of Reason*, London and New York: Allen Lane.

Posner, R.A. (1988) *Law and Literature: A Misunderstood Relation*, Cambridge, MA, and London: Harvard University Press.

—— (1990) *The Problems of Jurisprudence*, Cambridge, MA, and London: Harvard University Press.

Postema, G.J. (1986) *Bentham and the Common Law Tradition*, Oxford: Clarendon.

Pound, R. (1969 [1924]) *Law and Morals: The McNair Lectures 1923, Delivered at the University of North Carolina*, New York: Augustus M. Kelly.

Primoratz, I. (1989) *Justifying Legal Punishment*, Atlantic Highlands, NJ, and London: Humanities Press.

Raban, O. (2003) *Modern Legal Theory and Judicial Impartiality*, London: GlassHouse.

Rawls, J. (1955) 'Two Concepts of Rules', *Philosophical Review* LXIV (January): 3–32, reprinted in Acton (1969).

—— (1972) *A Theory of Justice*, London: Oxford University Press.

—— (1993) *Political Liberalism*, New York: Columbia University Press.

Raz, J. (1970) *The Concept of a Legal System: An Introduction to the Theory of Legal Systems*, Oxford: Clarendon.

—— (1975) *Practical Reason and Norms*, London: Hutchinson.

—— (1979) *The Authority of Law: Essays on Law and Morality*, Oxford: Clarendon.

—— (1986) *The Morality of Freedom*, Oxford: Clarendon.

—— (1994) *Ethics in the Public Domain*, Oxford: Clarendon.

Reznek, L. (1997) *Evil or Ill? Justifying the Insanity Defence*, London and New York: Routledge.

Richardson, J. and Sandland, R. (eds) (2000) *Feminist Perspectives on Law and Theory*. London: Cavendish.

Riddall, J.G. (1991) *Jurisprudence*, London: Butterworths.

—— (1999) *Jurisprudence*, 2nd edn, London: Butterworths.

Robinson, D. (1999) *Nietzsche and Postmodernism*, Cambridge: Icon Books UK and Totem Books USA.

Robinson, D.N. (1996) *Wild Beasts and Idle Humours: The Insanity Defence from Antiquity to the Present*, Cambridge, MA, and London: Harvard University Press.

Rommen, H.A. (1947) *The Natural Law: A Study in Legal and Social History and Philosophy*, trans. T.R. Hanley, St Louis and London: B. Herder.

Ross, A. (1958) *On Law and Justice*, London: Stevens & Sons.

Ross, W.D. (1930) *The Right and the Good*, Oxford: Clarendon.

Royle, N. (2003) *Jacques Derrida*, London: Routledge.

Rumble, W.E., Jr (1968) *American Legal Realism: Scepticism, Reform and the Judicial Process*, Ithaca, NY: Cornell University Press.

Sarat, A. and Kearns, R. (1996) *Legal Rights: Historical and Philosophical Perspectives*, Ann Arbor, MI: The University of Michigan Press.

Schauer, F. (1991) *Playing by the Rules*, Oxford: Clarendon.

Schmidt, J. (1996) *What is Enlightenment?*, Los Angeles and London: University of California Press.

Schopp, R.F. (1991) *Automatism, Insanity and the Psychology of Criminal Responsibility: A Philosophical Inquiry*, Cambridge: Cambridge University Press.

Shute, S. and Hurley, S. (1993) *On Human Rights: The Oxford Amnesty Lectures*, New York: Basic Books.

Simmonds, N.E. (1986) *Central Issues in Jurisprudence: Justice, Law and Rights*, London: Sweet & Maxwell.

Simmons, A.J., Cohen, M., Cohen, J. and Beitz, C.R. (1995) *Punishment: A Philosophy and Public Affairs Reader*, Princeton, NJ: Princeton University Press.

Singer, P. (1973) *Democracy and Disobedience*, Oxford: Clarendon Press.

—— (1991) (ed) *A Companion to Ethics*, Oxford: Blackwell.

—— (1993) *Practical Ethics*, Cambridge: Cambridge University Press.

Smith, J. (2002) *Smith and Hogan: Criminal Law*, London: Butterworths.

Smith, J.C. (1976) *Legal Obligation*, London: Athlone Press.

Solomon, R.C. (1988) *Continental Philosophy since 1750: The Rise and Fall of the Self*, Oxford and New York: Oxford University Press.

Sorrell, T. (ed.) (1996) *The Cambridge Companion to Hobbes*, Cambridge: Cambridge University Press.

Stacy, H.M. (2001) *Postmodernism and Law: Jurisprudence in a Fragmenting World*, Aldershot: Dartmouth.

Stephen, J.F. (1874) *Liberty, Equality, Fraternity*, London: Smith Elgard & Co.

Stewart, M.A. (ed.) (1983) *Law, Morality and Rights*, Dordrecht and Boston: Reidel.

Stoljar, S. (1984) *An Analysis of Rights*, London: Macmillan.

Sturrock, J. (1979) *Structuralism and Since: From Lévi-Strauss to Derrida*, Oxford and New York: Oxford University Press.

Suber, P. (1998) *The Case of the Speluncean Explorers*, London and New York: Routledge.

Summers, R.S. (1968) *Essays in Legal Philosophy*, Oxford: Blackwell.

—— (1971) *More Essays in Legal Philosophy*, Oxford: Blackwell.

—— (1984) *Lon L. Fuller*, London: Edward Arnold.

—— (1992) *Essays on the Nature of Law and Legal Reasoning*, Berlin: Duncker & Humbolt.

Szasz, T. (1960) *The Myth of Mental Illness*, New York: Harper & Row.

Taylor, C. (1989) *Sources of the Self: The Making of the Modern Identity*, Cambridge: Cambridge University Press.

Ten, C.L. (1980) *Mill on Liberty*, Oxford: Clarendon.

—— (1987) *Crime, Guilt and Punishment*, Oxford: Clarendon.

Tennant, N. (1997) *The Taming of the True*, London: Cavendish.

Thayer, H.S. (ed.) (1982) *Pragmatism: The Classic Writings*, Indianapolis and Cambridge: Hackett.

Thomson, J.J. (1990) *The Realm of Rights*, Cambridge, MA, and London: Harvard University Press.

Thoreau, H.D. (1983 [1849]) *Walden and Civil Disobedience*, New York and London: Penguin.

Toulmin, S. (2001) *Return to Reason*, Cambridge, MA, and London: Harvard University Press.

Tur, R. and Twining, W. (1986) *Essays on Kelsen*, Oxford: Clarendon.

Twining, W. (1973) *Karl Llewellyn and the Realist Movement*, London: Weidenfeld & Nicolson.

—— (ed.) (1986) *Legal Theory and Common Law*, Oxford: Blackwell.

Twining, W. and Miers, D. (1976) *How to Do Things with Rules: A Primer of Interpretation*, London: Weidenfeld & Nicolson.

von Hirsch, A. (1993) 'Censure and Proportionality', in A. Duff and D. Garland (ed.), *A Reader on Punishment*, Oxford: Oxford University Press.

Waldron, J. (1984) *Theories of Rights*, Oxford: Oxford University Press.

—— (ed.) (1987) *Nonsense upon Stilts: Bentham, Burke and Marx on the Rights of Man*, London: Methuen.

Walker, N. (1991) *Why Punish?*, Oxford: Oxford University Press.

Walker, N. and Padfield, N. (1996) *Sentencing: Theory, Law and Practice*, London: Butterworths.

Wasserstrom, R.A. (ed.) (1971) *Morality and the Law*, Belmont, CA: Wadsworth.

Weinreb, L. (1987) *Natural Law and Justice*, Cambridge, MA, and London: Harvard University Press.

West, D.J. and Walk, A. (eds) (1977) *Daniel M'Naghten: His Trial and the Aftermath*, Ashford: Gaskell Books, British Journal of Psychiatry.

Williams, G. (1987) 'Oblique Intention', *California Law Journal* 46: 417–21.

Williams, P. (1991) *The Alchemy of Race and Rights: Diary of a Law Professor*, Cambridge, MA: Harvard University Press.

Wolfenden Committee (1957) *Report of the Committee on Homosexual Offences and Prostitution* (Cmnd. 247) London: HMSO..

Wolin, R. (2004) *The Seduction of Unreason: The Intellectual Romance with Fascism from Nietzsche to Postmodernism*, Princeton, NJ: Princeton University Press.

Wollstonecraft, M. (1967 [1792]) *Vindication of the Rights of Women*, New York: W.W. Norton.

Woolhouse, R.S. (1988) *The Empiricists*, Oxford: Oxford University Press.

Wootton, B. (1981) *Crime and the Criminal Law*, London: Stevens & Sons.

Cases Index

Statutes Index

Index